12 Modern Philosophers

12 MODERN PHILOSOPHERS

Edited by

Christopher Belshaw and Gary Kemp

WILEY-BLACKWELL

A John Wiley & Sons, Ltd., Publication

This edition first published 2009
© 2009 Blackwell Publishing Ltd

Blackwell Publishing was acquired by John Wiley & Sons in February 2007. Blackwell's publishing program has been merged with Wiley's global Scientific, Technical, and Medical business to form Wiley-Blackwell.

Registered Office
John Wiley & Sons Ltd, The Atrium, Southern Gate, Chichester, West Sussex, PO19 8SQ, United Kingdom

Editorial Offices
350 Main Street, Malden, MA 02148-5020, USA
9600 Garsington Road, Oxford, OX4 2DQ, UK
The Atrium, Southern Gate, Chichester, West Sussex, PO19 8SQ, UK

For details of our global editorial offices, for customer services, and for information about how to apply for permission to reuse the copyright material in this book please see our website at www.wiley.com/wiley-blackwell.

The right of Christopher Belshaw and Gary Kemp to be identified as the authors of the editorial material in this work has been asserted in accordance with the Copyright, Designs and Patents Act 1988.

Library of Congress Cataloging-in-Publication Data

12 modern philosophers / edited by Christopher Belshaw and Gary Kemp.
    p. cm.
  Includes bibliographical references and index.
  ISBN 978-1-4051-5261-7 (hardcover : alk. paper) — ISBN 978-1-4051-5262-4 (pbk. : alk. paper)
1. Philosophy, Modern—20th century.   2. Philosophers, Modern.   I. Belshaw, Christopher.
II. Kemp, Gary, 1960 Oct. 15–   III. Title: Twelve modern philosophers.
  B804.A21 2009
  190—dc22

                                                                                2008026375

A catalogue record for this book is available from the British Library.

Set in 11.5/13pt Perpetua by Graphicraft Limited, Hong Kong
Printed in Singapore by Fabulous Printers Pte Ltd

1   2009

CONTENTS

ACKNOWLEDGMENTS

We have many people to thank. At Wiley-Blackwell, Nick Bellorini, Gillian Kane, and Liz Cremona have always had an unerring sense of what is better and what worse for this project, along with a less unerring sense, we're pleased to say, of time's passage. We had early encouragement from a number of philosophers in both the US and the UK. Without them, we might have faltered. Each of us would like to thank the other: neither would have got very far alone. And of course our deepest thanks are to the contributors who have provided these chapters, tolerated our sometimes pernickety comments and suggestions, and made the book more than possible.

The publishers gratefully acknowledge permission from the sources listed below to reproduce the photographs on the following pages:

16: Photo by Adele Skinner, courtesy of Douglas Quine.
34: Alec Rawls.
54: © Ena Bodin.
76, 94: © Sijmen Hendricks.
115, 216: Steve Pyke / Getty Images.
153: Robert P. Matthews / Office of Communications, Princeton University.
173: Martha Holmes / Time and Life Pictures / Getty Images.
232: © Rune Hellestad / CORBIS.

NOTES ON CONTRIBUTORS

Thomas Baldwin is Professor of Philosophy at the University of York. He is the author of *G. E. Moore* (1990) and *Contemporary Philosophy* (2001); he was also editor of *The Cambridge History of Philosophy 1870–1945* (2003) and *Reading Merleau-Ponty* (2007). He is currently the editor of the journal *Mind*.

Alexander Bird is Professor of Philosophy at the University of Bristol. He is the author of *Philosophy of Science* (1998), *Thomas Kuhn* (2000), and *Nature's Metaphysics* (2008), and researches is philosophy and history of science and medicine (he is a member of the British Association for the Advancement of Science), metaphysics, and epistemology.

Christopher Belshaw is a Senior Lecturer in Philosophy and Staff Tutor (Arts) with the Open University. He works mainly at the theoretical end of applied ethics. He is the author of *Ideas* (1998), *Environmental Philosophy* (2001), and *10 Good Questions About Life and Death* (2005). Another book, *Annihilation: The Sense and Significance of Death*, is forthcoming (2009).

José Luis Bermúdez is Professor of Philosophy at Washington University in St Louis, where he is also Director of the Center for Programs and Director of the Philosophy-Neuroscience-Psychology program. He is the author of *The Paradox of Self-Consciousness* (1998), *Thinking without Words* (2003), and *Philosophy of Psychology: A Contemporary Introduction* (2005). He is currently writing a textbook on cognitive science for Cambridge University Press.

Lori Gruen is Associate Professor of Philosophy and Feminist, Gender, and Sexuality Studies at Wesleyan University, where she also directs the Ethics in Society Project. She works at the intersection of ethical theory and ethical practice, with a particular focus on ethical issues that impact those often overlooked in traditional ethical investigations, e.g. women, people of color, non-human animals. She has published widely on topics in practical ethics including: animal ethics and mind, feminist ethics and politics, and philosophy of law. She is currently writing a book exploring the complex philosophical issues raised by our relations to captive chimpanzees.

Gary Kemp is Senior Lecturer in the Philosophy Department at the University of Glasgow. He works in the philosophy of logic and language, on Frege, Russell, Quine, and Davidson, and on aesthetics and philosophical themes in literature. He is the author of *Quine: A Guide for the Perplexed* (2005) and, with Tracy Bowell, of *Critical Thinking: A Concise Guide* (3rd edn. 2009).

A. R. Lacey was born in Birmingham in 1926. After studying Classics at Cambridge, he gained a PhD in ethics and then taught philosophy at Bedford College, London (1954–84) and King's College London (1984–2001). He specialized in ancient philosophy at first and later moved more toward modern philosophy. He has published *A Dictionary of Philosophy* (3rd edn. 1996), *Modern Philosophy: An Introduction* (1982), *Bergson* (1989), a translation of *Philoponous on Aristotle: Physics II* (1993), and *Nozick* (2001). He is now enjoying a quiet retirement in London and Bromsgrove.

Ernie Lepore is Professor of Philosophy at Rutgers University; he works in philosophy of language and mind and cognitive science. His most recent book is *Insensitive Semantics* (2004).

Kirk Ludwig is Professor of Philosophy at the University of Florida. He is co-author of *Donald Davidson: Meaning, Truth, Language and Reality* (2005) and *Donald Davidson's Truth Theoretic Semantics* (2007), with Ernie Lepore. He is editor of *Donald Davidson* (2003). He has published articles on a variety of topics in philosophy of language, philosophy of mind, epistemology, and philosophy of action.

Alan Malachowski is Honorary Lecturer in Philosophy at the University of East Anglia. His publications include: *Richard Rorty* (2002), *The New Pragmatism* (2008), *Reading Rorty* (ed., 2002), *Pragmatism*, 3 vols. (ed., 2004), *Richard Rorty*, 4 vols. (ed., 2002), and *The Cambridge Companion to Pragmatism* (ed., 2009).

Marie McGinn is Professor of Philosophy at the University of York. She is the author of *Wittgenstein and the Philosophical Investigations* (1997) and *Elucidating the Tractatus: Wittgenstein's Early Philosophy of Logic and Language* (2006), as well as articles on Wittgenstein, philosophy of mind, and skepticism.

A. W. Moore is Professor of Philosophy at the University of Oxford. His publications include *The Infinite* (2nd edn. 2001), *Points of View* (1997), and *Noble in Reason, Infinite in Faculty: Themes and Variations in Kant's Moral and Religious Philosophy* (2003). He has also edited three anthologies: *Meaning and Reference* (1993), *Infinity* (1993), and *Philosophy as a Humanistic Discipline* (2006), the last of which is a collection of essays by Bernard Williams, for whom he is a literary executor.

Jacob Ross is an assistant professor of philosophy at the University of Southern California. He is interested in, and works on, questions concerning normativity and rationality, along with a range of issues in ethics and metaethics.

Sonia Sedivy is Associate Professor of Philosophy at the University of Toronto. Her research focuses on philosophy of mind and perception, Wittgenstein, and philosophy of art, and her published papers range across these areas. She is currently completing a book that uses theory of perception and the later philosophy of Wittgenstein to address contemporary issues in theory of art.

Catherine Wilson is Distinguished Professor of Philosophy at the Graduate Center of the City University of New York. She is the author, most recently, of *Moral Animals: Ideals and Constraints in Moral Theory* (2004).

INTRODUCTION

CHRISTOPHER BELSHAW AND GARY KEMP

Our idea was simple. Philosophy as we practice it isn't well understood. We have wives, good friends, and colleagues in other departments who not only don't know what we do, but are almost afraid to ask. The subject hides its public face, and seems, often, intimidating, inbred, willfully obscure. So our idea was to invite one group of philosophers to discuss the thinking and writing of another group, to point out the importance and relevance of their work, and to direct the conversation to an audience not altogether, or even mainly, of insiders. This book, we hope, will help give our subject something of the recognition, and the status, that it deserves.

There are 12 philosophers represented here, all writing in English, and all of them active in the last third of the twentieth century. Some are now dead, others retired, still others with more good years ahead. They are all highly important figures in philosophy now: widely read, influential initiators of debate. Are they the top 12 philosophers of our time? Of course we make no such claim. But were someone to give a list of, say, the 20 key players, then, probably, the 12 here would be among them. They are not of a piece. Contemporary philosophy is considerably more diverse than it was a half century ago, and than it is commonly thought to be. And the writers represented here, though selected primarily for merit and not so much for variety, together deal in a range of subdisciplines. Anyone knowing something about most or all of them will know a fair bit about the subject as it is generally pursued today.

If, as we claim, philosophy is too little understood, where do people go wrong? Many think either that it deals with logic and arguments, or that it addresses and attempts to solve certain sorts of problems. Of course many think, arguably correctly, that these aspects coincide, and that it uses reason, logic, and arguments to solve, or attempt to solve, these particular problems. They think, generously, that its so dealing is useful, and the problems it addresses are big and important (and they might think this even without knowing in any detail what the methods or the content involve), or, less generously, that its concern with logic is obsessive, and its problems trivial, footling, mere playing with words. This mix of insights, half-truths, and outright misperceptions cannot just be dismissed. There is, we think, some obligation to explain what we do, and to point to its worth.

The Past

Go back to its beginnings, to Anaximander and Thales, Socrates, Plato and Aristotle, Epicurus and Zeno. If the philosopher was then a lover of wisdom, he was in many respects indiscriminately so, concerned with what there is in the universe, how these things work, and how within it and among them we should best live. His subject was continuous with what we'll now recognize as science on the one hand and religion on the other, as well as with horse-training, cookery, theatre criticism, and etiquette. Christianity slows things down, and filters all inquiry through God, or at least through bishops, and philosophy's second period of greatness follows, after a lengthy hiatus, in the aftermath of the Reformation and the Renaissance. Questions about the natural world are permitted and required, and while Descartes may have pretensions to answer many of them just on his own, Locke is content to see himself as an under-laborer, working alongside Boyle, Huygens, Newton, and other members of the Royal Society in a cooperative enterprise well suited to an increasingly bourgeois and meritocratic age. Science, then, begins to separate itself from philosophy, the one a hands-on or empirical investigation into how the world works, the other more clearly focused on conceptual inquiry. "What is phlogiston?" might be a question for the former, with "What is knowledge?" a concern of the latter. Hume, going on for a century later, takes this a stage further. Seemingly a skeptic and atheist in an undeniably more secular society, he asks us to turn our philosophical attention on ourselves, to look within and to construct a science of man. Rather than viewing us as rational beings, only contingently embodied, made in the image of God, Hume sees the human mind as itself a part of nature, to be explored by similar means, operating in accord with similar laws. This doesn't for long remain a new province for philosophy, however, for just as questions about the external world separate off to become science, so this probing of the internal landscape fairly soon gives rise to the further new discipline of psychology. Philosophy is fecund but not family-minded: its children are ready to make their own way in the world, and do so with its blessing. English-language philosophy – and this is perhaps predominantly philosophy if not just in England, then still mainly in the British Isles – having at least helped give rise to a range of other subjects – economics, linguistics, political science – is both purified and diminished, engaging with an increasingly narrow range of questions in, as ever, a limited number of ways.

There was, however, a certain pause when philosophy proved to be a most possessive parent. For if Hume saw the human mind as itself a part of nature, then Kant, at the end of the eighteenth century, argued that the mind must – in a sense that continues to be debated among Kant scholars – contain nature: it must be the source of the most abstract laws of nature if it is to know anything at all. A place was thus marked out anew for philosophy as the Queen of the Sciences, and Kant-inspired "idealist" philosophies dominated Germany and, to a lesser extent, Great Britain until the dawn of the twentieth century. But Kantian arguments are so thoroughly dense that, even if there is no definitive refutation at hand, there are vanishingly few card-carrying Kantians today (which is not to say there are few Kant *scholars*). And it never came close to winning the argument in Great Britain. Partly this has been due to the sheer effort required to sustain its formidable complexity, and partly it is because there were always other view-points being expressed, especially in the relatively practical subjects such as morality and society. For every T. H. Green or A. C. Bradley, for example, there was also a John Stuart Mill or Henry Sidgwick.

Some key developments

But even more decisively, the dawn of the twentieth century saw a new and contrary movement in Britain and, to lesser extent, Germany, which came to call itself analytic philosophy. The analytic philosophers accused the idealists of being, almost literally, caught up in their language. For Bertrand Russell and G. E. Moore and their followers, a new ideal of clarity rather than depth became the watchword, and this brought with it a new kind of optimism concerning what might be achieved – and not simply proclaimed – in philosophy.

Yet, perhaps paradoxically, this movement has in some respects contributed to philosophy's lack of popularity. For one of the things that puts people off analytic philosophy is the sheer difficulty of much of the writing; and this complaint is often accompanied by the protest that there is no need for this – why can't the philosopher simply put what he or she has to say in plain English, instead of this head-spinning jargon? Indeed, could it be that such language merely conceals an impoverishment of ideas? For, and this is asked by insiders and lookers-on alike, if there are genuinely philosophical questions to be asked, why are they not yet being answered? Thus the accusation that, bereft of its offspring, philosophy is no more than a series of footnotes to Plato. And thus too the still persistent image of the philosopher: Oxbridge, tweedy, port-passing, and insisting yet again both that people say precisely what they mean, and that what they mean is, from the point of view of its philosophical interest, mostly either confused or empty. Not a few of today's professionals were told, in their undergraduate days, that philosophy was merely an armchair game. No wonder, then, that the subject has relatively few friends.

To this there is a simple rebuttal, even if it will not silence everyone. A writer of a paper in, say, mathematics or biochemistry could write plain English just as well, but only at the cost of an indefensible expansion of what he or she writes. The same goes for philosophy. Definitions and principles that are well known among the intended audience may be left implicit, thereby condensing the argument. At bottom, it is no more mysterious than the practice in English of calling a child of your parent's brother or sister your "cousin." So although it's not surprising that philosophical writing is often impenetrable to the layperson, such is the price of theoretical advancement. This ideal of clarity – that everything philosophical is in principle translatable into the language of the street – is important to the self-image of the dominant trend in modern philosophy, and is also what sets it decidedly against some other traditions. When Martin Heidegger wrote of "*dasein*," or Jean-Paul Sartre wrote of the "for-itself," they presumably did not mean something that could in principle be defined literally in ordinary language; they meant something that would call for a special act of mind, an unusual conceptual leap of which there can at most be indirect proof (the language of religion, of course, sometimes has this character). Many philosophers do feel tugged in this direction at times – not only Sartre and Heidegger, but Wittgenstein, writing the concluding sections of his *Tractatus Logico-Philosophicus* in the German trenches of the First World War, or even Richard Rorty or John McDowell, both featured in this book, come to mind – but typically philosophers actively disdain that sort of word-making. At its worst, it is regarded as the mere naming, hence reification into a suitable object of study, of confusion.

Some would say that this is not simply a stylistic point, but a theoretical one. The schoolmaster's directive to "Be clear!" is of course well taken, but if the pupil asks "What do you mean?" there is little the schoolmaster can do by way of answer other than show some especially telling examples, hoping the pupil will catch on. By contrast, the model advanced by Russell and Gottlob Frege at the dawn of the twentieth century was, in effect, an analysis or theory of what clarity *is*. The bare bones of this ideal of clarity is the common part of Russell's and Frege's symbolic logics. It provides a certain anchoring for linguistic self-consciousness, and makes possible a newfound confidence both in the analysis of longstanding problems and in the articulate formulation of new problems and theories. Thus we find Rudolf Carnap in 1932 gleefully taking a sentence of Heidegger – "the nothing nothings" – and urging that this is merely a pseudo-statement, and literally nonsense.

This early ascendance of the new logic in philosophy – known as "logical positivism" – proved over-ambitious in its aims, and too ham-fisted in dividing sense from nonsense. Its leading early exponents – Ayer, Carnap, Wittgenstein – all spent their subsequent years backpedaling, in one way or another, from the claims of their youth (although only Wittgenstein rejected his earlier ideas completely). But logic itself retains its newfound status. In 1967 the Oxford philosopher Michael Dummett famously credited Frege with putting logic at the centre of philosophy, as well he might: logic based on the aforementioned system common to Russell and Frege can arguably represent all forms of reasoning, and is now part of the standard training that virtually all graduate students in philosophy receive. It is safe to say that the majority of books and articles in the field of philosophy – including the authors featured in this volume – are written in full consciousness of this development. Of course, only a small minority of those works explicitly employ the tools of symbolic logic; only when problems arise whose logical texture is too dense or otherwise hard to keep track of in terms of the ordinary idiom is the language of symbolic logic called for. Its influence is more often than not felt as a paradigm of clarity into which the philosopher's ordinary sentences could, if it came down to it, be translated.

The key figure in logic and its application in the latter half of the twentieth century is W. V. Quine, who is the first figure in our line-up. But as we look closer, we find the effect to be rather kaleidoscopic, not simply a blown-up version of the preceding bird's-eye view. Quine himself did not think of language as a determinate structure of propositions that only waited upon the philosopher to clarify; his actual position is considerably more complex. And others – not only the figures featured here, but writers such as Wittgenstein, Peter Strawson, John Austin, and Hilary Putnam – have borne various contentious relations to the simple view of philosophy as in some sense based on logic. Indeed, one of the aims of our book is to show that, beneath the easy uniformity imposed by certain words, the contemporary scene is abundantly diverse.

The Present

In many respects, philosophy flourishes today as never before. The past 50 years have seen a vast expansion: first, in the overall number of universities, and with it the production of graduates; second, in the number of philosophers employed, mainly within the universities, but increasingly, and as philosophers, in industry, think-tanks, medicine, the law; and third, the generation of philosophy publications – books, journals, encyclopedia entries, in print and on line. These factors are, of course, intimately related: we can say a little more about each, starting with the last.

Socrates wrote no books. Hume wrote several, but they veered more and more from mainstream philosophy, and, though he sought it, he never landed for himself a university position. Wittgenstein produced a slim volume early in his career and another, slightly less slim, at the end. But the intervening period was fallow, and he'd have been lucky, in the current climate, to hold onto his job. None of this is atypical. Until recently, people recognized as philosophers were either those whose writings, whatever their quantity and whatever their style, had created the right sort of stir, or those who held a university position, secure, undemanding, and who might produce a small handful of papers. All this has changed. Today's philosopher is almost certain to be employed by a university, as a philosopher, and will be subject to considerable pressure to generate a steady and measurable output. Our subjects here are or were near-lifetime professionals, well known and well regarded by their peers, makers of books and articles, active on the lecture and conference circuit, nurturers of young blood. And they are, or were, ambitious, not so much for themselves (though perhaps they've all been that) as for philosophy, taking it seriously, believing in it, and thinking its results worthwhile. One reason for calling them modern, for branding them with what some may see as an old-fashioned term, is just here, in this commitment to a sort of progress, and to philosophy as an aid to that progress. Another reason, connected but nevertheless distinct, is in their belief in ratiocinative processes – logic, argument, putting things as clearly as possible – as means to that progress. English-language philosophy may be hard, sometimes, to understand. But it takes no pleasure in this.

Consider the contrast between this ideally perspicuous, broadly analytical, and, as we are suggesting, forward-looking approach and what is often seen as its rival, that species of the discipline that we best know as continental philosophy. Through most of the twentieth century, if not before (for it's often said that the divide goes back to Kant), there's been both difference and hostility here, with us seeing them as wayward and indulgent mystifiers, and they in turn thinking of us as privileging form over content, pursuing logic and analysis to the end, but overlooking all the questions that matter. There is something in this: English philosophy was for a time unexciting, even complacent; and, in turning its back on what was offered to clarity by Frege and Russell, its European counterpart has been not only ambitious but garbled. There was a suspicion, particularly during the Cold War, of its being too frequently, and often unpersuasively, politicized, and more recently, a general wearying at its relativism, its constant repositioning and hunger for the new. In several of its current manifestations, continental philosophy seems both more pessimistic and more playful than its competitor.

Yet these differences are becoming perhaps less pronounced. Continental philosophy may have, even now, the greater cachet with the public – its best-known exponents could as reliably fill a hall as a middle-ranking rock star – but its overall influence is on the wane. Increasingly restricted to France and parts of Germany, losing its grip even in literature departments, repeatedly shaken or stirred by scandal, it is at the same time making real, though modest, inroads into the rival camp. One of our 12, Richard Rorty, went over to the other side mid-career, but he has nevertheless effected a certain *rapprochement*. Opposition between and within departments – and this has led sometimes to a complete rupture – is less obvious than it once was; and there are more conferences and journals that are other than unambiguously partisan. Perhaps both the mellowing and the decline of continental philosophy were inevitable; the permeability of European borders, the ease of travel, and the unstoppable spread of the English, or American, language all contribute to this. To put it crudely, with a globalized economy comes a homogeneity in thinking. The upshot is that what we are calling modern philosophy is, undeniably, in the ascendance.

That is broad brush. There are still more detailed questions about what this philosophy is concerned with and about how it is to be situated both within the academy and within the broader culture. The academy first.

Science

The relation that philosophy bears to science has long been very much a matter for philosophical dispute, and hence not a matter for anyone but philosophers to decide – it is not a matter for biologists, university bosses, or the voting public. Descartes saw the role of philosophy as providing a priori conceptual foundations, and some of the content, for physics. Early twentieth-century empiricists tended to see philosophy as hermetically sealed within the a priori, whereas science is wholly empirical or a posteriori. Quine saw philosophy as distinguishable from so-called empirical science only by degree, in the relative abstractness and generality of its subject-matter. And there are competing accounts of the "scientific method" – or, in some cases, a denial that there is any one such thing. But whatever the truth about these big issues, philosophy and science converge on more localized issues today than ever before. An assuredly incomplete list of such things includes: evolution, cosmology, consciousness, the interpretation of quantum theory, probability, decision theory, perception, semantics, pragmatics, the foundations of mathematics, evolutionary explanations of culture and morality. And it is not just a matter of a detached philosopher pontificating, like a priest, about how evolution, for example, is real; a philosopher interested in evolution is more likely to contribute to the mathematical modeling of gene populations, or discover and comment upon formalizations of evolutionary reasoning. All these things and more are discussed and furthered by philosophers as well as by scientists, and for the most part it would be idle to try to identify the philosophical threads running through them.

There is no one reason for this, though it is obvious in a general way that when a science is bedevilled with paradox or is counterintuitive, then a philosopher may be brought in. But recent developments have intensified this trend. In the 1950s and '60s, philosophy was under the spell of the late Wittgenstein and of the "ordinary language" philosophy of John Austin, Gilbert Ryle, and others. And in its more extreme forms it tended to hold that, insofar as a question is philosophical, it is not in any way scientific. But by the 1970s, a new breed of scientific philosophers had hatched, partly as a result of the widening of Quine's influence: Hilary Putnam, David Lewis, and many others who took the interpretation of natural science to be at the top of the list of philosophical concerns. And now today there is yet more incentive to think of philosophy as synergetically connected to science: to a much greater extent than before, the pressure to publish, to attend and participate in conferences, to win grants, and to impress the judges of the UK Research

Assessment Exercise collectively have the effect of encouraging activity that looks like progress, aspires to achievable objectives, and involves collaboration. In those respects, there is nothing like science.

Some of this might be wishful thinking. Scientists confidently build on what has come before, and their results get written down as items that students of the subject must learn. Perhaps philosophy can make such claims only when saying goodbye to newly christened domains; it may have been a philosophical task, for example, when Frege and others invented propositional logic, but the realization that it could serve as the basis of computer science led to practical questions about how to implement it, rather than any lingering philosophical questions. But philosophy can make, at least, a sort of negative process: for example, Cartesian dualism – Descartes's idea that the mind is a non-spatial entity that exists independently of the body – is now generally regarded as refuted. Yet it takes some philosophical reasoning to understand both the precise view and exactly what is wrong with it.

History and literature

Alongside its unsettled relation to science, there is need to consider philosophy's ambivalent relation to its own history. Whereas its continental counterpart is on the whole happy to be historically embedded, to see its endeavors as deriving from a particular time, and the concerns of that time, English-language philosophy is less certain of how to fathom its location in the bigger scheme.

On the one hand, there are those who, pursuing the science analogy, have simply no interest in philosophy's past, seeing it as a series of errors and confusions best left behind. On the other, in contrast, are the resolute antiquarians. Persuaded that the problems are unreal, all that is left is to chart the ways in which particular individuals, at particular times, went wrong. Most of us, however, are camped somewhere or other in the middle ground and, partly through training, partly through inclination, have some, but not an overriding, concern for history, either merely nodding toward its major figures or – more extreme – pursuing to some degree the procedures of rational reconstruction, holding that these figures had important things to say to us, but that, lacking the techniques of modern logic, they were unable to say them. Bernard Williams assiduously, and perhaps surprisingly, pursues such an end in his somewhat anomalous book on Descartes; but all of those represented here fall somewhere in this middle ground, taking philosophy's history seriously, but holding as well that it has a future.

A further respect in which the subject is at odds with the science model can be mentioned here. Throughout its career, philosophy has had an evident, even if not always acknowledged, close relationship to literature. From Plato on, a clear majority of its stars have been writers of elegance and finesse. This is, we suggest, neither a coincidence nor a suspect and regrettable victory of presentation over content. For if philosophical conversations are indeed the ones we need, and need at particular times, to have, rather than a take-it-or-leave-it issuing of discoveries or results, then it is near essential that its practitioners do what is required to get an audience on board. Otherwise they risk going unheard. So, even if there are from time to time suggestions that it should be a collaborative and self-effacing enterprise, modern philosophy is still, as we think is right, open to personality. And the writers here, as we hope will be clear, are more than able crafters of language. They work effectively alone, adopting different styles for different audiences. They are conscious of and careful with imagery and metaphor, and unafraid to reveal and make use of biographical details; thus Nagel's spider, Parfit's poetry, and Davidson's use of Shakespeare.

We now want to say something about the subject's main divisions, and to point to some of the ways that these are aligned with the writers we consider.

Metaphysics, Epistemology, and Philosophy of Mind

All three of these labels are liable to strike fear in the hearts of the relatively uninitiated; and to some extent their popular meanings are liable to mislead. We'll treat them gently and in order.

Metaphysics does not deal with the paranormal, the astrological, or self-help by dint of crystals and herbs. As the term itself implies, it is, broadly speaking, about a framework within which the physical world takes place. It is a step more abstract than physics itself. So a key concept is that of *possibility*; the physical world is as it is, but, we can ask, *could* it have been different? If so, in what sense? What are the constraints? Other concepts appertaining to the framework include existence, time, causation, object, properties – all these concepts are *used* in describing the world, but what about the concepts themselves? What about, as we can hardly help saying, the *natures* of these things? Metaphysics was frowned upon by the logical positivists; "metaphysics" had become a term of abuse. But the past 50 years have seen its triumphant resurrection. The connection with the philosophy of science is evident, but much of the activity has been inspired by the problems themselves, chiefly via the paradigm-resetting work of David Lewis and Saul Kripke in the 1960s.

Epistemology, or the theory of knowledge, is a venerable institution; it goes back at least to Plato, who posed its central question: What is knowledge? It remains a source of some embarrassment that this remains unanswered; but as so many answers, often highly sophisticated, have turned out to be dead ends, that in itself is generally counted as progress, as mentioned before. The attempts do offer an especially clear snapshot of the methods of philosophers. On the one hand, we have a theory: knowledge is X, where X is something informative (it would not do to propose, for example, that knowledge is what we have when we know something). On the other, we have what we call our intuitions; we think that this would be a case of knowledge, that that would not. Are they, as the theory predicts, cases of X, or not? It sounds simple: we want the X-cases to match knowledge cases, and the non-X-cases to match the non-knowledge cases. But, amazingly enough, no exact match has been found. Quine may have been at his wisest when he said that ordinary knowledge claims – the stuff of our intuitions as just sketched – are clouded by shifting interests that it would be unavailing if not impossible to sum up in a theory; perhaps, when doing philosophy, we should give up the word "knowledge" as a bad job. Nevertheless, the field remains very active. One of the most interesting attempts was proposed by Robert Nozick in the form of "truth-tracking"; today, much is made of the role that probability evidently plays in estimates of the status of possible states of knowledge.

The philosophy of mind is not about spiritual awakening, or about how to be smarter or more effective in interpersonal relationships. It is one area of philosophy that can be traced primarily to a single figure: René Descartes. Paying attention to a simple argument – "I think, therefore I am" – Descartes deduced that the mind is something that must be distinct from any physical thing. This is the celebrated thesis of Cartesian dualism mentioned earlier; he reasoned further that there is no barrier to its survival beyond the death of the body. There are serious problems with the thesis, most of which Descartes recognized and tried to solve, but for the most part unsuccessfully. Chief among these is the problem of the interaction between mind and body. I can cause physical events by willing, and they affect me through my perception of them; but if the mind has no physical properties, how are these things possible? It isn't, say most philosophers and psychologists nowadays. And so, since the 1950s, the race has been on to find a theory of the mind that grants the human brain its rightful place, and to explain the mentalistic concepts – thought, belief, perception, desire, and so on – in a way that is consistent with physicalism: the thesis that there is no stuff in the universe except what physics says there is. Jerry Fodor has been perhaps the prime mover in the development of the theory that the mind is in essence a computer. But Descartes-like doubts have re-emerged in more subtle forms in the work of Kripke and Nagel; John McDowell, meanwhile, advertises a cure for, rather than a refutation of, Cartesianism.

It used to be – before about the 1970s – that problems of these three sorts tended to be addressed through the lens of language, and the philosophy of language had more prestige than it does now. The "linguistic turn" attributed to Wittgenstein, Ayer, Carnap, and others tended to hold that all philosophical questions were really questions about language, and many – such as the questions of metaphysics – would disappear under linguistic analysis. Rorty has pointed out that, as in many such episodes in the history of our subject, that view held many contestable presuppositions, and proved a lot harder in practice to carry out. But turning to subjects more decidedly linguistic – meaning, reference, truth – the debates remain very much alive, and the question how to draw the line between what is and what isn't remains a pressing matter for philosophers of language. The views of Quine, Davidson, and Kripke slice through these issues in many ways, and remain required reading for those interested not only in philosophy of language, but also in metaphysics, philosophy of mind, and the theory of knowledge.

Ethics

An even more prominent aspect of late twentieth-century philosophy is the focus on moral and political philosophy and ethics. How is this to be explained? What needs first to be noted is a distinction between normative ethics, on the one hand, and descriptive ethics, or metaethics, on the other. Whereas the former is concerned with the content of moral dicta, with deciding what we should do, or how we should live, the latter puts the emphasis on form – do such dicta embody truths or tastes, can we get an ought from an is? – and so on. It's probably fair to say that the emphasis for 100 or so years now has been on the latter, and fair to say also that from early to the middle of the last century, the subject was at its most arid. Under the influence of positivism, subjectivist or emotivist accounts very much held sway, with all claims about what is good seen merely as disguised allusions to what we happen to approve of. Certainly, sustained challenges to that view, and with it the resurgence of normative ethics, is a very recent phenomenon, going back only to the 1960s or '70s. This shift hasn't always been well met, with considerable numbers insisting that it isn't for philosophy to tell us how to behave, and holding that that is the province, rather, of religion, appropriate societal pressure, or family upbringing. But, first, such claims are far from obviously true – we'd need a philosophical argument to implement the subject's boundaries; and, second, at least when speedily made, they reveal too little interest in why this resurgence has come about. It isn't difficult to explain. Religion's hold, social stability, and national and cultural boundaries have long made for a considerable degree of unity about the content of morality. Whether people have in fact agreed about what is to be done, or whether they've felt unable to articulate and push their disagreements isn't so relevant here: the upshot is at least (although there have of course been a number of notable exceptions) the appearance of a consensus.

This is no longer so. There is both less agreement and fewer scruples about giving disagreement its head. Moreover, university expansion and modernization have made for a much broader interface between academic and real-world concerns. Perhaps too we should see increasing democratization as generating an appetite for discussion rather than confrontation when there is a dispute as to what to do. Debates about homosexuality and censorship in the UK and about civil rights and the fallout from Vietnam in the US were among the first areas where philosophy was noticeably and effectively involved in revising the moral outlook. But of course there are many other issues – concerning bioethics, animal rights and welfare, the environment, business practices – that are now standard fare for philosophical analysis and comment. A conspicuous foregrounding of moral disagreement, with the term "ethics" – ethical investment, ethical foreign policy, research ethics – in particular having had a wholesale and seemingly successful makeover, is now part of contemporary style; and academic philosophy has both contributed to and capitalized on this, giving a sense that things are moving forward. Yet one of the surprises of modern times has been the resilience of religion. So moral debate doesn't involve just variant secular views but a confrontation of these views with faith, and, increasingly, faiths. What remains to be seen is whether this trend will be long-lasting or, like the late flowering of a consumptive, merely a blip. At present it acts somewhat like a brake, and is, for many, unnerving.

Peter Singer is, of course, of the philosophers represented here, the one who most keenly represents this trend, but others – Williams, Nagel, Rawls, Nozick – have, in their professional capacities, engaged systematically and significantly with some of the issues mentioned above. And Parfit ends his book on a highly optimistic note, pointing out that this secular ethics is very much in its infancy, and claiming for it that we might well have high hopes.

Philosophy and Culture

What now is the place for philosophy, and for the philosopher, in the wider culture? Anglo-American philosophy seems in many ways to be marginalized, and to have marginalized itself. It is doubtful whether even half the names in our 12 could be said to be familiar to readers of the *London* or the *New York Review of Books*. Contrast the position here with other disciplines: history, science, even economics have, within their major practitioners, several who have successfully turned outwards, balancing an academic career with writing for, and engaging with, the broader public. This is rare in philosophy. There is a handful of evident exceptions – Russell, Chomsky, Berlin, Ayer possibly, and some still remember Professor Joad – but they come mostly from an earlier time. Although Nagel has written an introductory book clearly aimed at a wider market, and Parfit published some of his work on cosmology in the *LRB*, today, in general, the serious and popular are kept apart.

This is curious. As we've noted, the subject itself is undergoing something of a revival both within the school and university setting, and, at least where moral philosophy is concerned, within the public eye. As we've also noted, there is a regrettable contrast here with continental philosophy, which appears well enough embedded within the intellectual milieu of mainland Western Europe, and has made not yet defunct forays into their equivalents in the UK and the US. But English-language philosophy is either self-effacing or ignored. Which is it, and why?

What might first suggest itself as an explanation, especially in light of the contrast just reiterated between Anglo-American and continental philosophy, is that there is a general anti-elitism, a mistrust of the intellectual, an overall leveling, that characterizes public life in both the US and, perhaps even more so, in the UK. This has increased markedly over the past half century, and reveals itself in the styles and content of TV and the press, constant pressures on public funding for libraries and the arts, and, we'd suggest, a simultaneous and non-coincidental increase in and skepticism about education. Can it be surprising that in such societies there isn't a dominant role for philosophy? Well, indeed, there's something in this, but three further factors, not unrelated, can help explain the particular position in which philosophy finds itself. First, the subject can, as we've allowed, appear to get nowhere. It can seem to involve endless and fruitless debate. Contrast science, where genuine and undeniable results are achieved. There is some stigma attached in hitching one's star to failure. Second, and related, there is the too blunt contrast that many are disposed to make between fact and opinion. The phenomenon here is fairly closely connected to what seems to be a general understanding, in the countries being considered, of the principles and procedures of democracy, and again with the adversarial system practiced in both the law and in politics. Perhaps over-enamored with the model of the market, the idea seems to be that we simply count heads on some contentious issue, rather than endeavor, collectively, to talk toward the truth. Thus it seems to many that where hard facts run out, we are left with mere opinion. So if philosophers cannot prove their point, they speak with no real authority. Third, again connected, there is the cult of the personality. Even when and where there is some interest in philosophical matters, it is more than likely that some well-known figure, perhaps already with a TV contract, will be consulted: a novelist, or politician, or celebrity chef.

This is a bleak picture, but there are already some signs that it is changing, and some recognition that philosophers do, in relation to this unsettlingly complex world, have a distinctive contribution to make. To further such change, there needs to be a wider acknowledgment, first, that strategies for clear thinking exist, are not innate, and can often but not unfailingly be taught. And, second, that such strategies can be usefully and fruitfully applied to a range of problems, some of them perhaps seemingly timeless, others among those which, for a variety of reasons, are peculiarly pressing today. Anyone doubting either the efficacy or relevance of philosophy needs only to look further into the works of the 12 philosophers represented here.

1 QUINE

A. W. MOORE

1 Introduction

Willard Van Orman Quine (1908–2000) is considered by many to have been the greatest analytic philosopher of the postwar period. He was born, raised, and educated, through to graduation, in Ohio. He did his graduate work at Harvard University, where he wrote a dissertation in formal logic. Most of his early work was likewise in formal logic, though the dissertation provided an indication of broader philosophical concerns that would stay with him throughout his career. In 1932 he was awarded a traveling fellowship to Europe. This gave him an opportunity to attend meetings of the Vienna Circle, a group of between 30 and 40 thinkers from a range of disciplines who met regularly in Vienna between the wars to discuss philosophy. This group was unified by the aim of making philosophy scientific, and to this end its members made special use of recent developments in logic with which Quine was very familiar. He subsequently spent time in Prague and Warsaw, and later described this period as intellectually the most rewarding of his life. This was principally because it brought him into contact with Rudolf Carnap, who was himself a member of the Vienna Circle and one of the foremost advocates of the logical positivism with which the Circle had come to be associated. Much of Quine's work can be seen as a response to Carnap's own version of logical positivism, parts of which Quine thoroughly espoused, parts of which he just as thoroughly opposed, and all of which had a deep and lasting influence on his philosophical career.

Apart from some short visiting positions around the world, Quine spent the whole of that career at Harvard, until his retirement in the mid-1970s. He was a prolific and exceptional writer, with a remarkable and distinctive style. That style was marked by elegance, wit, and clarity, as well as an extraordinary economy of expression. Two of his best-known and most influential books, *From a Logical Point of View* and *Word and Object*, appeared at a comparatively early stage in his career, in 1953 and 1960 respectively. (The first of these is a collection of essays that includes the two classics "On What There Is" and "Two Dogmas of Empiricism.") Although there were changes of mind in his many subsequent publications, these were invariably of a subtle nature, and the fundamental views for which Quine is famed had already received forthright expression in these two books. Much of his later work was concerned with developing and refining these views. Much of it was also a self-conscious exercise in the economy of expression to which I have already referred. The two books *Pursuit of Truth* and *From Stimulus to Science*, both of which appeared when he was in his 80s, and each of which is only 100 pages long, are astonishing compendia of all his main ideas. Their very concision means that they serve as poor introductions to his work, but, for aficionados, they are invaluable points of reference and much to be savored. They have also excited fascinating discussion about how far some of the shifts of emphasis and reformulations vis-à-vis his earlier work are really changes of mind of the sort I indicated above. However that may be, in common with the earlier work, they reveal Quine to be something rarely encountered in the analytic tradition: a systematic philosopher with a profound synoptic vision.

To understand that vision we need to return to Carnap.

2 Carnap's Logical Positivism

Logical positivism is a modified form of empiricism. Empiricism, in its purest form, is the doctrine that all knowledge is derived from sense experience. Logical positivists espouse something that is weaker than this in one significant respect, stronger in another.

It is weaker in as much as it concedes the existence of some knowledge that is not derived from sense experience – but only knowledge of a very special kind. Logical positivists draw a distinction between analytic truths and synthetic truths. Analytic truths are those whose truth depends on their meaning alone, albeit sometimes in recondite ways that take some working out. To understand an analytic truth is already to be in a position, at least in principle, to tell that it is true. Putative examples are trivial truths such as that all bachelors are unmarried, and mathematical truths such as that no square of a positive integer is exactly twice another. By contrast, synthetic truths are truths whose truth depends on something in addition to their meaning. Having understood a synthetic truth, one must rely on independent investigation to tell that it is true. A putative example is that water expands when it freezes. The logical positivists' position is that knowledge of analytic truths, and such knowledge alone, is an exception to the doctrine that all knowledge derives from sense experience.

In another respect logical positivists espouse something stronger than pure empiricism. For they espouse a doctrine with a semantic component as well as an epistemological component, that is to say a component that concerns meaning as well as a component that concerns knowledge. They insist that, unless a sentence expresses a truth that can in principle be determined in one of the two ways just indicated, or a falsehood whose negation can in principle be determined in one of these two ways, then it does not express a truth or a falsehood at all and is, to that extent, strictly meaningless. This so-called "verification theory of meaning" arguably casts each of the following sentences as strictly meaningless:

Every 24 hours each physical object in the universe doubles in size.
There is never any justification for killing another human being.
God moves in mysterious ways.

Carnap's own brand of logical positivism has one crucial further feature. He holds that the most fundamental of these distinctions, the distinction between the true and the false, is always drawn relative to some linguistic framework. By a linguistic framework, he means some systematic way of speaking about entities of a certain kind, such as the set of arithmetical rules that allow us to speak about positive integers. The decision whether or not to adopt any given framework is not itself a matter of truth or falsity at all, but rather a matter of the advantages and disadvantages of doing so. Thus, if we ask whether there is any positive integer whose square is exactly twice that of another, then we are asking an "internal" question within a particular framework. (As it happens, the answer in this case is "no." And this answer can be determined independently of sense experience: it is analytic.) If we ask whether we are right to accept the existence of positive integers in the first place, then we are asking an "external" question about whether we are right to adopt that framework. This takes us beyond the realm of the true and the false. But it is a legitimate question for all that. It is a question about how to speak, and, although there is no *truth* of the matter, there are important practical issues about the costs and benefits of speaking in this particular way.

In sum, then, Carnap holds the following package of ideas:

- a linguistic framework comprises rules for speaking about entities of some kind;
- within the framework there are truths about these entities;
- among these truths there are some, the analytic ones, whose truth depends solely on the rules of the framework (or, in other words, whose truth depends solely on their meaning);
- the truth of the rest, the synthetic ones, can be determined by appeal to sense experience, and *only* by appeal to sense experience;
- the decision whether to adopt the framework is not itself a matter of truth or falsity.

Very roughly, Quine accepts the core empiricism in this package of ideas, but baulks at the various modifications. What are his objections to these modifications? To answer this question, we need first to consider the particular form that his own empiricism takes.

3 Quine's Naturalism

Quine is a naturalist. That is, he holds that there is no higher authority, when it comes to determining the general character of reality, than what has in fact led us to our current broad consensus about its general character – which is to say, the methods and principles of the natural sciences, and paradigmatically of physics.

Such naturalism is not itself entailed by empiricism. True, natural scientists justify their findings by appeal to sense experience, as they would have to if empiricism were correct and if their findings had any claim to the title of knowledge. But empiricism does not entail that their findings do have any claim to the title of knowledge, still less that they have a unique claim to it. Even if physics is the best we can do in trying to derive a general systematic account of reality from our sense experience, it is not dictated to us by our sense experience. Our sense experience does not rule out alternative such accounts, say accounts whereby space has some very different geometry with corresponding implications concerning the shrinking and stretching of bodies as they move about, or accounts whereby reality is not fundamentally physical at all but fundamentally mental. Quine himself would be the first to insist on this. This is what he means when he says that physics is underdetermined by the evidence (*PT* §§41–3). Furthermore some people, if not Quine himself, will worry about the compass of physics, and indeed about the compass of the natural sciences more broadly. Such people may be perfectly happy to accept the findings of the natural sciences, at least provisionally. But they will urge that there are many matters on which these findings are silent and on which, say, the findings of the *social* sciences, or even such "self-evident truths" as appear at the beginning of the US Declaration of Independence, have as much right to count as part of "our current broad consensus about the general character of reality." None of the qualms that we might have, in light of these reflections, about privileging physics in the way in which Quine does, would be an obvious offence against *empiricism*. Quine's naturalism, to repeat, is not entailed by empiricism. Nevertheless, that is the context within which his own empiricism finds expression.

Why is Quine a naturalist? Partly because of the spectacular success that the natural sciences have enjoyed when it comes to predicting the future and thereby controlling and modifying the environment. But there is an even more basic reason. Ultimately, Quine does not think that there is any alternative. Physics *is* the best we can do, or at any rate is the best we have been able to do so far, in trying to derive a general systematic account of reality from our sense experience. It *must* therefore be our point of departure. It may not be our destination: in 100 years' time we may look back on our current scientific theories and see them as irremediably flawed in certain critical ways. But if so, then this will be because we have got there from here, and this in turn will be because we have done the only thing we can do starting from here, namely employ the procedures of currently accepted scientific methodology. If we were to step outside our current broad consensus altogether, in an effort to raise theory-neutral questions about how our current scientific theories stand in relation to reality, then we should have no basis for any further progress. In the famous image of the Austrian philosopher of science Otto Neurath (1882–1945) – an image that Quine himself often uses – we are in a boat and the only way in which we can rebuild the boat is by rebuilding it plank by plank, while remaining all the while afloat in it (*WO* 3).

Quine's naturalism, to repeat once more, does not follow from his empiricism. It is rather the reverse. Quine sees his empiricism as following from his naturalism. Thus he writes:

> It is a finding of natural science itself, however fallible, that our information about the world comes only through impacts on our sensory receptors. . . . Even telepathy and clairvoyance are scientific options, however moribund. It would take some extraordinary evidence to enliven them, but, if that were to happen, then empiricism itself . . . would go by the board. (*PT* 19–21)

Empiricism is itself an empirically testable theory then. It is not part of some philosophical propædeutic to scientific investigation. For Quine, there is no such thing.

That is why, in the quotation above, our sensory experience is itself construed in scientific terms, as "impacts on our sensory receptors." And this in turn connects with yet another part of Quine's overall vision: his physicalism. He holds that there are no facts, not even facts about our thoughts and experiences, that are not ultimately physical facts, that is facts about how things are physically (see section 7 below). Where exactly does *this* stand in relation to his naturalism? That depends on how "the physical" is construed. If the physical is construed in terms of our current physics, then Quine's physicalism is best seen as a further consequence of his naturalism, a consequence which, just like his empiricism, might have to be rejected in the light of evidence that challenged current physics itself. Quine sometimes construes the physical in this way. It is in this vein that he writes, "The science game is not committed to the physical" (*PT* 20). But if the physical is construed in a more regulative way, not in terms of current physics, but in terms of some *ideal* physics, then his physicalism is something closer to an evidence-insensitive methodological principle. And Quine sometimes construes the physical in *this* way. It is in this vein that he writes, in "Goodman's *Ways of Worldmaking*":

> If the physicist suspected there was any event that did not consist in a redistribution of the elementary states of his physical theory, he would seek a way of supplementing his theory. Full coverage in this sense is the very business of physics, and only of physics. (*TT* 98)

Either way, there is a special deference to physics, whereby, as Quine himself puts it, "nothing happens in the world, not the flutter of an eyelid, not the flicker of a thought, without some redistribution of microphysical states" (ibid.).

Now so far, there is nothing in Quine's vision that obviously distances him either from logical positivism in general or from Carnap's logical positivism in particular. Both his vision and the logical positivist vision are embellishments of empiricism. True, they are different embellishments. But we have seen nothing yet to bring them into conflict with each other. Logical positivists share Quine's respect for science. In my very first reference to the Vienna Circle (see section 1), I mentioned their aim of making philosophy scientific. Where, then, does the conflict lie?

4 The External/Internal Distinction and the Analytic/Synthetic Distinction

As far as Carnap's version of logical positivism is concerned, one useful way of broaching this question is to consider the very claim that there are fundamental particles of the sort postulated by current physics. What is Quine's attitude to this claim? He takes it to be a basic truth about reality (see section 7 below). He is not dogmatic about this. As we have seen, he concedes that current physics may eventually be rejected. But, pending any such rejection, all he *can* take this claim to be, granted his naturalism, is a basic truth about reality, neither more nor less. What is Carnap's attitude to the claim? He takes it to be, on the most natural way of construing it, a decision, or, better, the announcement of a decision, to adopt a particular linguistic framework, neither true nor false. This, certainly, is a point of disagreement.

The fact is that Quine sees no rationale for Carnap's distinction between external questions and internal questions. When the forces of the world impinge on people's surfaces, they hit back by making noises and marks on paper which record their conception of what is going on. And there are various dimensions of assessment for these noises and marks. Two in particular are pertinent to this issue. One is with respect to truth. The other is with respect to desiderata in the systems of classification involved: power, elegance, economy, user-friendliness, and suchlike. But there is neither need nor justification, in Quine's view, for keeping these separate; for seeing the latter as bearing on a choice of framework and the former as bearing on assertions made within the framework. If people respond to their sensory experience – the impacts on their sensory receptors – by claiming that there are quarks, or that there are positive integers, or that the number of quarks in the known universe is greater than some positive integer, then, in each case, they are simply asserting how they take things to be. Their classifications may have the aesthetic-cum-utilitarian virtues advertised above; and other classifications may have these virtues to a greater or lesser extent. But what these people have claimed is, in each case, straightforwardly true or false.

For similar reasons, Quine utterly repudiates the idea that there is a dichotomy between analytic truths and synthetic truths – a feature of logical positivism in all its guises, not just Carnap's version. In his celebrated essay "Two Dogmas of Empiricism" Quine identifies this idea as one of two dogmas that characterize "modern" empiricism and urges that there is no satisfactory way of effecting the dichotomy. We might suggest, for instance, that an analytic truth is one that would be true whatever reality was like; or that it could not be denied without self-contradiction; or that someone who genuinely took it to be false would thereby betray a misunderstanding of the language, whereas someone who genuinely took a synthetic truth to be false could simply be mistaken about reality. But, for Quine, these are variations on a single incoherent theme. They all presuppose that each individual truth has its own meaning, determining, by itself, what is required of reality to make that truth true.

Quine's view is that, when the forces of the world impinge on people's surfaces and they hit back by making noises and marks that record their conception of what is going on, they do so by making noises and marks that *collectively* record their conception of what is going on. None of their claims makes its own isolable contribution to the story that they have to tell. (This is the *holism* for which Quine is renowned and which he in turn finds in the work of the physicist and philosopher Pierre Duhem (1861–1941; TDE 41).) Suppose that, when the forces of the world impinge some more, these people find themselves reconsidering their earlier conception of what is going on. Perhaps they used to claim that all swans are white, and now they find themselves having what seems for all the world like an encounter with a black swan. There are all sorts of ways in which they might accommodate this unexpected sense experience. They might simply reject their earlier claim that all swans are white. They might continue to claim that all swans are white and dismiss this apparent counterexample as an illusion of some kind. They might continue to claim that all swans are white, *accept* that here is a black swan, and reject whatever principle precludes doing both of these things at once. There is much to be said for or against each of these options, for instance in terms of how easy each of them would be to implement given its various repercussions. But there is nothing in the meaning of any of the claims these people used to make, considered in isolation, to force them to take one option rather than another.

The real target of Quine's attack, then, is the idea that each individual claim stands in its own relations of confirmation and confutation with different possible courses of sense experience. This, indeed, is the second dogma that he identifies in his essay, though he also claims that "the two dogmas are . . . at root identical" (ibid.). An analytic truth would be a truth that was confirmed by *any possible* sense experience. For Quine that makes no sense. Any truth we accept, even the truth that all bachelors are unmarried, is just part of our overall story about how things are, and, had our sense experience taken a different course, it would have been a candidate for rejection. For instance, had we noticed a high correlation, but not an exceptionless one, between being unmarried and having some psychological trait, and had we found it more convenient to align bachelorhood with the latter rather than the former, then we might well have acknowledged a few married bachelors. Likewise, a synthetic truth would be a truth that was confuted by some possible sense experience. But that too makes no sense for Quine. Any truth we accept could be preserved in the light of any possible evidence if we made suitable compensating adjustments to the rest of what we accept, most obviously if we dismissed the evidence as illusory.

It is natural to protest, in the bachelor example, that had we ventured, on those grounds, "There are some married bachelors," then we would simply have been changing the meaning of the word "bachelor." Indeed, in later writings Quine himself talks in similar terms. Commenting on the case of a "deviant logician" who tries to flout the law of non-contradiction by accepting something of the form "This is how things are and this is not how things are," Quine urges that such a person merely evidences a non-standard use of language – say, an idiosyncratic use of "not." "Here, evidently, is the deviant logician's predicament," writes Quine: "when he tries to deny the doctrine he only changes the subject" (*PL* 81). In "Two Dogmas of Empiricism," however, his position is less compromising, and the idea that each bit of language has its own monadic meaning which it might retain or lose through any change of doctrine is itself part of what is under attack.

In repudiating the dichotomy between analytic and synthetic truths, Quine is not denying that there are associated distinctions of degree. He readily concedes that, among the claims we currently accept, some would be more resistant to rejection than others. To use the eponymous metaphor of his book *The Web of Belief*, these claims are closer to the centre of the web of what we currently accept than the other claims are, and hence more directly connected to more of the rest of the web. So their rejection would necessitate more rejections elsewhere. And the more of the web we reject, the harder it is for us to maintain our grip on what we come to accept. Hence Quine's "maxim of minimum mutilation" (*PT* 14). The fact remains that the distinction of the kind which the logical positivists recognize, and which is deliberately designed to mitigate their empiricism, is anathema to Quine. His empiricism is of a purer form. He holds that *all* knowledge is derived from sense experience – albeit no individual item of knowledge is derived from any individual episode of sense experience.

5 The Indeterminacy of Translation

One consequence of these views, and one of Quine's best-known theses, is what he calls the indeterminacy of translation. This is the thesis that there can be two ways of translating from one language into another which are incompatible with each other even though neither is incompatible with anything that the speakers of the two languages are disposed to say or do; and, furthermore, that there is no fact of the matter, in such a case, concerning which way of translating is correct (though there may be pragmatic factors, such as simplicity, to tell in favor of one over the other).

To see how this thesis is related to the views just being canvassed, imagine yourself engaged in a project of radical translation. That is, imagine yourself trying to compile a bilingual dictionary for English and the language of some people with whom neither you nor any other English speaker has had any prior contact. And suppose that you have got as far as speculating, perhaps on excellent grounds, that one of the sentences they accept as true can be translated as "All swans are white." Now suppose that you see, for the first time, a group of them encountering a black swan, though this does not stop them from accepting the sentence in question as true. There are all sorts of hypotheses you might form. Perhaps they allowed for this possibility all along and your translation was imperfect. Perhaps they are dismissing this sense experience as an illusion. Perhaps they have started using one of the terms in their sentence in a new way, say the term that they previously used to denote swans. Perhaps they operate with some bizarre logic. To be sure, some of these hypotheses will come to mind much more naturally than others, depending on what exactly these people go on to say and do. But if Quine is right about the holistic interdependence of the claims they make, and of the claims you make, then *in principle* all of these hypotheses, and more besides, can, with suitable compensatory adjustments elsewhere, be kept alive. And this in turn will allow for incompatible ways of translating from their language into English.

There is a less severe example, due to Quine himself, which shows how the choice of a system of classification likewise allows for latitude in translation. The example is less severe in that it concerns differences of translation that impact only at the level of words, not of whole sentences (where they cancel out). Quine imagines a word in the alien language, "gavagai," whose use is akin to the use of "rabbit" in English. He urges that "gavagai" might just as well be rendered, not as "rabbit," but as "undetached part of a rabbit" (*WO* ch. 2). Again, nothing that the speakers of the alien language say or do can rule out this extravagant rendering if suitable compensatory adjustments are made elsewhere. Thus, suppose there is an alien construction which is naturally translated as "There are exactly two —s here." And suppose this construction is combined with the word "gavagai" to yield a whole sentence *S* which the speakers of the alien language accept as true when, and only when, there are exactly two rabbits manifest. Then this might seem decisive against a rendering of "rabbit" as "undetached part of a rabbit." For when there are exactly two rabbits manifest, there are many more than two undetached parts of a rabbit manifest. In fact, however, it is not decisive against that rendering. For the original construction might itself be translated differently. It might be translated, however artificially, as "There are exactly two —s here, unless —s are undetached parts of a rabbit, in which case there are exactly two rabbits here." Because these differences do not impact at the level of whole sentences – the two rival translations of *S* are in *some* sense equivalent, each amounting to the claim that there are exactly two rabbits present – Quine sometimes calls the indeterminacy that this example illustrates the indeterminacy of reference rather than the indeterminacy of translation (e.g. *PT* §20). It is a less radical indeterminacy. But the lessons to be learned are essentially the same.

And what of Quine's insistence that there is no fact of the matter in these cases concerning which way of translating is correct? He means this quite literally. Recall that, for Quine, the only facts are physical facts, facts about how things are physically (see section 3 above). The physical facts of these cases, including all the facts about how speakers of the alien language interact with their environment, do not themselves rule out any of the rival translation schemes. The whole point, in a way, is that we have the conceptual resources to discriminate more finely than the facts themselves can.

To be sure, this raises the question of why Quine thinks that the facts "stop" where they do. For, as we noted earlier, they themselves already discriminate more finely than the evidence can: thus Quine's insistence that physics is underdetermined by the evidence (section 3 above). Many critics have wondered why Quine allows the facts to go beyond the evidence but not all the way to settling these differences of translation. The key, once again, is Quine's naturalism. To determine the general character of reality, beyond the evidence, is the very business of the natural sciences, and above all of physics. To determine the best way of translating from one language into another is not.

6 Quine's Conception of Philosophy I: Metaphysics

At the beginning of the previous section I described the indeterminacy of translation as "one consequence" of Quine's naturalistic recoil from Carnap's logical positivism. Another is his particular conception of philosophy.

Analytic philosophers often conceive of philosophy as an undertaking of a very different kind from any of the natural sciences. They do not see it as their business, as it is the business of natural scientists, to discover and state truths about reality, but rather to analyze and to clarify the concepts that are used in discovering and stating truths about reality, and to understand the very nature of the scientific enterprise – its aims, its scope, its limits, and its methodology. Philosophy, particularly in the guise of metaphysics or epistemology, serves as a kind of propædeutic to the natural sciences.

Quine, as we have seen, is deeply opposed to this conception (section 3 above). His naturalism itself already precludes the idea that there is either room or need for any such propædeutic to the natural sciences. And his rejection both of Carnap's distinction between external questions and internal questions and of the dichotomy between analytic truths and synthetic truths blocks two of the most obvious suggestions about how philosophical practice and scientific practice, on this conception, differ (one of these suggestions being that, where philosophers are principally concerned with answering external questions, natural scientists are principally concerned with answering internal questions; the other being that, where philosophers are principally concerned with establishing analytic truths, scientists are principally concerned with establishing synthetic truths).

For Quine, again as we have seen, there are some related distinctions of degree (section 4 above). But those are all there are. Philosophers, no less than natural scientists, are engaged in the broad project of determining the general character of reality. Insofar as they have a distinctive contribution to make to this project, then it is simply a matter of their operating at a particularly high level of generality. Metaphysics is no different in *kind* from physics.

Or at least, such is the case where metaphysics is a legitimate enterprise at all. Towards the sort of metaphysics that purports to be concerned with truths that utterly transcend sense experience, Quine has straightforward logical positivist antipathy. The logical positivists' verification theory of meaning (see section 2 above) is one part of their doctrine that he thoroughly applauds – subject, of course, to the crucial proviso that it be construed in a suitably holistic way, and not at the level of individual claims.

There is a delicious example of Quine's utter impatience with empirically unconditioned flights of linguistic fancy which I cannot resist quoting, since the quotation is a personal favorite of mine. In a collection of essays on Quine's work entitled *The Philosophy of W. V. Quine*, Henryk Skolimowski makes a series of needling proposals about Quine's ideas, from a broadly unsympathetic point of view, about which he himself comments, "I can anticipate Professor Quine's response to my proposals. He is likely to say that he doesn't know what I mean by my assertions about the spiral of understanding as corresponding to the walls of our cosmos" (*PQ* 489). Quine's response, published in the same book, is mischievously caustic:

> Skolimowski predicts that I will pretend not to understand what he means by his "assertions about the spiral of understanding as corresponding to the walls of our cosmos." I am tempted, perversely, to pretend that I do understand. But let us be fair: if he claimed not to understand me, I would not for a moment suspect him of pretending. (*PQ* 493)

What examples are there, then, of the distinctive, highly general tasks that it is the prerogative of philosophers to undertake? One very typical example is to determine whether physical objects are three-dimensional objects that endure through time, or four-dimensional objects with temporal parts. The former view is pretty much the view of common sense. The latter view assimilates physical objects to what we ordinarily think of as their "histories," where these extend into the future as well as into the past; and it means that physical objects divide up into different "periods." Quine himself favors the latter view (*WO* §36). A closely related and equally representative example is to determine whether propositions concerning the future are (already) true or false. Quine's view, consonant with his four-dimensionalism, is that they are. What is particularly striking, especially in light of the pragmatism that motivates Carnap in his approach to what he takes to be external questions, is the way in which Quine at one point argues for his view by unashamedly adverting to its *ethical* pay-off. He writes:

> Consider the following dilemma. Conservation of the environment is called for by the interests of people as yet unborn, and birth control is called for by the menace of overpopulation. On the one hand, thus, we are respecting the interests of people as yet unborn, and on the other hand we are denying them the very right to be born. Observe, then, how the four-dimensional view resolves the dilemma.

On that view, people and other things of the past and future are as real as those of today, where "are" is taken tenselessly as in "Two and two are four." People who will be born *are* real people, tenselessly speaking, and their interests are to be respected now and always. People who, thanks to birth control, will not be born, are a figment; there are no such people, not even tenselessly, and so nobody's right to life has been infringed. (*Q* 74–5; emphasis in the original, punctuation slightly adapted)

7 Quine's Conception of Philosophy II: Ontology

Perhaps the most characteristic philosophical questions, however – on Quine's conception – are questions in ontology: questions about what exists and, more fundamentally, about what it is to exist. As far as the latter are concerned, Quine's view is that to exist is to be among the entities postulated by some true theory, or, as he more frequently puts it, to be among the entities to which some true theory is "ontologically committed"; and that a theory is ontologically committed to just the entities that must exist in order for it to be true. In a way this is trivial, as Quine himself would be the first to concede (though it non-trivially precludes existence beyond the purview of any theory). It sounds somewhat less trivial when Quine hones what he means by saying that an entity must exist in order for a theory to be true. He means that the entity must be among the things about which the theory makes explicit generalizations, once it has been suitably formalized (where an explicit generalization is any claim of the form "Everything is thus and so"). Anyone versed in modern logic will recognize this account as the purport of Quine's famous slogan "To be is to be the value of a variable" OWTI 15).

As for what actually does exist, that, we now see, is a question to be answered, in part, by determining which theories are actually true. So it is a question largely for natural scientists; but not exclusively for them. For there is also the issue of how any given theory is best formalized. This is an issue that is more philosophical. Typically it will involve what Quine calls "semantic ascent" (*WO* §56): the shift from talking in certain terms to reflecting on those terms instead. To revert once again to the example of the positive integers (see section 2 above), the issue will be not whether there are any positive integers satisfying this or that condition, but whether we do well to include the term "positive integer" and all the apparatus that goes with it as part of the formalization of the theory. This is *precisely* the kind of shift that

Carnap takes to be constitutive of ceasing to ask internal questions, within a linguistic framework, and instead asking external questions, about that framework. But although Quine takes it to be a characteristically philosophical kind of move, he does not think that moves of this kind are only ever made by philosophers, still less that moves made by philosophers are only ever of this kind. Moreover – and this is the crucial point of disagreement between him and Carnap – he thinks that, provided all goes well, the results of the exercise will be, not just decisions about how to speak, but insights into how things are (see section 4 above). The differences between what philosophers will have contributed to these insights and what natural scientists will have contributed to them are all, still, differences of *degree*.

Quine's own preference, both on aesthetic and on pragmatic grounds, is for theories that postulate as few entities as possible. He describes this preference as "a taste for desert landscapes" (OWTI 4). It aligns him to William of Ockham, who is famously credited with the slogan known as Ockham's razor, that "*entia non sunt multiplicanda praeter necessitatem*" ("entities are not to be multiplied beyond necessity"). And it means that, if he could, Quine would gladly endorse formalizations of scientific theories that did *not* include the term "positive integer" and all the apparatus that goes with it. As it is, he reluctantly acknowledges that a good deal of heavy-duty mathematics – not just arithmetic – is indispensable to current physics. He concludes, against his own instincts, but in strict accord with his ontological principles, that positive integers exist.

In some cases, parsimony can be achieved through what might be called creative doubling. This occurs whenever we acknowledge entities of one kind by identifying them with entities of some other kind that we already acknowledge. For an example of this, we can turn to a section of *Word and Object* with the remarkable title "The Ordered Pair as Philosophical Paradigm" (§53). No great philosophical significance attaches to the *content* of this example: quite the opposite! But in its structure, it serves as a particularly clear illustration of the phenomenon in question. The relevant background to the example is Quine's belief that, over and above whatever other entities exist, there are also sets of these entities. This in turn rests on his conviction that set theory is part of the heavy-duty mathematics that occurs in the best formulation of current physics. Thus, given any two entities a and b, there is also their *pair set* $\{a, b\}$, the set whose members they are. This is not the same as their *ordered pair* $<a, b>$. The latter differs from the former in one crucial respect: the order matters. Thus, whereas $\{a, b\}$ is the same entity as $\{b, a\}$, $<a, b>$ is not the same entity as $<b, a>$. Suppose, then, that we acknowledge ordered pairs as well as pair sets. (Quine gives reasons for doing so.) Does this mean that we are thereby acknowledging entities of an entirely new kind? Not necessarily. The defining characteristic of ordered pairs is that the identity of each should be determined, asymmetrically, by the identity of its two elements, where what "asymmetrically" signals is that the contribution made by the "first" element to determining the identity of the ordered pair should be different from that made by the "second." But there are sets that satisfy this condition, albeit not the elements' pair sets: consider, for example, in the case of the two elements a and b, the set $\{ \{a\}, \{a, b\} \}$. (This is the pair set of the singleton $\{a\}$ and the pair set $\{a, b\}$, where the singleton a is the set whose only member is a.) We can therefore identify ordered pairs with sets that we already acknowledge. Not that $\{ \{a\}, \{a, b\} \}$ is unique in this respect. There are many identifications we could adopt. It does not matter which we adopt, so long as we are clear about it – and faithful to it.

How is this a "philosophical paradigm"? In as much as it exemplifies a tactic that we can exploit in a range of cases, many of them of far greater philosophical interest than this. Thus consider minds. Many people think that these are quite distinct from any physical objects; and hence that mental states and processes are logically independent, if not causally independent, of any physical states and processes. (If this were so, it would threaten Quine's physicalism (see section 3 above).) Suppose, however, that physical states and processes always at least *accompany* mental states and processes, and that they exhibit a complexity that correlates perfectly with the complexity of the mental states and processes themselves. Then, Quine says, we can identify the latter with the former, which in turn means that we can identify minds themselves with physical objects (brains perhaps). This will clearly be of great philosophical significance. Not that we shall be revealing what minds "really are" in some deep metaphysical sense – any more than we were revealing what ordered pairs "really are" in some deep metaphysical sense. It is a piece of legislation, designed to help us systematize and formalize, in as elegant and economical a way as possible, our theories about what is going on. That is, it contributes, as does all good philosophy on Quine's conception, to our best account of the general character of reality.

8   Quine's Influence

I said at the outset that Quine is considered by many to have been the greatest analytic philosopher of the postwar period. Certainly, his brand of naturalism is the apotheosis of the naturalistic spirit that has been so characteristic of analytic philosophy during the past half-century. To what extent he created that spirit, and to what extent he reflected it, are less important than how successfully he refined and propagated it. His influence has been manifest in more particular ways too: in the many doctrines that he advanced that have since been adopted by countless others; in the many questions that he raised that have since been addressed by countless others; and in the many techniques that he introduced that have since been exploited by countless others. There is also his highly influential philosophical style, where by "style" I mean something that embraces not just his prose style (which is in fact inimitable) but his conception of how philosophy should be done. Here, special mention should be made of the extent to which he brought an appreciation of the value and use of formal logic to analytic philosophy.

As is the case with any great philosopher, however, his influence has been marked no less by rebellion among his successors than by discipleship. Thus many of his specific proposals about meaning, to take one central example, have been subjected to sustained and vigorous counter-argument. And, even when philosophers who have disagreed with him have not been particularly concerned to justify their disagreement, they have felt obliged to register it. It would be virtually inconceivable nowadays for an analytic philosopher to make pivotal but uncritical use of the analytic/synthetic distinction – something that was commonplace before Quine's onslaught.

Several of Quine's students went on to become great philosophers in their own right. Two notable examples are Donald Davidson and David Lewis. Davidson in particular was something of an acolyte. Although he had many extremely important ideas of his own, they were ideas that made sense only in a broadly Quinean framework – and his disagreements with Quine, fascinating and instructive though they were, could be viewed as disagreements of detail. Lewis's case is somewhat more complex. He is renowned for a philosophical thesis that appears radically un-Quinean: that there are infinitely many possible worlds apart from the actual world, or in other words that there are infinitely many spatio-temporally unified cosmoses of a piece with, but quite independent of, the one which we inhabit. In one respect, at least, this thesis *is* radically un-Quinean. For it does not so much as make sense without a distinction between what is necessarily true and what is contingently true (between what is true in all possible worlds and what is true merely in some possible worlds, including our own); and this distinction is either the same as the distinction between what is analytically true and what is synthetically true or at any rate close enough to it to succumb to Quine's strictures. In another respect, however, Lewis shows his Quinean credentials. For, although his commitment to all of these possible worlds hardly seems to betoken a "taste for desert landscapes," it is a reluctant commitment, exactly of a piece with Quine's own commitment to positive integers. Lewis holds that appeal to possible worlds is indispensable to the smooth running of systematic philosophy; and hence, to echo the phrase that I used at the end of the previous section, that it contributes to our best account of the general character of reality. We should not lose sight of the irony, which is itself a testament to Quine's influence, that even this most un-Quinean of theses is accepted only because of what its proponent sees as due allegiance to a basic methodological principle of Quineanism.

References

From a Logical Point of View: Logico-Philosophical Essays [*LPV*]. New York: Haper & Row; 1st edn. 1953; 2nd edn. 1961.

From Stimulus to Science [*FSS*]. Cambridge, MA: Harvard University Press, 1995.

"Goodman's *Ways of Worldmaking*," repr. in *Theories and Things*.

"On What There Is" [OWTI], repr. in *From a Logical Point of View*.

Philosophy of Logic [*PL*]. 1st edn. Englewood Cliffs: Prentice-Hall, Inc., 1970; 2nd edn. Harvard: Harvard University Press, 1986.

Pursuit of Truth [*PT*]. 1st edn. Cambridge, MA: Harvard University Press, 1990; 2nd edn. 1992.

Quiddities: An Intermittently Philosophical Dictionary [*Q*]. Cambridge, MA: Harvard University Press, 1987.

"Reply to Henryk Skolimowski," in L. E. Hahn and P. A. Schilpp (eds), *The Philosophy of W. V. Quine* [*PQ*]. La Salle, IL: Open Court, 1986.

Theories and Things [*TT*]. Cambridge, MA: Harvard University Press, 1981.

The Web of Belief, co-authored with J. S. Ullian. 1st edn. New York: Random House, 1970; 2nd edn. 1978.

"Two Dogmas of Empiricism," repr. in *From a Logical Point of View*.

Word and Object [*WO*]. Cambridge, MA: The MIT Press, 1960.

A selection of other works by Quine

Methods of Logic. 1st edn. New York: Holt, 1950; 4th edn. Cambridge, MA: Harvard University Press, 1982.

Ontological Relativity and Other Essays. New York: Columbia University Press, 1969.

Selected Logic Papers. New York: Random House, 1966.

Set Theory and Its Logic. 1st edn. Cambridge, MA: Harvard University Press, 1963; 2nd edn. 1969.

The Roots of Reference. La Salle: Open Court, 1974.

The Ways of Paradox and Other Essays. New York: Random House, 1966.

2 RAWLS

THOMAS BALDWIN

John Rawls (1921–2002) was the most important political philosopher of the latter half of the twentieth century. His major work, *A Theory of Justice* (1971), gave a new impetus to political philosophy, providing a fresh approach which transformed familiar debates. It is still the starting point for contemporary discussion.

1 Life

Rawls grew up in Baltimore and entered Princeton University in 1939; after graduating in 1943 he served in the US Army, and he was in the Pacific in August 1945 when a nuclear bomb was dropped on Hiroshima, an act he later condemned as a great wrong.[1] After the war, he returned to Princeton and completed a PhD in philosophy in 1950. In 1952 he was awarded a Fulbright scholarship which enabled him to spend the year 1952–3 in Oxford. He returned to the USA to an academic position at Cornell, where he taught from 1953 until 1959. The Cornell Philosophy Department was then strongly influenced by Wittgenstein's work, and Rawls's writings from this period show this influence. In 1959 he moved to Harvard, first just for one year, and then, after a two-year spell at MIT, for the rest of his career. The dominant philosopher at Harvard at this time was W. V. Quine, whose influence can also be seen in Rawls's writings. The publication of *A Theory of Justice* in 1971[2] brought him both fame and controversy; and his work thereafter was largely taken up with defending, refining, revising, and extending the position he had there advanced. He was appointed James Bryant Conant University Professor at Harvard in 1979. He retired in 1991, but continued to teach until incapacitated by a stroke in 1995.

Despite his fame, Rawls was an exceptionally modest individual. He shunned both public debates and public honors (I once arranged for him to be offered an honorary degree by Cambridge University, but to the consternation of the University authorities he declined the offer). His wish to avoid special treatment is exemplified by the following story: "[I]t somehow came up in conversation with an administrator at Harvard that he was a vegetarian. 'But you've gone to all those dinners without ever telling anyone,' she exclaimed. Rawls's response was that he was not that interested in food and preferred not to make a fuss – he simply left the meat on the plate."[3] His general attitude to life is, I think, captured in the following passage:

> It is a mistake to believe that a just and good society must wait upon a high material standard of life. What men want is meaningful work in free association with others. . . . To achieve this state of things great wealth is not necessary. In fact, beyond some point it is more likely to be a positive hindrance, a meaningless distraction at best if not a temptation to indulgence and emptiness. (*TJ* 257–8)[4]

2 Justice, Fairness, and Reciprocity

"Justice," says Rawls, "is the first virtue of social institutions" (*TJ* 3: 3), by which he means that it is the most important condition of their worth. So, for Rawls, a theory of justice is a theory of *social* justice, and Rawls explains that the social institution he primarily has in mind is a society, conceived as a "self-sufficient association of persons" who constitute "a cooperative association for mutual advantage" (*TJ* 4: 4). Rawls's societies are, however, not voluntary associations. Membership of a Rawlsian society is involuntary: as he puts it in his second major work, *Political Liberalism*, "we enter only by birth and exit only by death" (*PL* 135–6). Thus, although it is sometimes possible for people to change their society by emigration, it is an important constraint on a theory of justice that this possibility should not be thought of as an excuse for discrimination. The rules of Rawls's societies define the basic normative relationships between their members, the rights, and duties which constitute "the basic structure of society" (*TJ* 7: 6). Rawls takes it that societies are responsible for protecting these rights; so it is in principle legitimate for them to exercise the coercive power necessary to fulfill this responsibility (*TJ* 240: 211). Rawls's societies are, therefore, *political* societies, or, as we would normally put it, *states* – especially given his assumption that they occupy "a definite geographical territory" (*TJ* 126: 109). An oddity of Rawls's writing, however, is that he makes almost no explicit use of the term "state;" this is because he takes it that use of the term brings with it a conception of a state's sovereignty which has no legitimate application.

Justice is not simply the first virtue of political societies, it is also, Rawls says, a moral virtue (JR 208). What brings morality into the story is the way in which moral considerations determine the fundamental "principles of justice" by reference to which the basic structure of a society is appraised: "[T]he principles of justice may be thought of as arising once the constraints of having a morality are imposed upon rational and mutually self-interested parties who are related and situated in a special way" (JF 63). This constraint of "having a morality" does not imply adherence to some specific moral code. Instead Rawls has a more formal value in mind, which he initially calls "fairness," and this gives him the phrase "Justice as Fairness" which is the title of his most famous paper. But its significance needs some elucidation. "Justice *as* fairness" is not an identity, the thesis that justice *is* fairness (*TJ* 12–13: 11); instead, Rawls's thought is that the principles of justice are to be understood as principles whose adoption by those who are to be bound by them is the outcome of a fair procedure:

> The question of fairness arises when free persons, who have no authority over one another, are engaging in a joint activity and among themselves settling or acknowledging the rules which define it and which determine the respective shares in its benefits and burdens. A practice will strike the parties as fair if none feels that, by participating in it, they or any of the others are taken advantage of, or forced to give in to claims which they do not regard as legitimate. (JF 59)

As this passage indicates, according to Rawls it is fundamental to justice that its requirements be ones which those who are to be bound by them can regard as collectively self-imposed through a procedure which is fair because the choice of the principles which define these requirements is arrived at in a way which is open, inclusive, non-coercive, and impartial. In *A Theory of Justice*, Rawls describes these aspects of a fair procedure as "The Formal

Constraints of the Concept of Right," and he applies it to "the choice of all ethical principles and not only for those of justice" (*TJ* 130: 112).

A few years later[5] Rawls modified his position, placing fairness on a level with justice (the difference between them being that fairness applies to voluntary institutions and justice to involuntary ones) and arguing that what is fundamental to both is "reciprocity," the mutual recognition by persons of each other as free and equal. In part, this is just a change in terminology; compare the following passage from his later paper "Justice as Reciprocity" with the second sentence quoted above from "Justice as Fairness":

> A practice will strike the parties as conforming to the notion of reciprocity if none feels that, by participating in it, he or any of the others are taken advantage of or forced to give in to claims which they do not regard as legitimate. (JR 208)

As we shall see, however, reciprocity enters into Rawls's theory in other ways, so there is also some substance to this change. But what is most important about this change is Rawls's explicit acknowledgment that reciprocity is the fundamental value which informs his political philosophy:

> It is this requirement of the possibility of mutual acknowledgment of principles by free and equal persons who have no authority over one another which makes the concept of reciprocity fundamental to both justice and fairness. (JR 209)

What now needs elucidation is the conception of freedom involved in the recognition of persons as "free and equal." For Rawls, freedom is not the familiar ability to do as one likes without restriction; instead, it is a moral status with three fundamental aspects.[6] First, to be free is to be a responsible agent, someone capable of appreciating reasons for action and taking responsibility for what they do. Rawls takes it that this capacity is grounded in "the moral power to have a conception of the good," by which he means both that one has "a conception of the good," that is, some fundamental values and attachments from which one gets one's sense of identity, and that one has the ability to appraise these values and attachments critically. This moral power both defines the second aspect of our freedom and grounds its third aspect, which is that people are "self-originating sources of valid claims." What Rawls means by this is that each person has a fundamental moral status which implies that their interests merit equal consideration in the determination of rights and duties, the basic structure of society. Reciprocity is then the mutual recognition of each other as "free and equal" in this sense. As will be apparent, this freedom is the freedom of someone whose capacity to construct a meaningful life of their own entitles them to full and proper consideration when moral and political questions are at stake; and recognition of this status is the ethical value which informs Rawls's moral and political theory.

3 The Original Position

As we have seen, Rawls maintains that the requirements of justice are determined by principles which the members of the society would agree to impose upon themselves in a hypothetical situation which respects their recognition of each other as free and equal. In *A Theory of Justice* Rawls famously fills out this hypothetical "original position," as he calls it, by having us imagine ourselves placed behind a "veil of ignorance" which prevents us from knowing anything distinctive about ourselves, our situation, and our society, and then inviting us to select fundamental principles for a society in which we are to live. One might think that assuming ourselves to be in this state of ignorance would leave us quite unable to make a rational choice of principles. But Rawls holds that we are to imagine ourselves as having unlimited knowledge of general truths about the world and also knowledge of the "primary social goods" of human life, which he takes to be rights, opportunities, wealth, and self-respect. Furthermore, we are to assume that our motivations in the original position are those of people who are "rational and mutually disinterested" (*TJ* 13: 12), by which he means that they act to promote their own self-interest without any concern, positive or negative, for the interests of others. In the light of these positive characterizations of the original position, he argues, it is possible to demonstrate that there are two fundamental principles for social cooperation which it would be rational for persons within the original position to adopt and which thereby constitute fundamental principles of justice. First, that each person has a right to the most extensive scheme of basic liberties compatible with everyone else having a right to similar liberties; second, that social and economic inequalities are to be arranged in such a way that positions of power and status are open to all, and differences in wealth and income arise only through distributive systems which work to the advantage of everyone, and especially to the advantage of the least well-off members of society (*TJ* 60–1: 53).

These principles are obviously contentious and I will say a good deal more about them. But my first concern here is with the way in which Rawls characterized the original position. His idea was that by combining the veil of ignorance with the assumption of self-interested rationality, he could induce the rational choice of principles which promote anyone's interests. This was a clever idea, but an immediate source of unease about it is that it undermines the aim of presenting the principles of justice as the agreed outcome of a procedure which respects the value of reciprocity. For because the veil of ignorance obscures all the differences between people, there is no question of imagining people in the original position coming to an *agreement* concerning the principles which it would be rational to adopt. Instead, the standpoint is just that of "one person selected at random" (*TJ* 139: 120) whose rational judgment is bound to be the same as that of anyone else. So the original position with its veil of ignorance is not a model of an ideal social contract; instead, it models the role of an ideal legislator. But that role brings with it a very different conception of justice and morality, founded not on the fundamental value of reciprocity but on that of impartial sympathy.

This objection invites the question why Rawls does not take it that reciprocity is one of the primary social goods which the parties to the original position are assumed to take into account. The answer to this is that Rawls believed that by means of his account of the original position, he represented the value of reciprocity, and thereby ensured that the principles of justice thus chosen would express this value (see *PL* 305–6). John Harsanyi, the American economist and social philosopher, in effect showed, however, that this belief is mistaken.[7] Harsanyi argued that the distributive principle which is the rational choice for a self-interested person behind the veil of ignorance is the utilitarian principle that goods such as wealth should be distributed in such a way as to give each person the best chance of maximizing their welfare. This conclusion, however, is not that which Rawls wanted to reach: his second principle of justice implies that wealth should be distributed in a way which is most beneficial to the least advantaged members of society, and Rawls argues that this principle is preferable to Harsanyi's utilitarian principle precisely because it affirms the value of reciprocity within society (*TJ* 102: 88). Yet, on the face of it, Harsanyi's principle is that which is implied by Rawls's own original position argument because of the emphasis there on rational self-interest. Rawls rejects this conclusion on the grounds that the rational strategy to be adopted in the original position is the "maximin" strategy of minimizing the risk of faring badly; for, he argues, when a reflective person make his choice of principles, he has to allow for the possibility that he is designing "a society in which his enemy is to assign him his place" (*TJ* 152: 133). We can certainly agree that if this possibility is to be assumed to be likely, then self-interest dictates that maximin would be the rational strategy. But Rawls explicitly denies that this eventuality is to be assumed to be likely; hence, given the unlimited general knowledge of the world which is assumed to be available in the original position (*TJ* 137–8: 119), the reflective person motivated by rational self-interest has no good reason to adopt a maximin strategy. He should aim to maximize his expected goods in the light of his knowledge of the world and thus opt for Harsanyi's principle.

In *A Theory of Justice* Rawls systematically uses his conception of the original position to present his theory of justice. If the argument above is correct, this was a mistake. But it does not follow that the thesis which motivated the conception of the original position, namely that the requirements of justice are determined by principles which would be agreed by parties who recognize each other as free and equal, is also a mistake. Instead, what is required is some other way of working out the implications of taking reciprocity to be the fundamental value by reference to which social and political institutions are to be appraised. There are important suggestions to this effect in the literature, but I shall not pursue them here.[8]

There is, however, a separate issue here, namely how a merely hypothetical agreement can be supposed to determine the requirements of justice in the actual world. After all, Rawls himself remarks that "we cannot say that a particular state of affairs is just because it could have been reached by following a fair procedure. . . . A fair procedure translates its fairness to the outcome only when it is actually carried out" (*TJ* 86: 75). The way Rawls proposes to deal with this problem, nonetheless, is to maintain that justice, and morality in general, just are concepts whose application in the actual world depends upon their application in hypothetical situations in which the requirements of reciprocity are fulfilled. The basis for this claim is the thesis that justice and morality are expressions of human reason, and that the way in which their requirements are identified is by means of an abstract "construction" which focuses on the ideal of a society whose members recognize each other as free rational agents:

> Apart from the procedure of constructing these principles, there are no reasons of justice. Put in another way, whether certain facts are to count as reasons of justice and what their relative force is to be can be ascertained only on the basis of the principles that result from the construction. ("Kantian Constructivism in Moral Theory," *CP* 351)

Rawls calls this position "Kantian constructivism" because it is inspired by Kant's account of the role of practical reason in determining the moral law; but Rawls is careful to distance himself from the metaphysical aspects of Kant's conception of practical reason – his philosophy is a naturalized Kantianism.

4 Basic Liberties and the First Principle of Justice

In *A Theory of Justice*, Rawls stated his first, fundamental, principle of justice as the principle that each person has a right to the most extensive scheme of basic liberties compatible with everyone else in their society having a right to similar liberties. In *Political Liberalism*, he modified this principle, substituting "a fully adequate scheme of basic liberties" for the earlier talk of "the most extensive scheme" of them (*PL* 291). What lies behind this change is Rawls's acceptance of H. L. A. Hart's criticism of the principle as originally formulated. Hart had argued that Rawls's talk of the "most extensive scheme of liberties" was unsatisfactory, since what is important as far as justice is concerned is the identification and protection of basic liberties, not their maximal extension, whatever that might be.[9] Rawls agreed with Hart on this point and modified his first principle accordingly to affirm that justice requires the protection of "a fully adequate scheme of basic liberties which is compatible with a similar scheme of liberties for all" (*PL* 291).

This revised principle raises the question of which liberties belong to a "fully adequate scheme," and this cannot be separated from the question why this principle is the fundamental principle of justice in the first place. One of the odd features of *A Theory of Justice* is that Rawls does not address this question until he gets to the final chapter of the book, where he argues that liberty gets its priority from "the central place of the primary good of self-respect" (*TJ* 543: 476[10]) because "the basis for self-esteem in a just society is not then one's income share but the publicly affirmed distribution of fundamental rights and liberties" (*TJ* 544: 477). Although this claim is intelligible, it is not well integrated into the main structure of his theory and it does not settle what rights and liberties are fundamental. It is, therefore, no surprise that in *Political Liberalism*, as well as reformulating the first principle of justice, Rawls provides a much better rationale for its priority and content. Since, as we have seen, freedom includes "the moral power to have a conception of the good," the recognition of each other's freedom will lead people to value the liberties which enable them to exercise this power. For Rawls there are two such basic liberties: liberty of conscience and freedom of association (*PL* 310–13). It is clear that these liberties are indeed essential to the capacity to construct a life of one's own which Rawls takes to be central to our freedom. But Rawls holds that there is another group of basic liberties, the "political" liberties associated with participation in democratic institutions, which are not further requirements of the "moral power to have a conception of the good." Instead, he argues, they are to be justified by reference to another fundamental moral power which is characteristic of members of a just society: "the sense of justice" (*PL* 302).

Rawls introduced the conception of the "sense of justice" in *A Theory of Justice* in the course of a subtle account of the development of moral sensibility. He argues that a sense of justice, a disposition to act in accordance with the requirements of justice, is the result of a kind of reciprocity:

> Because we recognize that [other persons] wish us well, we care for their well-being in return. Thus we acquire attachments to persons and institutions according to how we perceive our good to be affected by them. The basic idea is one of reciprocity, a tendency to answer in kind. Now this tendency is a deep psychological fact. Without it our nature would be very difficult and fruitful social cooperation fragile if not impossible. (*TJ* 494–5: 433)

This form of reciprocity is not the reciprocity of "justice as reciprocity," but they are closely related because the "tendency to answer in kind" implies that where people find themselves treated as free and equal they are likely to treat others in the same way and in this way develop a sense of justice. Hence we are to think of the sense of justice as a normal disposition of anyone who has grown up in a reasonably just environment. For this reason, Rawls holds, it is a basic moral power, one that is central to our willingness to act towards others in "reasonable" ways, just as our capacity for a conception of good is central to our self-interested "rationality."

Rawls's account of the development and role of a sense of justice is plausible and valuable. But it does not follow that a sense of justice is the ground for the status of political liberties as basic liberties which are essential constituents of a fully adequate scheme. For a sense of justice is essentially a disposition to fulfill the requirements of justice, whatever they are, and it does not of itself dictate what these requirements are to be even if it is dependent upon our "tendency to answer in kind." Instead, it seems to me, the status of these political liberties follows from an aspect of justice as reciprocity concerning which Rawls says surprisingly little in this context – namely, equality. It is central to Rawls's theory that justice is the working out of the recognition of each other as "free *and equal*" (my italics); and the route from the recognition of each other as equal members of political society to some form of representative democracy which includes universal political liberties is familiar and well established. What is fundamentally wrong with Plato's elitist constitution in the *Republic* is not that it violates the sense of justice of its citizens, but that it divides up humankind into groups with different ethical status. To recognize each other as free and equal is precisely to reject any such division and for this reason to demand equal political rights for all.

There is, however, a different kind of equality whose importance Rawls does acknowledge in this context, namely that the basic liberties identified by the first principle should be of "equal worth" to all members of society. The main anxiety here arises from the effects of social and economic differences between people. In *A Theory of Justice*, Rawls argued that this anxiety is adequately addressed by his second principle of justice, which implies that these differences are only legitimate where they are of benefit to the least advantaged members of society. But he later accepted the need to provide a separate way of substantiating the equal worth of liberty: in *Justice as Fairness* (2001), his late restatement of his theory of justice, he remarks:

> This principle [i.e. the first principle of justice] may be preceded by a lexically prior principle requiring that basic needs be met, at least insofar as their being met is a necessary condition for citizens to understand and to be able fruitfully to exercise the basic rights and liberties. (*JF* 44 n. 7)

5 Social and Economic Inequalities and the Second Principle of Justice

I turn now to the second principle of justice, that social and economic inequalities are to be arranged in such a way that positions of power and status are open to all and differences in wealth and income arise only through distributive systems which work, if not to the advantage of everyone, at least to the advantage of the least well-off members of society. This principle has two clauses, one concerning social inequalities, the other economic ones; Rawls says that the social clause takes priority over the economic clause, and I shall discuss them in this order.

The substance of the social clause is that justice requires that there be "fair equality of opportunity," by which Rawls means that "those with similar life abilities and skills should have similar life chances" (*TJ* 73: 63). The familiar method of realizing this requirement is through education, and Rawls holds that school systems should be organized so as to remove class barriers; in his later work, he also maintains that basic healthcare needs to be assured for all, which addresses a further cause of unequal opportunities (*LP* 50). Rawls recognizes, however, that one's life chances are also profoundly shaped by one's family; hence, he asks (*TJ* 511: 448), does justice require that the family be abolished? In *A Theory of Justice* he replies that once we take account of the economic clause of his second principle, the differences between different families should be sufficiently mitigated to avoid this conclusion. This reply seems fair enough, though it is striking that he does not appeal to his first principle of justice to defend the family via a right to privacy, as would be normal today. Rawls returned briefly to the issue of the family in his late writings.[11] Again, his concern is with equality of opportunity, but now with a different focus on the traditional roles of women as wife and mother insofar as these tend to make it impossible for them to enjoy the same opportunities for fulfilling and rewarding careers as men. For Rawls, this situation is inherently unjust; the only fair division of labor between men and women in the family is a voluntary one.

The economic clause of Rawls's second principle of justice, generally known as the "difference principle," states that systematic differences in wealth and income are justified only where they work to the advantage of the most deprived section of society (*TJ* 75: 65). In applying this principle, Rawls starts from the belief that the economy of a just society will be organized as a free market, given the greater efficiency of a market economy as compared with a command economy and also its compatibility with the basic liberties of the first principle and the requirements of fair equality of opportunity (*TJ* 272: 240–1). In endorsing a market economy, however, Rawls emphasizes that socialist systems of collective or cooperative ownership are not ruled out; the choice between these and a system of private ownership, or some combination of them, should be a pragmatic matter (*TJ* 280: 248). Whatever system is adopted, however, Rawls maintains that "income and wages will be just once a (workably) competitive price system is properly organized and embedded in a just basic system" (*TJ* 304: 268). Hence differences in wages will reflect "features of jobs that are significant on either the demand or the supply side of the market, or both," such as "Experience and training, natural ability and special know-how" (*TJ* 305: 269); but if the system is in other respects just, then these differences will also be just. Indeed, the situation is for Rawls a paradigmatic case of pure procedural justice (*TJ* 304: 267).

The anxiety to which this account gives rise is that it dissipates Rawls's initial egalitarian presumption by permitting those with scarce skills to bargain hard for disproportionately large salaries. Rawls will reply that within a just society people will not be motivated to press their claims in this way: for they should be assumed to be committed to the ideal of constructing a society in which any systematic income differential from which one benefits oneself is only a means of bringing greater benefits to others, especially the most deprived section of society (*JF* 64, 76–7). Furthermore, Rawls's conception of a just distributive system includes provision for redistributive taxation which aims "gradually and continually to correct the distribution of wealth and to prevent concentrations of power detrimental to the fair value of political liberty and fair equality of opportunity" (*TJ* 277: 245). Thus Rawls's hope is that once these points are taken into account, the resulting system is that which has the best chance of enabling the most deprived groups of society "to make intelligent and effective use of their freedoms and to lead reasonable and worthwhile lives" (*LP* 114). One may not be altogether persuaded by this line of thought; but it would be a great mistake to read Rawls as an apologist for contemporary capitalist society. In his late writings he emphasizes the difference between the kind of "property-owning democracy" he favors and "welfare-state capitalism," the kind of political economy characteristic of contemporary Britain and the USA (he later remarks that it was "a serious fault" of *TJ* that it failed to emphasize this contrast; see *JF* 139 n. 5). Welfare-state capitalism permits "very large inequalities in the ownership of real property . . . so that control of the economy and much of political life rests in few hands;" hence although "welfare provisions may be quite generous and guarantee a decent social minimum covering the basic needs, a principle of reciprocity to regulate economic and social inequalities is not recognized" (*JF* 138). By contrast, in a property-owning democracy, the aim is not simply to assist those who need help, but to disperse wealth and capital in order to "put all citizens in a position to manage their own affairs on a footing of a suitable degree of social and economic equality" (*JF* 139). Rawls ends with the hope that in a system of this latter kind, the problem of social exclusion, or the "underclass" as he calls it, will be addressed insofar as it can be:

> Under these conditions we hope that an underclass will not exist; or, if there is a small such class, that it is the result of social conditions we do not know how to change, or perhaps cannot even identify or understand. When society faces this impasse, it has at least taken seriously the idea of itself as a fair system of co-operation between its citizens as free and equal. (*JF* 140)

Rawls's difference principle has attracted more critical attention than all the rest of his work put together. I have already mentioned, and endorsed, Harsanyi's criticism of Rawls's attempt to derive the difference principle from his original position. But I take this to be primarily a criticism of Rawls's conception of the original position; it does not settle the question whether one should favor the difference principle over the utilitarian approach favored by Harsanyi. Rawls's objection is, of course, that utilitarianism fails the test of reciprocity since it does not protect the claims of the most deprived from being set aside in favor of greater benefits to other, better off, social groups (*TJ* 33: 29). But this argument is disputable: utilitarians will argue that, given the diminishing marginal utility of wealth, the goal of maximizing average welfare will direct a society to prioritize improvements in the situation of the most deprived. And when one considers the detail of Rawls's proposed policies for implementing his difference principle, as sketched above, it is hard to see anything incompatible with the implications of an enlightened utilitarianism. A more fundamental criticism of Rawls's difference principle came from his Harvard colleague Robert Nozick.[12] Nozick argued that the way in which this principle seeks to direct the distribution of wealth and income conflicts with the fact that wealth and income are personal property which it is not society's legitimate business to redistribute in order to achieve a particular pattern of distribution. Personal property is a personal "entitlement" over which society has no legitimate claim without the consent of the property-holder. Rawls's reply is that personal entitlements arise only within a just system of property rights (*JF* 72–3) and that there is nothing wrong with a system which uses taxation to constrain property holdings in order to achieve a just distribution of wealth and income (*JF* 51–2). The only condition under which such interference would be wrong is if the property rights in question were to derive from the exercise of basic liberties to acquire, hold, and transfer property. Rawls, however, denies that there are any such basic liberties (*JF* 114).

Nozick's criticism of the very idea of distributive justice is therefore misguided. But Rawls himself is guilty of a comparable mistake in suggesting that his own difference principle follows directly from the fact that a person's "native talents" are undeserved. Rawls argued that because one has no underived moral entitlement to one's native talents, it is appropriate for society to be organized in such a way that everyone benefits from their use, especially those who have not been favored by the natural lottery which distributes them. These talents may therefore be viewed, he says, as "a social asset to be used for the common advantage" (*TJ* 107: 92), and in this way, he holds, "we are led to the difference principle" (*TJ* 102: 87). Rawls's use of the phrase "social asset" here was unfortunate, since it suggested that there is social ownership of personal abilities; but that unintended meaning can be set to one side. The important question concerns the relationship between the difference principle and the fact that native talents are not deserved. The fact that native talents are undeserved certainly removes a Nozick-inspired objection to the difference principle. But the converse implication does not hold: the fact that native talents are undeserved implies next to nothing about the just distribution of the goods people produce by making use of their talents. It is, for example, entirely consistent with a utilitarian distributive principle. Rawls's intuitive argument for the difference principle was, therefore, a mistake.

6 The Rawlsian State

Rawls conceives of his two principles of justice as providing the foundations for the network of rights and duties which constitutes the basic structure of a just society. So the Rawlsian state (if one can so speak) is essentially an implementation of these principles: the first principle frames the state's constitution and legal system, while the second principle sets policy goals for the legislature. An important implication of the first principle is that the state is to be neutral as between the varied religious and ethical beliefs of its citizens except for those which conflict with the conception of justice as reciprocity, which is fundamental to the state itself. Thus there can be no established church or other faith: against defenders of confessional states, however tolerant, Rawls argues that it is unjust that those who do not share the official faith of their society should be disadvantaged with respect to the state's political institutions. When it comes to the implementation of the second principle of justice, however, the Rawlsian state is far from neutral. The first clause of the principle implies that the state should actively promote equality of opportunity in the fields of education, employment, and so on; and the difference principle implies that the state must take an active role in promoting a property-owning democracy in which ownership of wealth and capital is dispersed.

What is not covered by the principles of justice is the duty of citizens to obey the laws of their state insofar as it is just. Since membership of one's society is not voluntary, Rawls accepts that the fundamental ground for this duty cannot be a contractual obligation (*TJ* 335–6: 295–6). Instead, he says, it rests upon a "natural duty of justice," understood as the duty "to comply with and to do our share in just institutions where they exist and apply to us" (*TJ* 334: 293). For Rawls this natural duty is justified by the line of thought that is central to his conception of justice as reciprocity: in thinking about the rules which would be agreed by the members of a society whose members recognize each other as free and equal, he argues, we can see that these rules, whatever they are, would include the higher-order requirement to comply with whatever rules are agreed. (*TJ* 334–5: 295). It is, however, one thing to accept a duty to obey the law where the law is indeed just; but what about where it is unjust? Rawls was writing *A Theory of Justice* during the 1960s, when the civil rights campaign led by Martin Luther King was at its height. It is not surprising, therefore, that Rawls added a discussion of civil disobedience to his account of political obligation, despite the fact that in doing so he was no longer dealing with the basic structure of an ideally just society, but was instead dealing with the requirements of justice in a situation in which there is serious injustice. Whereas traditional social contract theorists such as Locke had taken it that the appropriate response to extreme injustice ("tyranny") was rebellion and the removal by force of the existing state, Rawls argued that a political society which recognizes the inescapable fallibility of its own political institutions should allow that there can be justified acts of disobedience which aim not to overthrow the state, but to correct serious existing injustice: "Indeed, civil disobedience (and conscientious refusal as well) is one of the stabilizing devices of a constitutional system, although by definition an illegal one. . . . By resisting injustice within the limits of fidelity to law, it serves to inhibit departures from justice and to correct them when they occur" (*TJ* 383: 336). Hence: "So understood a conception of civil disobedience is part of the theory of free government" (*TJ* 385: 338). This was an important insight, previously propounded informally by Thoreau, Gandhi, and King, but here for the first time built into an account of the moral structure of a reasonably just state.

7 Political Liberalism

During the 1980s Rawls came to acknowledge the "fact of reasonable pluralism," the fact that even among well-informed and well-intentional thinkers there are irresolvable disagreements concerning the foundations of morality between Kantians (such as himself), utilitarians, intuitionists, and adherents of the great variety of religious beliefs. Although he held that these disagreements do not entail skepticism, either about morality or about moral theory, they do imply that the public vindication of the requirements of justice that is needed to ground the stable allegiance of citizens to their society should not require the adoption of any one general ethical theory such as the Kantian theory he himself held. As a result, Rawls was led to think that political philosophy requires the detachment of a "political conception of justice" from any underlying ethical theory and his second major book, *Political Liberalism* (1993), was his attempt to present a conception of this kind. This required a significant change in his philosophical perspective from that of *A Theory of Justice*; but in many other respects the change is not great, since Rawls retained much of the substance of his theory.

In *Political Liberalism*, Rawls still holds that the conception of justice is a "moral conception" which applies to social institutions, but he now takes it that the moral requirements in question are the implications of values which are essentially political. And instead of relying on his "Kantian" constructivism to develop these implications, Rawls recasts his account of the justification of political judgments as "political constructivism." This is the thesis that the requirements of justice can be justified by reference to "public reason," the project of constructing publicly defensible rules for social cooperation among reasonable persons even if they have very different ethical beliefs. In this sense, "Political liberalism, then, aims for a political conception of justice as a freestanding view" (*PL* 10). Despite these changes, however, Rawls's general approach remained much the same, though he is now more concessive concerning the details of his principles:

> Accepting the idea of public reason and its principle of legitimacy emphatically does not mean, then, accepting a particular liberal conception of justice down to the last details of the principles defining its content. We may differ about these principles and still agree in accepting a conception's more general features. (*PL* 226)

By detaching his theory from comprehensive ethical theories, Rawls aimed to be neutral with respect to such theories. Nonetheless, he also holds that political constructivism can work only among the adherents of "reasonable" ethical theories. But what does "reasonable" mean here? One aspect is manifest in the doctrine of "reasonable pluralism," where what is reasonable is what is defensible in the light of the evidence and thus meets the standards of theoretical reason (*PL* 56); Rawls's pluralist thesis is that more than one ethical theory is reasonable in this sense. But there is another aspect based on practical reason which concerns the willingness of people to be "reasonable" with respect to one another. Here reasonableness is just reciprocity:

> Reasonable persons, we say, are not moved by the general good as such but desire for its own sake a social world in which they, as free and equal, can cooperate with others on terms all can accept. They insist that reciprocity should hold within that world so that each benefits along with others. (*PL* 50)

In this sense, then, reasonable ethical theories are those which affirm the value of reciprocity. This conclusion is not surprising, but it shows how even when Rawls was aiming to advance a freestanding political conception of justice, he retained his commitment to "justice as reciprocity."

8   The Law of Peoples

Right from the start, Rawls had envisaged that his theory of justice should be applicable to international affairs (JF 49); but in *A Theory of Justice* he provided only a very brief sketch of this application in which he claimed that it would just lead to the standard principles of the law of nations (*TJ* 378: 332). Towards the end of his life, however, he returned to this issue, and his last major piece of writing, *The Law of Peoples* (1999), was an extended discussion of justice in international affairs. As the title of the book indicates, Rawls takes it that international affairs are best conceived as dealing with relationships between "peoples," rather than nations, societies, or states. This terminology is potentially misleading, since whereas we normally speak of, say, the Kurds and Basques as peoples, Rawls takes it that a "people" will have a constitutional government with jurisdiction over an established territory, which the Kurds and Basques lack. It is in fact relations between states that Rawls is concerned with, but for the purpose of exposition, I will stick with his term.

As one would expect, Rawls employs within international affairs much the same approach he had used in domestic affairs. The aim is to frame principles of justice, a "Law of Peoples," to regulate relationships between members of a just international society, the "Society of Peoples." These principles are to be thought of as founded upon the fundamental value of reciprocity:

> Thus, the criterion of reciprocity applies to the Law of Peoples in the same way it does to the principles of justice for a constitutional regime. This reasonable sense of due respect, willingly accorded to other reasonable peoples, is an essential element of the idea of peoples who are satisfied with the status quo for the right reasons. (*LP* 35)

Not surprisingly, therefore, Rawls proposes that the Law of Peoples can be thought of as the rules which would be agreed to in a hypothetical original position in which the parties think of themselves as representing a people and coming to an agreement behind a veil of ignorance as to "the basic terms of cooperation among peoples who, as liberal peoples, see themselves as free and equal" (*LP* 33). As ever, we do not have to endorse the details of this to appreciate his general line of thought. Instead the focus needs to be on the proposed Society of Peoples and its Law.

One thing which is striking about Rawls's Society is that he allows that it includes "decent" peoples which, despite not being wholly just liberal societies, respect basic human rights and the rule of law internally and refrain from aggressive war externally. It might at first appear that this represents a significant retreat from his defense of liberal politics. But Rawls argues that just as liberal political principles call for the toleration of non-liberal associations which pose no threat to others, a liberal Society of Peoples should tolerate decent peoples even if their constitution is in some respects illiberal (*LP* 59–60). This situation is, he argues, what we should expect of a "realistic utopia." The Society is a "utopia" insofar as its basic principles represent the implications, rational and reasonable, of the basic value of reciprocity (*LP* 17–18); but it is also "realistic" insofar as it acknowledges the fact of reasonable pluralism and the resulting diversity of decent peoples who subscribe at the level of international affairs to liberal principles (*LP* 18).

What then are the principles of international justice, the "Law of Peoples"? As before, Rawls largely reiterates existing principles of the law of nations (*LP* 37) and maintains that peoples are free and equal members of the Society of Peoples, with a right to self-defense, a duty not to intervene in the affairs of other peoples, and a duty to honor human rights internally. These points can be regarded as broadly equivalent to Rawls's first principle of (domestic) justice. But what is the international analogue of the second principle of justice which deals with social and economic inequalities? All that Rawls offers here is a duty of assistance: "Peoples have a duty to assist other peoples living under unfavorable conditions that prevent their having a just or decent political and social regime" (ibid.). Rawls thinks of this duty as primarily owed to "burdened peoples" which "lack the political and cultural traditions, the human capital and know-how, and, often, the material and technological resources needed to be well-ordered" (*LP* 106). The aim, then, is to help such societies establish the conditions under which they can become well-ordered so that they can develop decent political institutions and a reasonably self-sufficient economy (*LP* 110–11). Rawls notes also the importance of ensuring that the terms of trade and other economic relations between peoples are fair (*LP* 42–3); but all this is very different in spirit from the difference principle. He argues, however, that interventions to promote economic equality between peoples are likely to be ineffective, since the level of material prosperity of a people is primarily a matter of its own cultural traditions and values (*LP* 117). This claim is questionable. But Rawls has a further and better point, that it is essential to respect the independence of decent free peoples (ibid.). This point, however, shows that his approach to justice in international affairs was misconceived.

Rawls takes it that justice in international affairs "simply extends" the ideas which inform his theory of justice for political societies (*LP* 123). Yet whereas he accepts that political societies should have a government with coercive powers (*PL* 136), he rejects the suggestion that the Society of Peoples needs a world government with coercive powers (*LP* 36). Rawls is right about this last point; but this fundamental difference between the two cases indicates that an understanding of international justice cannot be achieved by the simple extension to international affairs of a theory of justice for political societies. At this point, therefore, Rawls's program falters.[13] But this weakness does not undermine his great achievement, which has been nothing less than the revival of political philosophy in the latter part of the twentieth century.

Notes

1 "Fifty Years after Hiroshima," reprinted in *CP*.
2 The original 1971 edition of *A Theory of Justice* runs to 600 pages. In 1999 Rawls brought out a revised edition of the book for which the text was reset, with the result that the page numbers are different. I give page references in the form "(*TJ* x: y)," where "x" denotes the page number in the 1971 edition and "y" that in the 1999 edition. Some significant differences between the editions are mentioned in the notes.
3 I take this story from Brian Barry's obituary of Rawls in the *Financial Times* November 28, 2002.
4 This passage is an addition in the revised edition.
5 The change is made in his 1971 paper "Justice as Reciprocity," reprinted in *CP*. *TJ* was also published in 1971, but in the book, much of which had in fact been written many years earlier, Rawls sticks with the earlier approach of "justice as fairness."
6 See "Justice and Fairness: Political not Metaphysical," in *CP*, esp. pp. 404–8.
7 Harsanyi put his criticisms of Rawls very clearly in J. Harsanyi "Can the Maximin Principle Serve as a Basis for Morality? A Critique of John Rawls's Theory," *American Political Science Review* 69 (1975): 594–606. This paper reformulates arguments which Harsanyi had published earlier and which Rawls discusses in *TJ*.
8 The most important proposal is that advanced by T. M. Scanlon; see his "Contractualism and Utilitarianism," in A. Sen and B. Williams, eds., *Utilitarianism and Beyond*, Cambridge University Press: Cambridge, 1982.
9 See H. L. A. Hart, "Rawls on Liberty and Its Priority," *University of Chicago Law Review* 40 (1973): 534–55; repr. in N. Daniels, ed., *Reading Rawls*, Blackwell: Oxford, 1975, pp. 230–52.
10 This and the next passage are altered in the revised edition of *TJ*; indeed, in this edition the whole section, §82, is considerably altered.
11 See "The Idea of Public Reason Revisited" in *CP*, esp. pp. 595–601. Rawls is here responding to Susan Okin, *Justice, Gender and the Family*, Basic Books: New York, 1989.
12 See *Anarchy, State and Utopia*, Blackwell: Oxford, 1974, esp. ch. 7.
13 For extensive discussion of Rawls's account of international justice, see R. Martin and D. A. Reidy, eds., *Rawls's Law of Peoples*, Blackwell: Oxford, 2006.

References

Collected Papers [*CP*]. Cambridge, MA: Harvard University Press, 1999.

"Fifty years after Hiroshima," *Dissent* (1995): 323–7; repr. in *Collected Papers*, pp. 565–72.

"Justice as Fairness" [JF], *Philosophical Review* 67 (1958): 164–94; repr. in *Collected Papers*, pp. 47–72.

"Justice as Fairness: Political not Metaphysical," *Philosophy and Public Affairs* 14 (1985): 223–52; repr. in *Collected Papers*, pp. 388–414.

Justice as Fairness: A Restatement [*JF*]. Cambridge, MA: Harvard University Press, 2001.

"Justice as Reciprocity" [JR], in S. Gorowitz, ed., *John Stuart Mill: Utilitarianism, with Critical Essays*. Bobbs-Merrill: Indianapolis, 1971; repr. in *Collected Papers*, pp. 190–224.

"The Idea of Public Reason Revisited," *University of Chicago Law Review* 64 (1997): 765–807; repr. in *Collected Papers*, pp. 573–615.

"Kantian Constructivism in Moral Theory," *Journal of Philosophy* 77 (1980): 515–72; repr. in *Collected Papers*, pp. 303–58.

The Law of Peoples [*LP*]. Cambridge, MA: Harvard University Press, 1999.

Political Liberalism [*PL*]. New York: Columbia University Press, 1993.

A Theory of Justice [*TJ*]. Oxford: Oxford University Press, 1971; rev. edn. 1999.

3 DAVIDSON

ERNIE LEPORE AND KIRK LUDWIG

1   Introduction

Donald Davidson (1917–2003) was born in Springfield, Massachusetts, and raised, from 1924, in Staten Island, New York. He was educated both as an undergraduate and a graduate at Harvard University. After a stint in the US Navy during the Second World War, which interrupted his graduate education, he returned to Harvard to complete a dissertation on Plato's *Philebus* in 1949. He went on to become one of the most important philosophers of the second half of the twentieth century.

Davidson's work is difficult, even by the standards of analytic philosophy. He was a systematic philosopher, but his work is presented in a series of short, cryptic, densely argued, though elegant essays. Together they form a mosaic out of which emerges a deeply unified picture of the nature of the mind–world relation, a picture that rejects root and branch the central problematic of the modern tradition, that our understanding of the world must be built from the inside out, that is, from the first person point of view. The central tenet of Davidson's philosophy is that the standpoint from which to understand thought, language, and knowledge is the third person point of view, the point of view from which we understand language and communication.

Virtually everything else in Davidson's work grows out of or is woven into this central idea.

Davidson is best known for his work in the philosophy of language, and especially the theory of meaning, the philosophy of action, and the philosophy of mind. His work in each of these areas was connected with his work in the others. In the first of these areas he is best known for his suggestion that we can explain what it is for words to mean what they do by considering their systematic contributions to the truth conditions of sentences containing them, and his linking our understanding of them to their use as seen from the standpoint of the interpreter of another. This is to treat the third person standpoint as primary in the task of understanding language and its interconnections with thought, and it is the linchpin of Davidson's philosophy. In the second of these areas, he is best known for his view that ordinary explanations of what we do, ordinary action explanations, are both causal and rational in character, that is, they cite a cause for an action which justifies it from the point of view of the agent. This forms a part of the framework for understanding the task of interpreting language use, as that involves centrally conceiving of the other as a rational agent. In the third area, he is best known for an important argument for a novel form of non-reductive materialism called *anomalous monism*, according to which each particular mental event is a physical event, yet mental event types are not the same as physical event types. This argument rests on Davidson's account of the nature of rational agency.

In the following, we approach Davidson's mature philosophical outlook through its ontogenesis, for insight into influences on it and the context of its development help to illuminate its underpinnings, its historical context, and its influence. No fully adequate account of Davidson's contributions can be given in a short space. We trace main lines of development and provide an overview of the place of Davidson's philosophy in the larger tapestry of twentieth-century analytic philosophy.

2   The Sources of Davidson's Philosophy

The two main springs of Davidson's philosophical work were his interest in the nature of human agency and in the nature of language. Though initially separate, they later became intertwined, in a way characteristic of much of Davidson's work. Both interests were sparked during his early years at Stanford, where he moved in 1951 from his first job at Queens College in New York. When he arrived at Stanford, he had no philosophical project. He began a collaboration with Patrick Suppes and J. J. C. McKinsey on decision theory (the theory of what choice, as revealed in behavior, reveals about preference and belief). This is one source of his interest in the philosophy of action, and it played, as we will see, an important role in the development of his project in the theory of meaning. The other source of his interest in the philosophy of action was his dissertation advisee Dan Bennett, who spent a year in England with Elizabeth Anscombe and Stuart Hampshire, and returned to write a dissertation on the philosophy of action. In reading and thinking about the dissertation, Davidson came to believe that it was a mistake to hold that the properties of reason explanations prohibited them from being causal explanations, in contrast to the then orthodoxy in philosophy, in a period in which Wittgenstein's influence was still pervasive. An invitation from the philosopher Mary Mothersill to present a paper at the American Philosophical Association in 1963 led to his extraordinarily influential essay, "Actions, Reasons, and Causes," in which Davidson argued against the dominant orthodoxy. Taking an agent's reasons for action to be given by what he wants and what he believes he can do to get what he wants, Davidson argued that ordinary explanation of human action is a variety causal explanation: an agent's reasons for an action both minimally justify the action from the agent's point of view and cause it to come about. Along the way he cleared up some deep-seated confusions about the relation between causes, events, and their descriptions, which was to prove central to his later argument for anomalous monism. Davidson's view quickly became orthodoxy.

During this period, McKinsey, an early contributor to the development of quantified modal logic, invited Davidson to co-author a paper for the *Library of Living Philosophers* volume on Rudolph Carnap's method of intension and extension in semantics. Carnap was a central figure in the logical positivist movement in the 1930s and 1940s and had a great influence on the development of analytic philosophy in the twentieth century. When McKinsey died before the project got started, the task fell to Davidson. Working on his contribution, while teaching the philosophy of language, stirred an interest in the theory of meaning and especially in the problem of how to understand sentences attributing beliefs and other so-called propositional attitudes.

There were two problems which reflections on the semantics of belief sentences rendered salient.

The first was the question of how we understand complex expressions on the basis of the words that make them up and rules governing their arrangements. This is the problem of giving a compositional account of the meaning of complex expressions, that is, a compositional meaning theory. It is not at all obvious how to give such a theory, and beliefs sentences in particular present a special problem. A sentence such as "Galileo believed that the earth moves" is clearly understood on the basis of understanding its significant parts. We do not have to learn such sentences one by one, and we understand without difficulty sentences of this form we have never encountered before. But what role exactly is the sentence "the earth moves" playing? It is not used in the way it is in a sentence such as "the earth shines and the earth moves." For this sentence to be true, both "the earth shines" and "the earth moves" must be true. But "the earth moves" does not have to be true in order for "Galileo believed that the earth moves" to be true, and we may obtain a false from a true sentence by replacing "the earth" with a co-denoting term (e.g., "the third planet from the sun"), in contrast to "the earth shines and the earth moves." This makes it look as if the words after "believed that" are functioning differently than they do in other contexts.

Carnap's solution, following Frege, involved assigning to expressions both an extension (a referent, set of things it is true of, or a truth value) and an intension (roughly a sense or meaning). In belief reports, it is the intensions of the terms in the complement clause that are active, on Carnap's view, for beliefs have to do with how people see things rather than with just what the things are. And since the meaning of "the third planet from the sun" differs from that of "the earth," we cannot expect substituting the first for the second to preserve the truth of a belief report.

Davidson came to think, however, that there were significant difficulties with Carnap's account of belief sentences (and with Fregean accounts more generally). In particular, he came to doubt that the Frege–Carnap approach to attitude sentences was compatible with the requirement that we understand belief sentences on the basis of grasping a finite number of semantical primitives and rules for their combinations. This requirement renders salient the real difficulties involved in coming to a proper understanding of the compositional structure of natural languages (see "Theories of Meaning and Learnable Languages," *ITI* 3–15).

The second problem that reflection on the semantics of belief sentences rendered salient was the question of how to tell when a proposed account of the compositional structure of a natural language sentence was correct. The solution to both problems came together.

In November 1954, Davidson presented a paper on Carnap's method of intension and extension at the University of California, Berkeley. In the audience was the great Polish logician Alfred Tarski, who was on the faculty. Afterwards, Tarski gave Davidson a copy of his article "The Semantic Conception of Truth and the Foundations of Semantics."[1] This led Davidson to Tarski's groundbreaking technical paper on truth, "Wahreitsbegriff."[2]

Tarski provided an axiomatic definition of a truth predicate for a formal language which was demonstrably extensionally correct, that is, which enabled one to prove for each sentence of the object language (the language for which the truth predicate was defined) a sentence in the metalanguage (the language of the theory) which says under just what conditions it is true, for each of the infinity of sentences of the object language. This was an important breakthrough, for, in providing a formal, consistent definition of truth, Tarski created a demonstrably consistent foundation for application of the concept of truth in logic and the foundations of mathematics, and paved the way for a systematic study of semantics in connection with the languages dealt with by logicians and mathematicians.

Davidson's retrospective remarks show clearly how these various threads came together in his program in the theory of meaning:

> [W]hen I understood ["Wahreitsbegriff"] it really turned me on. Still, I might not really have appreciated it if I hadn't done that stuff on decision theory. I had an appreciation for what it is like to have a serious theory, and I think the other people who were working in philosophy of language didn't have an appreciation for what it was like to have a serious theory. . . . Tarski, who knew what a serious theory was like alright . . . didn't have much philosophical interest. . . . I saw how to put these two things together. It came to me as if the heavens had opened and then I started to write a whole bunch of things. (*PR* 253)

Davidson saw Tarski's work as a providing a way of bypassing many of the traditional problems of the theory of meaning. Properly deployed, it would provide an account of the compositional structure of language and a standard for the correctness of an account of the logical form of a complex expression – namely, integration into a theory of the language as a whole which locates the role of the words in the relevant expression in a theory of their role in any other grammatical construction in which they can appear.

What was Tarski's accomplishment? He provided a criterion of adequacy for a truth definition for a formal language and showed how to construct a definition of a truth predicate that met the adequacy condition. He called the adequacy condition Convention T. It requires an adequate truth definition to be formally correct and to have as theorems all sentences of the form (or of a form analogous to) (T),

(T) *s* is T if and only if *p*

where "is T" is the truth predicate being defined, "s" is replaced by a description of an object language sentence in terms of its significant parts, and "*p*" is replaced by a sentence of the metalanguage that translates s. (S), for example, is an instance of (T) (a "T-sentence").

(S) "La neige est blanche" is T iff snow is white.

This guarantees that s is in the extension of "is T" if and only if it is true, because if "p" is a translation of s, then it is true iff s is. The definition can be stated in the form of a set of base and recursive axioms that provide "truth conditions" for every object language sentence. The base axioms apply to primitive expressions. The recursive axioms apply to expressions built up out of others, and ultimately out of the primitive vocabulary.

Davidson's interest was in meaning, rather than truth. But he saw a way of exploiting the structure of an axiomatic truth theory in Tarski's style in pursuit of a meaning theory. For if in (T) "p" translates s, replacing "is T if and only if" with "means that" yields a true sentence. Furthermore, the canonical proof of the T-sentence (a proof that draws intuitively only on the content of the axioms) will reveal the structure of the sentence relevant to stating meaning-giving truth conditions for it, and, thus, exhibit how we can understand the sentence on the basis of its parts and their mode of composition. In this way the truth theory can do duty for a compositional meaning theory.

Further modifications are required to extend a truth theory of the sort Tarski developed to a natural language in which we must accommodate context sensitivity, such as inflection for tense, and expressions like "I" and "now," and the adequacy condition must be correspondingly modified. But seeing how this is done in detail is not necessary to get the main idea about how a truth theory is to aid in meeting the goals of a compositional meaning theory.[3]

The final piece in Davidson's program fell into place when W. V. O. Quine, the most influential American philosopher of second half of the twentieth century, visited the Center for Advanced Study in the Behavioral Sciences at Stanford as a fellow in the 1958–9 academic year, while on leave from Harvard University. At the time, Quine was preparing the final version of the manuscript of *Word and Object*, his *magnum opus* on the relation of language to reality, which Davidson agreed to read. Davidson and Quine had known each other since Davidson's days as an undergraduate at Harvard. But Davidson's interests in the philosophy of language developed largely after he had left Harvard, and it was during the year that Quine was at Stanford that he had his greatest influence on Davidson. "When I finally began to get the central idea," Davidson later wrote, "I was immensely impressed; it changed my life" (IA 41).

The methodological centerpiece of *Word and Object* is the project of radical translation. The "radical translator" approaches the task of understanding another speaker without any prior knowledge of the speaker's meanings, beliefs, or other psychological attitudes. He restricts himself to the speaker's dispositions to verbal behavior in response to stimulus in constructing a translation manual for him and thus isolates the empirical content of a theory of translation. Translation manuals alike in empirical content were judged to capture all the meaning facts which there were. In his "Epistemology Naturalized," Quine explains the ground for this conclusion as follows:

> The sort of meaning that is basic to translation, and to the learning of one's own language, is necessarily empirical meaning and nothing more. . . . Language is socially inculcated and controlled; the inculcation and control turn strictly on keying of sentences to shared stimulation. Internal factors may vary ad libitum without prejudice to communication as long as the keying of language to external stimuli is undisturbed. Surely one has no choice but to be an empiricist so far as one's theory of linguistic meaning is concerned.[4]

This conception of the ground of meaning facts had an enormous impact on Davidson. Davidson "thought it was terrific," and reported: "I sort of slowly put what I thought was good in Quine with what I had found in Tarski. And that's where my general approach to the subject came from" (*PR* 258).

The earlier work on decision theory played an important role in this synthesis. Davidson brought two morals from the study of decision theory to bear on the theory of meaning. The first was that "putting formal conditions on simple concepts and their relations to one another, a powerful structure could be defined," and the second was that the formal theory itself "says nothing about the world" and that it is interpreted by its application to data to which it is applied (IA 32). Tarski's work provided the essential framework for developing a formal theory. Quine's resolutely third person approach to meaning provided Davidson with an important restriction on the evidence in relation to which the formal theory was to be interpreted.

If we take truth as basic and use axioms which employ metalanguage terms that interpret object language expressions in giving their (object relative) truth conditions (e.g., for any x, "rot" in German is true of x iff x is red), then the truth theory illuminates in the proof of T-sentences the compositional structure of language. We connect meaning with its basis in speakers' behavior and interactions with their environment and other speakers by treating a formal truth theory as an empirical theory whose empirical content is located in how it would be confirmed for a speaker or speech community. Illumination of its theoretical concepts is sought not in reductive analyses, but rather in showing how evidence can be marshaled in support of a theory of interpretation for a speaker. In this way we make clear holistically, in Davidson's words, "what it is for words to mean what they do."

Here we have three reorientations of the philosophical project of illuminating meaning. First, there is the introduction of the truth theory as the vehicle for the meaning theory. This aims to extract the resources of a theory that deals just with the extensional properties of expressions, their referents, extensions, or truth values, all that we want by way of a compositional meaning theory. It does this by putting certain constraints on a theory dealing with these things aimed at guaranteeing that, from appropriate theorems, we can "read off" what a sentence means. If successful, this shows that the traditional ontology of senses, intensions, properties, relations, and propositions is not necessary for a compositional meaning theory. Second, there is the eschewing of the traditional project of providing a reductive analysis of "is meaningful" in favor of a looser and more holistic form of conceptual illumination as represented by the application of the theory as a whole to the evidence as a whole. Third, there is the restriction of the evidence in terms of which the theory is to be interpreted to what is available from the third person point of view absent any assumptions about the (detailed) psychology or meanings of the speaker.

This project in the theory of meaning became intertwined with the project in the philosophy of action in two ways. The first was through the application of the methodology of uncovering the logical form of action sentences, which resulted in Davidson's important contributions to the logic of adverbial modification ("The Logical Form of Action Sentences") and to the logic of singular causal statements ("Causal Relations"). The second was through the application of the body of theory developed in understanding human agency to the problem of interpretation. To understand this, we must consider in more detail Davidson's recasting of Quine's project of radical translation as "radical interpretation" and the relevant portions of his work in the philosophy of action. This will lead us into the developments of Davidson's work in the philosophy of mind and in epistemology.

3 Radical Interpretation

Central to the radical interpreter's project is the confirmation of a Tarski-style axiomatic truth theory for the speaker's language. But, though this is central, in Davidson's account, to the enterprise of interpretation, it is not all that the interpreter aims to do. He must also use the truth theory to interpret speaker utterances, and he must fill in the picture of the speaker as a rational agent responding to his environment and others. Speaking is an activity embedded in a form of life appropriate for rational agents. As Davidson puts it at one point, "[a]ny attempt to understand verbal communication must view it in its natural setting as part of a larger enterprise" (*PR* 151). This means that understanding what people mean by what they say must be fit into and made coherent with a larger theory of them as rational, linguistic beings.

The nexus between the project of interpreting another's language and of interpreting his attitudes lies in identifying, as an intermediate stage in interpretation, attitudes toward the truth of sentences. Such attitudes, Davidson assumes, can be identified ultimately on the basis of purely behavioral evidence. In the first phase of his work on radical interpretation, "hold true" attitudes toward sentences took center stage. A hold true attitude toward a sentence s is a belief that s is true. A speaker holds true a sentence s on the basis of two things: first, what he believes the sentence means, and, second, what he believes to be so. If a sentence s means that p, and a speaker believes that p, then (at least generally or typically, Davidson assumes) the speaker will hold true s. If we can identify the belief on the basis of which a speaker holds true a sentence s, then we can say what it means (on that occasion). If we can say what it means, we can identify the content of the belief on the basis of which he holds it. The trick is to figure out from observation of the relations between the speaker and his environment how to break into the circle. There is no way to do this without the aid of an additional principle governing the relation of a speaker's attitudes toward his environment. Since there must be (on Davidson's view) a way of doing it, whatever principles are needed are justified by their necessity for interpretation – "the alternative being that the interpreter finds the speaker unintelligible" (*PR* 157).

Davidson invokes the Principle of Charity (following Quine) to solve the problem of breaking into the circle of belief and meaning. The Principle of Charity says that the interpreter should treat his subject as largely right about his environment and as largely rational in his behavior. The Principle of Charity aims to fix one factor, namely, belief, in order to get at meaning, by holding that it is a constitutive principle of interpretation that a speaker's beliefs about his environment are largely correct. Then from correlations between hold true attitudes and conditions in the environment, we tentatively identify the contents of the speaker's underlying beliefs and so what the sentences he holds true on their basis mean. Those conditions then also give the target truth conditions for the sentence in a truth theory for the language. For example, from correlations such as,

S holds true "It's snowing" at t iff it is snowing at t

we infer tentatively, where "L" designates S's language, that

For any speaker x, and time t, "It's snowing" is true in L at t for x iff it is snowing at t

is a theorem for a truth theory for L which meets an appropriate analogue of Tarski's Convention T. We then project axioms for the theory that fits as best as possible the data we get of this form to develop a theory of interpretation for the speaker.

The Principle of Charity also requires us to find the other, so far as possible in the light of his behavior and interactions with others and his environment, to be a rational agent. This means that we must find his attitudes largely arranged in patterns that make for both theoretical and practical rationality, and which connect them in coherent ways with his intentions as revealed in his choice behavior. This provides an important constraint on the development of an interpretation theory, and it is a point of connection between Davidson's work in the philosophy of action and in his project of understanding language and linguistic communication. For the detailed exploration of the structure of the norms which govern attribution of propositional attitudes on the basis of behavior is the project of the philosophy of action. We accordingly turn next to the development of Davidson's views on agency.

4 Action, Agency, and Rationality

"Actions, Reasons, and Causes," as we noted above, championed the view that ordinary action explanation is causal explanation of a special sort, namely, a sort which cites causes which also show minimally what was to be said for the action from the agent's perspective. The was in contrast to the dominant view at the time that reasons for actions cannot be causes of them but rather explain actions by showing how they fit into a larger pattern of behavior or a pattern of social relations. This was motivated in large part by what were thought to be, in principle, objections to reasons being causes of actions, and we will turn to Davidson's response to one particularly influential objection below.

An action explanation, according to Davidson, is successful when it indicates what he called a primary reason for the agent's action. A primary reason consists of a belief and pro attitude (a term that covers any propositional conative or motivational state, such as desires, wants, urges, and the like). The pro attitude is directed toward actions of some type, and the belief is to the effect that the action the agent performed was of that type. This applies both to actions done for their own sake and for the sake of further things. Often, explanations of actions do not cite a full primary reason, but they nevertheless explain because they give enough information in the context for the primary reason to be inferred. If we explain someone's buying flowers by saying it is his wedding anniversary, it is easy to fill in the rest of the story about his beliefs and desires with respect to his action, given common knowledge. A primary reason shows something about what was to be said for the action from the agent's point of view, for it tells us that the agent thought it was of a type which he wanted to perform. From the primary reason we can construct a practical syllogism showing what was to be said for it:

Action A is of type F
Actions of type F are desirable (insofar as they are of type F)

Action A is desirable (insofar as it is of type F)

The first premise is supplied by the belief and the second by the desire. It is natural then to take the primary reason cited in explanation of an action also to be what causes it.

The most influential objection to this idea was that the relation between reasons and actions could not be causal because there was a logical connection between the reasons for an action and the action. This is because the concept of an action is the concept of a piece of behavior that can be made intelligible by reasons. If one is blown off a cliff by the wind, it is something that happens to one but not something one does, and it follows one had no reasons for it. If one jumps off, by contrast, it is something one does and it follows that one had a reason for doing it. Hume had argued convincingly that the causal relation connects independently existing events, and so that it holds between things contingently. It was then thought that the logical relation indicated above between actions and reasons precluded reasons from causing actions.

The objection, however, is unsuccessful. First, that one has a reason to do something does not entail that one will, and any given action may have been motivated by a great variety of different primary reasons. So there is in fact no entailment from the specific primary reason cited to explain any action and the occurrence of the action, or vice versa. Second, and more fundamentally, objection rests on the conflation of an event with its descriptions. The causal relation holds between events, but logical relations hold between descriptions of events. The fact that two events were picked out by way of descriptions which were logically related would not in itself show that they did not stand in the causal relation, for any two events standing in the causal relation admit of descriptions which are logically connected. Thus, for example, "The cause of B caused B" may be true despite the fact that from "something is the cause of B" it follows that "B exists."

This point is relevant to our thinking about the relation between the reasons we have and what we do. For if events stand in the causal relation in virtue of contingent laws that connect events of those types, the fact that there are some logical connections between actions and reasons (at least to the extent that no behavior can be an action unless it has its reasons) suggests that in understanding why reasons are causes of our actions, we may need to shift from the vocabulary of reasons to the vocabulary of physics. This presages Davidson's later argument for anomalous monism, to which we will turn shortly.

Actions are for Davidson bodily movements – where this is construed broadly to include any bodily changes (see "Agency"). This includes even mental actions, given Davidson's thesis that every mental event is a physical event, and the assumption that mental events are identical with physical changes in the body. Events are particulars, changes in objects, and, hence, can be described in various ways. It follows that reasons are reasons for an action under a description, for reasons focus on desirable features of actions. It is not surprising then that many of our descriptions of actions are in terms of their effects. For example, "Booth killed Lincoln" describes a bodily movement of Booth in terms of an effect of it which Booth saw as desirable, Lincoln's death. It tells us he did something to cause Lincoln's death, though it leaves open exactly what it was.

In an influential paper on the problem of weakness of the will ("How is Weakness of the Will Possible?"), Davidson developed a model of practical reasoning based on the observation that reasons relate to actions under descriptions. Specifically, Davidson argued that practical reasoning is similar to probabilistic reasoning in the sense that it involves assembling reasons for something which those reasons do not entail. That the sky is red at night may make it probable that the weather will be fair in the morning. That the barometer is dropping may make it probable that the weather will not be fair. But it cannot be that it is both probable that the weather will be fair and probable that it will not be. So these probability statements must be understood as relativized to their supporting evidence. Similarly there may be reasons in favor of and against an action under different descriptions. The action cannot be both good and bad. So the judgments made on the basis of reasons must be conditioned by the reasons, by the features they focus on, and by their relative weights. In probabilistic reasoning, we follow the rule of total evidence: the best judgment is the one that is made on the basis of all of one's evidence. Similarly, there is in practical deliberation a parallel principle of rationality, the principle of continence: the better course of action is the one that wins out in the light of all our relevant reasons, each receiving its appropriate weight.

This is the key to seeing how weakness of the will is possible and why it appears not to be. When we come to a decision as a result of practical deliberation, even if it is based on all our relevant reasons, it is still a conditional judgment. But when we act, we thereby express an unconditional judgment that that action is best. If we are rational, the unconditional judgment is based on our all-things-considered conditional judgment about what it is best to do. We act incontinently, or display weakness of the will, when we choose an act, and so judge unconditionally that it is best when our all-things-considered judgment favors another. The appearance of its impossibility, Davidson thinks, arises from two plausible principles: first, that what we do shows what we most want, so that if we want to do A more than to do B, and both are open to us, then we do A intentionally rather than B if we do either, and, second, that if someone judges doing A to be better than doing B, he wants to do A more than B. These principles apparently rule out doing something intentionally other than what one judges best, all things considered. But once we see that there is a distinction to be drawn between the unconditional judgment that something is best expressed in action and the all-things-considered judgment that something is best which is the result of practical deliberation, the appearance of inconsistency is removed.

In later work Davidson associated the unconditional judgment with intention, and argued against intentions being reducible to other sorts of states, either beliefs or desires, or to any special kind of action. On this view, an intention is a sort of pro attitude, but differs from desires and other pro attitudes that are the input to practical deliberation in being directly tied to commitments to act. Reasons for belief and reasons for intending are quite different, but reasons for acting and intending are (or almost always are) the same. Intentions can be formed prior to actions or simultaneous with them. When we act with an intention or intentionally, the intention brings about the action.

5   Non-reductive Materialism

Davidson's work in the philosophy of action laid the foundations for his influential argument for anomalous monism ("Mental Events").

Anomalous monism is the combination of two theses. The first is that each particular mental event is identical with a particular physical event. The second is that there are no strict laws connecting the physical with the mental – "psychophysical laws," as Davidson called them. The second implies that there are no type-type identities between mental and physical events; that is, that no mental event type is a physical event type. This is in striking contrast to the traditional view according to which, if the mental is nothing over and above the physical, it is because mental event types are just physical event types. Davidson's position is a form of non-reductive materialism: materialism (hence monism of substances rather than dualism) because it holds there are only material bodies, and non-reductive because it holds that mental types are not reducible to physical types. The argument has three main premises:

1 The principle of the nomological character of causality: If two events stand in the causal relation, then there are descriptions of them under which they are subsumed by a strict law.
2 The principle of causal interaction: every mental event stands in the causal relation with some physical event which is not also a mental event.
3 The anomalousness of the mental: there are no strict psychophysical laws.

A strict law is one that "there is no improving in point of precision and comprehensiveness" (*EAE* 223). The laws of physics, for example, aim to be strict laws, which form a closed comprehensive system for its domain that is as precise as is possible. If we assume that an event is physical iff it is subsumed by a strict physical law, and that there are just mental and physical events, then it follows, given (1)–(3), that every mental event is identical to some physical event though no type of mental event is identical to any type of physical event. For, as every mental event causally interacts with some physical event (2), every mental event is linked with a physical event by a strict law (1). But the law cannot be a psychophysical law (3). It must, given our other assumptions, therefore be a physical law. Thus, every mental event has a description under which it is subsumed by a strict physical law and is, hence, physical.

The crucial assumption is the third, the anomalousness of the mental. Davidson's argument for this is cryptic and difficult. The central thought is that for two descriptions to be suitable for appearance in a law, they must be suited for one another. Suppose (following Nelson Goodman) we define "grue" to apply to anything which is green and observed before midnight, or which is not observed before midnight and is blue. Then consider the two generalizations from observation: all emeralds are green; all emeralds are grue. Both fit all our evidence, but we only think the first is confirmed by its instances and projectable to the future and unobserved instances. But this is *not* just because "grue" is a predicate unsuited for appearance in a strict law. For, if we define "emerire" to apply to anything which is an emerald if observed before midnight and otherwise a sapphire, we can see that "all emerires are grue" is as well supported and projectable as either "all emeralds are green" or "all sapphires are blue." The question then arises when predicate pairs are suitable for appearing in laws, and, moreover, in strict laws. Many ordinary rough laws, such as that windows break if you throw bricks at them, we know to admit of exceptions, and they are often called *ceteris paribus* (other things being equal) laws. To turn these into strict laws, to make them more precise, we must often shift to the vocabulary of physics. The concepts of physics are a family of concepts governed by a set of constitutive principles – principles that tell us, roughly speaking, what constitutes something's falling under a basic physical kind, so that they fix the subject matter of the physical. Davidson holds that strict laws must draw their concepts from a family of concepts governed by constitutive principles.

Once this assumption is in place, the argument depends only on one further claim, namely, that the constitutive principles governing the application of psychological concepts are fundamentally different from those governing the application of physical concepts. They are so because the application of psychological attitudes to an agent is governed by the requirement that the agent be found by and large rational in his thought and behavior (the second component in the Principle of Charity). This is directly tied to agents being capable of acting and so of having their behavior explained in a way that shows it rational to some degree from the point of view of the agent. While this does not mean that agents must be perfectly rational, it does mean that understanding them as agents requires finding in them a pattern of attitudes which make sense of them as doing things for reasons, and so the attribution of any given attitude (belief, desire, or intention) requires fitting it into a pattern of others that exhibits them has having logical relations and roles in relation to which behavior falls into an intelligible pattern. These principles do not govern attributions of fundamental physical concepts, however, because physical concepts do not apply to objects or states in virtue of any contents that they have, but rational relations hold between states in virtue of their contents. Thus, the physical and the mental make up two distinct families of concepts governed by different sets of constitutive principles. Given Davidson's assumption that strict laws must draw on predicates from the same family of concepts, it follows that there cannot be any strict psychophysical laws.

6 Epistemological Consequences of Radical Interpretation

We return now to the project of radical interpretation and the morals to be drawn from reflection on it. If we take the radical interpreter's position to be conceptually basic in the sense of being the standpoint from which to articulate the basic structure of the concepts of a theory of a speaker, then what the interpreter has to assume about his subject matter can be taken to be constitutive of it and not merely to be expressing some aspect of the epistemic limitations of the radical interpreter's position. Davidson's fundamental assumption is that the radical interpreter's position is basic in this sense. This leads directly to a number of important theses about the mind–world relation and our epistemic position with respect to our own minds, the minds of others, and the external world. The central observation is that in order for a radical interpreter to bring to bear the evidence he has on the theory structured by the concepts of meaning, truth, and agency, he must see his subject as (a) knowing what he thinks, (b) knowing what he means, and (c) knowing what is going on around him in the world. Why? Suppose we can, as Davidson assumes, identify a speaker's hold true attitudes, i.e., his beliefs about which of his sentences are true, on the basis of behavioral evidence. Suppose that we can determine which hold true attitudes are prompted by conditions in the environment and which conditions prompt them. Hold true attitudes are the product of how the speaker thinks the world is and what he thinks his sentences mean. As noted above, it seems that the only way to break into this circle is to assume that the speaker is right about his environment. Provided that we assume further that he knows what his sentences mean and what he believes, he will hold true sentences which are about conditions in the environment that prompt those hold true attitudes. If we identify correctly those prompting conditions, then we can read off what the sentence means and at the same time what belief it expresses.

But this all rests on the assumptions that the speaker is by and large right about the world, his own thoughts, and what he means. And if Davidson's fundamental assumption is correct, it follows that it is constitutive of what it is to be a speaker that one is mostly right about the external world, one's own thoughts, and what one's words mean.

The importance of this conclusion can hardly be overemphasized. If it is right, then we have a transcendental guarantee of knowledge of our own minds, the minds of others (for they must be accessible through the interpreter's procedure), and the external world. We secure this without having to explain how it is that we justify our beliefs on the basis of evidence, for knowledge in each of these domains emerges as a fundamental condition on having the capacity to speak and think at all. The traditional philosophical conundrums about how knowledge of the world and other minds is possible is resolved not so much by meeting the challenges head on, but by sidestepping them, by refusing the challenge as posed in favor of a roundabout guarantee of what was wanted but could not be got through reflection on our supposed impoverished evidential base in sensory experience. Given this transcendental guarantee, we are in a position then to evaluate individual beliefs by how well they cohere with our overall picture of the world, which is guaranteed to be largely right. To the extent to which a belief is not in line with most of what we believe, especially about the most basic things made available through perceptual experience, we have reason to think it not likely to be true. Conversely, to the extent to which a belief coheres well with most of what we believe, appropriately weighted by its connections with perceptual experience, we have reason to think it likely to be true. This does not mean that experience is an epistemic intermediary between believers and the world. It is a causal intermediary only. Its importance has to do with its being a causal intermediary between conditions in the environment and thoughts prompted by them which are, in virtue of that, about them.

This highlights another consequence of Davidson's position. Since radical interpretation reads into the contents of someone's environment directed beliefs the conditions that prompt them, and this expresses a constitutive feature of belief, belief is essentially relational – even general beliefs, because what concepts a speaker has, on this view, depends on what conditions in the world are systematically prompting his beliefs. Thus, Davidson is committed to a form of what is called externalism about thought content, the view that among the conditions that determine what the content of a thought is are conditions which are external to the thinker.

The result is a profoundly anti-Cartesian theory of mind and a profoundly anti-empiricist theory of knowledge. It is anti-Cartesian in rejecting the first person point of view as methodologically fundamental and in consequence in rejecting the view that the contents of the mind are what they are and are available to their subject independently of his embedding in the world. It is anti-empiricist through rejecting the traditional empiricist theory of knowledge and content according to which sensory experience is our ultimate evidence for the nature of the world and the source of our ideas, i.e., our concepts. The latter view, in its twentieth-century embodiment in the doctrines of the logical positivists, held that the meaning of a sentence was to be sought in the sensory conditions under which it could be confirmed or disconfirmed. The objectivity of thought is secured by its contents being determined by the distal objects in our environment which would form the basis for an interpretation of us. This secures us against idealism and relativism at the same time: against idealism by making the mind depend on the world rather than vice versa, and against relativism by guaranteeing a common intersubjective world that thought is about. Knowledge of the world and others is not seen as based on knowledge of oneself, but all three are seen as essential to the possibility of any of the others and are grounded in our nature as linguistic beings.

7 Davidson's Place in Twentieth-Century Philosophy

Davidson's mature philosophy, though it rejects it, developed out of the empiricist tradition. Seeing how this happened sheds light on its place in philosophy in the twentieth century. Carnap was the largest influence on Quine, as Quine was on Davidson. Two central doctrines shaped Carnap's views. The first was that there was a sharp division between the analytic and the synthetic, that is, between sentences (putatively) true in virtue of meaning (such as "All bachelors are unmarried") and those true in virtue of matters of contingent fact (such as "There are more bachelors in New York than in Montana"). The second was that the content of contingently true sentences was to be sought in their method of verification in sensory experience. Quine got his fundamentally empiricist outlook from Carnap. But he rejected both the analytic/synthetic distinction and the assignment of empirical meaning to sentences one by one, as opposed to in whole theories, styling these in the title of a famous article, "Two Dogmas of Empiricism."[5] The rejection of the analytic/synthetic distinction for Quine was tantamount to the rejection of the distinction between the a priori and the a posteriori. Thus, the traditional view of philosophy as an a priori discipline and its pretension to provide a foundation for the pursuit of science falls by the wayside.

Philosophy becomes distinguished from the disciplinary sciences only in dealing with more general categories. Philosophical theorizing becomes subject then to how well it fits in with the rest of our empirical theorizing about the world. It is in this light that Quine's approach to the theory of meaning and language is to be understood. Quine was skeptical of the analytic/synthetic distinction because he was skeptical about how well grounded the concept of meaning it relied on was. He set out to replace it with something more scientifically respectable in *Word and Object*.[6] Quine's fundamental starting point is the observation that "language is a social art" and it is this that motivates the stance of the radical translator. For, it follows from the essentially social character of language, Quine argues, that evidence for its acquisition and deployment must be intersubjective, and, hence, recoverable from overt behavior. In a conservative extension of the traditional empiricism theory of meaning, which keyed content to sensory experience, Quine then keyed sameness of meaning to sameness of response to patterns of physical stimulus of the sensory surfaces. This extrudes the traditional subjective basis of content in the empiricist tradition, sensory experience, to the sensory surfaces and renders it in principle intersubjectively available. A key change in Davidson's approach is that he takes it one step further by pushing the basis of shared meaning out to distal events and objects in the environment. In so doing, he rejects the last vestige of empiricism in Quine's philosophy – the third dogma of empiricism.

Davidson was a synoptic and original thinker and he dealt with large themes, though this is easily obscured by his concentration of the essay form and his compressed style and intensely analytical approach. Whether or not it is ultimately judged to be successful, his development of a unified response to the largest problems of the philosophical tradition, of mind, world, and self, which I have tried to bring out in the above, and the way in which he brought into his work so many different strands of influence and combined them, is an enormously impressive achievement. The strands of his own influence have been multifarious, and they are still developing. It is too early to tell what Davidson's place in the history of philosophy will be, the final place of his work in the development of historical patterns of thought. But it is hard to imagine what the landscape of contemporary philosophy would have been like without him.

Notes

1 Alfred Tarski, "The Semantic Conception of Truth and the Foundations of Semantics" *Philosophy and Phenomenological Research* 4/3 (March 1944): 341–76; repr. in Simon Blackburn and Keith Simmons (eds.), *Truth*. Oxford: Oxford University Press, 1999, pp. 115–43.

2 In Alfred Tarski, *Logic, Semantics Metamathematics*, 2nd edn., trans. J. H. Woodger, ed. John Corcoran. Indianapolis, IN: Hackett, 1983, pp. 152–278.

3 See E. Lepore and K. Ludwig, *Davidson; Meaning, Truth, Language and Reality*. Oxford: Oxford University Press, 2005; see also Lepore and Ludwig, *Davidson's Truth-Theoretic Semantics*. Oxford: Clarendon Press, 2007.

4 "Epistemology Naturalized," in *Ontological Relativity and Other Essays*. New York: Columbia University Press, 1969, p. 81.
5 "Two Dogmas of Empiricism," repr. in *From a Logical Point of View: Logico-Philosophical Essays*. New York: Haper & Row; 1st edn. 1953; 2nd edn. 1961.
6 *Word and Object*. Cambridge, MA: The MIT Press, 1960.

References

An extensive bibliography of primary and secondary material, compiled by Davidson himself, is contained in Lewis Edwin Hahn (ed.), *The Philosophy of Donald Davidson, Library of Living Philosophers* XXVII. Chicago: Open Court, 1999.

"Actions, Reasons and Causes," *Journal of Philosophy* 60 (1963); repr. in *Essays on Actions and Events*.

"Agency," in Robert Binkley, Richard Bronaugh, and Ausonia Marras (eds.), *Agent, Action, and Reason*. Toronto: University of Toronto Press, 1971; repr. in *Essays on Actions and Events*.

"Causal Relations," *Journal of Philosophy* 64 (1967); repr. in *Essays on Actions and Events*.

Essays on Actions and Events [*EAE*], 2nd edn. Oxford: Clarendon Press, 2001.

"How is Weakness of the Will Possible?," in Joel Feinberg (ed.), *Moral Concepts*. Oxford: Oxford University Press, 1970; repr. in *Essays on Actions and Events*.

Inquiries into Truth and Interpretation [*ITI*], 2nd edn. Oxford: Clarendon Press, 2001.

"Intellectual Autobiography" [IA], in Lewis Edwin Hahn (ed.), *The Philosophy of Donald Davidson: Library of Living Philosophers* XXVII. Chicago, IL: Open Court, 1999.

"The Logical Form of Action Sentences," in Nicholas Rescher (ed.), *The Logic of Decision and Action*. Pittsburgh, PA: University of Pittsburgh Press, 1967; repr. in *Essays on Actions and Events*.

"Mental Events," in Lawrence Foster and J. W. Swanson (eds.), *Experience and Theory*. London: Duckworth, 1970; repr. in *Essays on Actions and Events*.

Problems of Rationality [*PR*], with introduction by Marcia Cavell and interview with Ernest LePore. Oxford: Clarendon Press, 2004.

A selection of other works by Davidson

"A Coherence Theory of Truth and Knowledge," in D. Henrich (ed.), *Kant oder Hegel?* Stuttgart: Klett-Cotta, 1983; repr. in E. Lepore (ed.), *Truth and Interpretation: Perspectives on the Philosophy of Donald Davidson*. Oxford: Basil Blackwell, 1986, and in *Subjective, Intersubjective, Objective*.

"Adverbs of Action," in Bruce Vermazen and Merrill B. Hintikka (eds.), *Essays on Davidson. Actions and Events*. Oxford: Oxford University Press, 1985; repr. in *Essays on Actions and Events*.

Decision-Making: An Experimental Approach, with P. Suppes. Stanford: Stanford University Press, 1957; repr. 1977, Chicago, IL: University of Chicago Press, Midway Reprint Series.

"First-Person Authority," *Dialectica* 38 (1984); repr. in *Inquiries into Truth and Interpretation*.

"The Individuation of Events," in Nicholas Rescher (ed.), *Essays in Honor of Carl G. Hempel*. Dordrecht: D. Reidel, 1969; repr. in *Essays on Actions and Events*.

"Intending," in Yirmiahu Yovel (ed.), *Philosophy of History and Action*. Dordrecht: D. Reidel, 1978; repr. *Essays on Actions and Events*.

"Knowing One's Own Mind," in *Proceedings and Addresses of the American Philosophical Association* 61 (1987): 441–58; repr. in *Subjective, Intersubjective, Objective*.

"Laws and Causes," *Dialectica* 49 (1995); repr. in *Truth, Language and History*.

"The Method of Truth in Metaphysics," in P. A. French, T. E. Uehling Jr., and H. K. Wettstein (eds.), *Midwest Studies in Philosophy 2: Studies in the Philosophy of Language*. Morris: University of Minnesota Press, 1977; repr. in *Inquiries into Truth and Interpretation*.

"Moods and Performances," in A. Margalit (ed.), *Meaning and Use*. Dordrecht: D. Reidel, 1979; repr. in *Inquiries into Truth and Interpretation*.

"A Nice Derangement of Epitaphs," in E. Lepore (ed.), *Truth and Interpretation: Perspectives on the Philosophy of Donald Davidson*. Oxford: Basil Blackwell, 1986; repr. in *Truth, Language and History*.

"On Saying That," *Synthese* 19 (1968); repr. in *Inquiries into Truth and Interpretation*.

"On the Very Idea of a Conceptual Scheme," *Proceedings and Addresses of the American Philosophical Association* 47 (1974); repr. in *Inquiries into Truth and Interpretation*.

Plato's "Philebus." New York: Garland Publishing, 1990.

"Quotation," *Theory and Decision* 11 (1979); repr. in *Inquiries into Truth and Interpretation*.

"Radical Interpretation," *Dialectica* 27 (1973); repr. in *Inquiries into Truth and Interpretation*.

"Rational Animals," *Dialectica* 36 (1982); repr. in *Subjective, Intersubjective, Objective*.

"Reply to Quine on Events," in E. Lepore and B. McLaughlin (eds.), *Actions and Events: Perspectives on the Philosophy of Donald Davidson*. Oxford: Basil Blackwell, 1985; repr. in *Essays on Actions and Events*.

Subjective, Intersubjective, Objective [*SIO*]. Oxford: Clarendon Press, 2001.

"The Structure and Content of Truth" (The Dewey Lectures 1989), *Journal of Philosophy* 87 (1990): 279–328.

"Thinking Causes," in John Heil and Alfred Mele (eds.), *Mental Causation*. Oxford: Clarendon Press, 1993; repr. in *Truth, Language and History*.

"Thought and Talk," in S. Guttenplan (ed.), *Mind and Language*. Oxford: Oxford University Press, 1975; repr. in *Inquiries into Truth and Interpretation*.

"Three Varieties of Knowledge," in A. Phillips Griffiths (ed.), *A. J. Ayer Memorial Essays: Royal Institute of Philosophy Supplement* 30. Cambridge: Cambridge University Press, 1991; repr. in *Subjective, Intersubjective, Objective*.

"True to the Facts," *Journal of Philosophy* 66 (1969); repr. in *Inquiries into Truth and Interpretation*.

Truth, Language and History, with Introduction by Marcia Cavell. Oxford: Clarendon Press, 2005.

"Truth and Meaning," *Synthese* 17 (1967); repr. in *Inquiries into Truth and Interpretation*.

Truth and Predication. Cambridge, MA: Belknap Press, 2005.

"Two Paradoxes of Irrationality," in R. Wollheim and J. Hopkins (eds.), *Philosophical Essays on Freud*. Cambridge: Cambridge University Press, 1982, pp. 289–305, repr. in *Problems of Rationality*.

"What Metaphors Mean," *Critical Inquiry* 5 (1978); repr. in *Inquiries into Truth and Interpretation*.

WILLIAMS

CATHERINE WILSON

Bernard Williams (1929–2003) was the pre-eminent British moral philosopher of the twentieth century. His educational background was exemplary, his career progress smooth. Williams took a first-class honors degree in Classics at Balliol College, Oxford, went on to fellowships at All Souls and New College, and then to posts in London and Cambridge, where he became Knightsbridge Professor of Philosophy in 1967 and then Provost of Kings College in 1979. He moved to the University of California, Berkeley in 1988, before returning to Oxford as the White's Professor of Moral Philosophy in 1990. To the wider public he was known as the Chair of the Committee on Obscenity and Film Censorship, which held sessions in the late 1970s. He was married twice, to distinguished women in each case, first to Shirley Brittain, a journalist and later a politician, and then to the philosophy editor Patricia Skinner; he had three children. Williams was knighted in 1999.

Williams was unmistakably an analytical philosopher, a mapper of entailment relations, a discoverer or manufacturer of distinctions, an inventor and sometimes a solver of conceptual puzzles. The subjects of his work ranged from philosophical logic, to the history of philosophy, to ethics and political philosophy. He published a number of papers on conditionals, inference, and the logical consistency of beliefs in the *Proceedings of the Aristotelian Society* and the *Philosophical Review* in the 1960s and 1970s, and he composed a last book, *Truth and Truthfulness* (2002), on language and its uses, directed against postmodernist philosophers who deny that truth is either a possible property of any of our representational schemes or a desirable property of beliefs. His commitment to analysis informed his monograph *Descartes*, published in 1978. Williams distinguished sharply and influentially in its introduction between the history of ideas and the history of philosophy as distinct literary genres. To write about Descartes from the former perspective, motivated by historical curiosity, was to try to understand and to explain what Descartes meant. Such an inquiry necessarily yielded, if properly done, Williams declared, "an object essentially ambiguous, incomplete, imperfectly done" (*D* 10). To write about Descartes from the latter perspective, motivated by purely philosophical curiosity, was to aim for "the rational reconstruction of Descartes's thought, where the rationality of the construction is essentially and undisguisedly conceived in a contemporary style" (ibid.). This required the presentation of Descartes's arguments in modern-day logical form and the assessment of their formal validity. Williams did not invent this approach to the texts of the past, and it was strongly opposed by historians who believed it could only introduce distortions into interpretation to treat a seventeenth-century philosopher as our contemporary. Yet Descartes was perhaps exceptionally well suited to this treatment, insofar as he intended in his *Meditations* to produce a single sustained argument, with lemmata and a *quod erat demonstrandu*, analogous to a mathematical proof.

Williams's fame rests, however, on his contributions outside philosophical logic. He was unusual within his academic cohort, moreover, for at least four reasons. First, his first book *Morality* (1972), a survey of some conventional topics in ethics and metaethics, including the meaning of "good," subjectivism and relativism, utilitarianism, and amoralism, that prefigured much of his later work, opened with the claim that "[w]riting about moral philosophy should be a hazardous business." He went on to observe that "most moral philosophy at most times has been empty and boring," that most "analytical" or "linguistic" moral philosophy was "peculiarly empty and boring," and that "contemporary moral philosophy has found an original way of being boring, which is by not discussing moral issues at all." Williams wanted to come to grips with the problems of personal life experienced acutely by the artist, one such problem being the threat of the futility of his efforts, and philosophy was evidently an art form for him, as well as a discipline oriented to a kind of truth. He wanted to write about the emotions of everyday life, including emotions that even philosophers of the emotions have tended to avoid discussing, including ambition, shame, and disenchantment.

Second, not only was Williams widely read in fiction, conversant with art history, and something of an expert on opera, but, unlike most of his contemporaries, he made frequent references in his writings to literary works. Made-up examples, he maintained, that philosophers present to themselves and their readers, "will not be life, but bad literature." Good literature, though not life, was closer to life, and he tried for social and psychological verisimilitude in all his made-up-for-the-philosophical-occasion illustrative examples, some of whom were suicidal, alcoholic, unfaithful, or lost in the jungle – along with "tawdry fascist bosses," tycoons, and bureaucrats. He was as comfortable discussing Greek morality by reference to Homer's Ajax as he was discussing the value of life by reference to Janacek's superannuated Elena Makropoulos, or alienation from one's family by reference to Henry James's Owen Wingrave. His most notable fictional character, portrayed in his classic essay "Moral Luck," was a version of the painter Paul Gauguin.

A third feature that sets Williams apart from many analytic philosophers was his love of the archaic and his fascination with the exotic and the exaggerated. He was, as a result, a powerful and intuitive historian of philosophy. He knew intimately the Homeric epics and classical drama, but he also shared certain concerns with the mid-twentieth-century existentialists and their forerunners; his views about projects, commitment, and contingency were Sartrean; his mistrust of moral experts was reminiscent of Dostoyevsky and Nietzsche. He believed that contact with radically other minds – with the strangeness of their concepts – had a liberating and fertilizing effect on the philosophical imagination as it applied itself to contemporary problems.

Finally, Williams did not shrink from confident, some would say overconfident, generalization, insisting that prescriptive moral theory was incapable of systematization. Much analytical moral philosophy of the second half of the twentieth century is organized around the main schools of Kantianism, utilitarianism, and contractualism, and the task of the philosopher is often taken to be the criticism and modification of proposals and formulations of the various schools. Kantians maintain that there are objective moral duties that are binding upon all rational creatures endowed with the powers of agency and control over their own behavior without exception, that these duties are corrective of their natural inclinations, which tend to be wayward and self-seeking, and, in some cases at least, that these duties have a certain logical form that fits them to be discovered by reflection. Utilitarians insist as well that the content of morality is objective, only their starting point is not the rationality and will that Kantians insist on, but the susceptibility of human beings to pain and pleasure, and their aversion to the former and attraction to the latter. They conceive morality not so much as a set of duties and obligations, but as a set of rules and policies, which can be determined by calculating the pains and pleasures that are likely to be consequent on various courses of action. Contractualists, finally, assert that the content of morality is not fixed in advance. Morally correct rules and policies, as well as duties, are just those that reflect the compromises that rational and feeling, but also self-interested beings that have the power to help or harm one another, can and will agree to once they are in possession of reasonably accurate information about the world.

At the end of *Descartes*, Williams concluded that Cartesian dualism was untenable, but he ventured a version of dualism related to Descartes's own that informed much of his later writing. He looked with some admiration on Descartes's ambition to lay down the concepts and methods of a complete system of empirical knowledge, guided by a few rules and principles of inquiry and absolutely free of bias and prejudice. But Williams denied that moral knowledge could be obtained and organized in parallel fashion. He questioned the extent to which we might gain "any conception of the world that will be independent of our peculiarities and the peculiarities of our perspective." What he called "an absolute conception of reality" – a theory of physical nature and of the generation of our perceptions of it different from all "local or distorted" representations of the world – could, he thought, perhaps be attained eventually by science. First person thoughts, however, said Williams, could never be fitted in to this absolute conception because, insofar as we think in a language, what our thought means is indeterminate, as Quine had argued in his paper on the indeterminacy of translation (*D* 297ff.). Williams's rejection elsewhere of all aspirations towards a scientific account of morality, such as he deemed utilitarianism to be, and his constant emphasis on the undecidability of certain moral dilemmas by contrast with the eventual decidability of scientific problems and puzzles, reflected this dualism. In the various papers that went to make up the collections *Problems of the Self* and *Moral Luck*, as well as in his monograph *Ethics and the Limits of Philosophy*, Williams explored the consequences of his view that neither first person reflection nor philosophers' theorizing could produce objective moral knowledge. Although much of his work was dedicated to challenging the view that philosophy could produce an objective theory of human agency and the moral requirements pertaining to it, his writings nevertheless presented a certain distinctive picture of our agency and of the moral pressures to which it responded – and against which it sometimes struggled.

So Williams rejected the basic assumptions underlying the main schools of moral philosophy, and expressed his skepticism over attempts to specify the criteria of moral rightness. "There cannot be," he declared in his Preface to

Moral Luck, "any very interesting, tidy or self-contained theory of what morality is, nor, despite the vigorous activities of some present practitioners, can there be an ethical theory, in the sense of a philosophical structure which, together with some degree of empirical fact, will yield a decision procedure for moral reasoning" (*ML* ix–x). Philosophy, he thought, "should not try to produce ethical theory, though this does not mean that philosophy cannot offer any critique of ethical beliefs and ideas . . . [I]n ethics, the reductive enterprise has no justification and should disappear. . . . Practical thought is radically first-personal. It must ask and answer the question 'what shall *I* do?'" (*EL* 19–21). And the answer to that question, he argued, is importantly personal. For what I do is not only the result of *my* deliberations, it will involve changes in the world of which I am the cause. Williams was not, however, exclusively a philosopher of private life. He was passionately concerned in real life with politics, and while he harbored a kind of skepticism, or perhaps merely pessimism regarding economic and sexual equality, he could be equally scathing about the absurdities of capitalism and the class system.

In what follows, I will discuss Williams's most significant philosophical contributions in moral theory falling under the headings of personal identity, his rejection of external reasons, his criticisms – developed in parallel with the economist Amartya Sen – of utilitarianism, his discussion of moral luck, and his skeptical views regarding convergence in ethics at the limit of inquiry.

1   Personal Identity

Williams took the view that "bodily identity is always a necessary condition of personal identity" (*PS* 1). In making this claim, he set himself against a long tradition in the history of philosophy that began with Locke. Locke had argued in Book II, chapter 23 of his *Essay Concerning Human Understanding* that to be the same person – the being to whom various things had happened, and the being who was responsible for its voluntary actions, deserving praise and blame, punishment and reward for them, what was necessary, and all that was necessary – was the preservation of a substantial set of memories. Locke was in fact arguing against the Cartesian posit of a special mental substance constituting the self in which these memories inhered; he thought they might inhere in physical substance. But his point was that the psychological requisites of personhood could inhere in any body, and could in principle jump or be transferred from any body into any other if God allowed or facilitated this. The personhood of A could be imposed upon the body of B, by merely removing B's memories and introducing A's in their place. Consciousness of one's good and evil deeds, not the mere involvement of one's body in them, was, in other words, necessary and sufficient for moral responsibility.

The Lockean conception was allegedly vindicated by thought experiments such as the following: Suppose your mind were transplanted into another body and another person's mind transplanted into your body. Who would you rather be tortured? Clearly, you would prefer that torture go with your old body, not your old mind in its new body. But other thought experiments, as Williams pointed out, do not sustain the Lockean thesis. Rather, we tend to think of the "I" that undergoes various processes as a body that can pass through different mental states. We mind the announcement, for example, that we will be tortured, even if we are informed that we will be unconscious when it happens and not remember it, or that we will have another person's memories implanted in us. Williams argued that what we respond to and recognize as the identifying features of persons could not even be imagined to survive transplantation into the body of another. Voice and expression are crucial elements of personality and depend on the constitution of the body; hence it is virtually impossible to imagine oneself transported into a body of the opposite sex. (Persons who have undergone sex change operations who are happy in the new role are not exactly counterexamples; for such cases only show that the ordinary and usual identification with the body can be disturbed — and rectified.) To love a person, Williams insisted, is closer to loving a particular body than to loving a set of narratable memories and dispositions, for these same memories and dispositions would hardly be lovable in a coarse, uncoordinated frame, unless that is the sort of body one happens to love.

A self, for Williams, was a certain body, with a past, and a particular relationship to it. Being a self implied being capable of deep or shallow attachments to other persons, a liability to retrospective emotions of pride, shame, and regret, as well as being a source of agency in the world. Central to Williams's thought was the notion of a project. Selves, he said, are "inevitably future oriented," and they accumulate or fashion combinations of ambitions, hopes, plans, and efforts, that occupy their attention and command their effort. Projects provide a reason for living; they are the conditions of there being a future for any one of us, for "unless I am propelled forward by the conatus of desire, project, and interest, it is unclear why I should go on at all; the world, certainly, as a kingdom of moral agents, has no particular claim on my presence or, indeed, interest in it" (*ML* 12). Without projects of an importance so great that their pursuit can sometimes override moral considerations, Williams maintained dramatically and controversially, there can't be enough "substance or conviction" in one's life to compel allegiance to life itself.

Because projects are various, in the sense that so many are eligible for adoption, and personal, in the sense that ordinarily no one cares about their fulfillment as much as the agent whose projects they are, there is no unique answer to the question "How is it best to live?" no way, as Williams put it, to fill the entire rectangle of life-space. We do not, contrary to what the utilitarians maintained, organize our lives so as to maximize pleasure and minimize pain, and ethical behavior and practice is not to be identified with behavior and practice that will in fact maximize aggregate happiness and minimize aggregate pain. Rather, we desire to produce, accomplish, and experience certain things and these desires and their objects change over the course of a lifetime, sometimes in response to opportunities unexpectedly afforded and pathways that turn out to be blocked. We want certain outcomes; we want to produce them, and to have these outcomes depend on our efforts and our desires to produce them. But we live in a world of limited information, and uncertainty, and there are limits to what we can do to ensure the outcomes we desire, in part because of the unpredictable ways in which others react and things turn out. We have no clear idea how to maximize pleasure – which is in any case not the same thing as happiness, or general satisfaction with one's life and how things have turned out – and even less idea how to organize society so as to minimize as much pain as possible for the greatest number. However, "the fact that there are restrictions on what we can do is what makes us rational. Not to know everything is . . . a condition of having a life" (*EL* 57). Further, we have to understand our present projects as those of a person at least some of whose projects have changed in the past and whose future projects will change.

Personal identity, Williams concluded, is tied to the body, is both fixed and fluid, and depends on the representation, veridical and illusory, of the future imaginary. Its role in decisive moral argument is accordingly limited. Williams was skeptical about a common procedure in moral argument, namely the use of "role reversal" thought-experiments and the invitations offered by Rawls and his followers to consider policies from the point of view of anyone affected by them. Williams seemed to doubt that the results of such exercises could be valuable. In the first place, whatever I am doing when I try to imagine myself with the body, voice, expressions, history, emotions, and experience of someone whose situation is remote from mine has no success conditions attached to it, and to suppose it a valid and indeed unique test for political policies seems absurd. In the second place, he pointed out, role-reversal tests might legitimate abominations because they are so superficial. A Nazi might enthusiastically maintain that, if he were a Jew, he ought to be killed; that such sacrifices are necessary to save the world (*EL* 84).

Contractualism, considered as a theory able to furnish criteria for the just or the right, faltered in his view on the psychological impossibility of the thought-experiments it required.

Often, Williams argued, I am so rooted, as a member of a culture, in certain practices, the analogues of personal routines and habits of individuals that are almost invulnerable to revision, that even if alternative modes of organizing my society are "available" to me, in the sense of being represented in certain philosophical texts, they may not be available to me in more than a nominal sense. For the Greeks, Williams maintained, a world without slavery was simply unthinkable, even if it was a genuine misfortune, or at least a piece of bad luck, to be a slave (*SN* 125). Radical social change, the implication is, of *this* society into another one may be as unthinkable and therefore as impossible as would be *my* transformation into another person.

Williams's treatment revived the Nietzschean problem about promising: my future desires, ambitions, and preferences will depend on what I do now, as well as on chance and necessity, but I cannot predict exactly how. The institution of promising seems to demand performance of what was promised regardless of what happens; but how can I bind myself to some performance in an unknown future? Williams did not try to solve this problem theoretically; he indicated rather the importance in human life of both vows and escapes, broken promises. He implicitly agreed with some contemporary psychologists that impulsive, emotion-driven action is often experienced as highly rewarding, and that opportunities to indulge in it might be the conditions of what the subject himself would consider to be a happy life. This point alone was sufficient to distance him from the major traditions of ethics.

2   The Rejection of External Reasons

An old problem in moral philosophy is whether an action can be obligatory for an agent, and whether he has reason to perform it, even if he does not feel bound by the putative obligation, and does not feel that he has a reason to perform it. Henry James's character, Owen Wingrave, whose military family presents him with many reasons for going to war that Owen cannot accept as reasons, furnished a key example (*ML* 106–7), consistent with Williams's notion of the self as the one who projects values into the world insofar as he desires and strives, and feels the force of various kinds of "musts" in his life. Both Kantianism and utilitarianism imply the existence of agent-external obligations and reasons for action. In both ethical frameworks, however, it is difficult to give an account of why real agents should act in accord with such allegedly objective and impartial reasons, and how they can be motivated to do so if they profess to be unmoved or even horrified by the duties urged on them as ineluctable. Observation of Kantian duties may be held to be a condition of rationality, or even agency, but why must I care whether philosophy deems me to be rational or an agent?

Moralists frequently argue that we have objective reasons to act benevolently or beneficently towards others even when we fail to acknowledge those reasons, or when so acting would impose unwanted sacrifices on us. Such agent-transcendent reasons lie, they maintain, in the fact that no one, including myself, is objectively more important than anyone else, or in the fact that altruistic action can make the world overall a better place. Williams pointed out how difficult it is to establish that an agent N has a reason to do X, when that agent does not want to do X. It is often difficult to see that one ought to act in ways that are manifestly in one's own interest, let alone in other's interests, and urging an agent that he or she will be better off in the future for pursuing some course of action need not result in the agent's accepting the persuader's urgings as a reason to do that thing. My future self is no more and no less worthy of consideration than my present self, some philosophers claim, but at any given moment I may care disproportionately about one or the other, and to insist that I *ought* to give each temporal segment of my life equal weighting, or that I *may* or *may not* discount the future, is to make prescriptions, not to demonstrate objective obligations to care or not to care. Admittedly, it might be considered to be in Robinson's real interests, Williams agreed, to stop drinking, whether Robinson acknowledges it or not, but how are we to give a general criterion for the existence of a real as opposed to a subject-acknowledged interest?

To relate real interests to basic norms of human functioning seems too narrow; the notion of "what's good for N" depends on the particular person N. It is not identical with her preference set, but neither can it be the same as what's good for anyone and everyone. Even if one could define objectively the notion of being "good for N" or for N's having an unrecognized reason to do X, it is difficult to generate a right on the part of others to coerce N for her own good, or a duty of N to act in her real, unrecognized interests. Perhaps, Williams suggested, we have a right and a duty to inform, educate, or attempt to persuade people not to do things manifestly contrary to their real interests, but not to interfere with them. Yet, he said, we seem entitled to take steps to prevent suicidally depressed Susan from killing herself, even if information and education will not help convince her that it is not in her real interests to end her life now.

Williams considered the psychological remoteness of external reasons to impact negatively on both Kantianism and utilitarianism. The former posits duties towards oneself and towards others that are entirely independent of inclinations; the latter insists that there are rules of utility maximization that agents ought to obey whether they are motivated to or not. Where utilitarianism is concerned, Williams argued, it is a paradox of sorts that we do not necessarily wish that our *real* interests, as opposed to those that are transparently evident to us, be furthered. At the same time, we do not wish our mere preferences, preferences that are not in our interests, to be furthered. A benevolent and well-informed administration cannot, then, aim to satisfy either our real or our apparent interests; insofar as these diverge, it will make us miserable in one case and ruin us in the other. To the extent that our perceived interests can be brought into line with our real ones through education, the problem is solvable, but it is a feature of the human condition that a gap between the two can open at any moment and that it cannot be entirely closed.

Where Kantianism is concerned, the greater the contrast between objective moral requirements and subjective inclinations is made out to be, the less grounded our moral emotions appear to be, and the less reason we have to be moral. Kant had to invent a special emotion, Williams points out, "reverence for the moral law," to explain why we do not merely recognize but also obey the moral law. Having done so, one might observe, he failed to explain why this emotion operates so sporadically, or how the "radical evil" he saw as effacing it is consistent with the existence of transcendental duties. As Kant saw it, moral requirements do not stem from "my position in the world, my character, my needs," or even from "others' demands on me, but only from my own autonomous noumenal will; consequently, I cannot be forced into a position in which I do something morally incapable of justification." Obligations can trump obligations, but morality, whether we like it or not, can never be trumped by anything non-moral that we consider important. To sustain these claims, Kant needed an elaborate metaphysics, remote from the experience of everyday moral agency, one transcending, Williams insisted, the limits of philosophy. Williams's daring appeals to the hazardous situations of life and literature were intended to show up the vacuity of the metaphysics of morals.

3 Against Utilitarianism

There were further problems with utilitarianism, according to Williams. The chief difficulty with taking the general welfare as the criterion of the right is not only that we are self-interested and psychologically incapable of considered the welfare of others as on a par with our own; it is, rather, that we do not frame our own projects according to utilitarian criteria and we do not even prefer that others around us do so. We do not want to be involved with people who think in calculating, utilitarian ways about overall outcomes, but with people who are generous, affectionate, forceful, resolute, creative, and happy, and who form strong personal relationships. Rule utilitarians, when they insist that some spontaneous, emotion-driven, or highly partial actions, or indeed some merely dutiful ones, are justified or required on the grounds that, if everyone did likewise, the world would be a better place, are guilty of "one thought too many" (*ML* 18). Williams conceded, nevertheless, a need for explicitness and clarity in public codes, which had to be reconciled with being able to live "that worthwhile kind of life which human beings lack unless they feel more than they can say, and grasp more than they can explain."

Risk and effort, not pleasure, are what we often seek – at least according to Williams's psychological anthropology. Further, the informed perspective I take on my own experience-set, and how I came to have it, may be different from the perspective I would take if I were uninformed. The prospect of being hooked up to a nirvana machine can rightly be judged appalling, even if the experience of being hooked up to a nirvana machine would not be appalling. What's wrong with being hooked up to a nirvana machine is not that my experiences are in that case in any way suboptimal, for I could even be given the experiences of risk and effort by the machine, but that something fundamental to me – my shaping my own plans and projects, and my exerting my agency with respect to them – is objectively missing, however things seem to me. Here Williams seemed to endorse the notion of external reasons and real interests lying outside a subject's accessible motivation-set, but the nirvana machine is of course a special case.

A related flaw in utilitarianism, in Williams's view, was that it did not take into account the fact that actions of mine are experienced not as performed by someone, that someone happening to be identical with me, but as flowing from me. As such, it assigns us, implausibly, a form of "negative responsibility" whenever we fail to act so as to improve the overall condition of the world. Am I required, as some utilitarians claim, to bring about all states of affairs within my powers that, judged impersonally, contain less overall suffering and greater happiness than those states of affairs resulting from my refusing to act or doing something else instead would? William denied that anyone could show, from a metaethical perspective, that I am impersonally required to bring such states about. He further raised the possibility that I may be personally and blamelessly unable to act in an optimizing way. In his

"Jim in the Jungle" thought-experiment, an agent is given a choice between shooting one prisoner out of a group of 20 and letting all 20 prisoners be shot by someone else. This decision can be made, legitimately, in various ways, he maintained, but not simply by asking which state of affairs is overall the worse outcome – 1 dead or 20? (*ML* 38).

According to Williams, in such dilemmas, one must ask oneself not simply how many dead people there should be after I act, but rather "Can *I* be the one who deliberately kills someone, even if it is to prevent a large scale horror?" and "Can *I* be the one who shrank back from killing someone when I could have prevented a large-scale horror?" (Imagine that the mothers of young children amongst the group plead with me to overcome what they see as my cowardice or fastidiousness, and to sacrifice one to save the lives of the rest.) My being involved in it is as much a part of the situation as the effects on the 20 being considered. And this would be so, one might add, even if I were offered amnesia for the event, and did not have to live with the memory of what I had done or refused to do, for I would still have been the one who did or refused to do something. However, Williams did not draw the reverse conclusion that any act that we approve should be one we are prepared to do ourselves. We should not demand of politicians, he thought, that they be personally willing in principle to carry out unappealing acts they deem politically necessary. Such aversive acts might include fighting on the front lines, interrogating suspects, and spying, which are normally delegated to others who have a taste for them. Williams's criterion here was surprisingly practical and even utilitarian: imposing such a demand would restrict the political role to the most brutal contenders for offices and appointments.

4 Moral Luck and Regret

Some schools of ancient philosophy propounded the view that a good person cannot be harmed; the good person's only true interests, they maintained, are in his or her own upright conduct. The losses of things the ordinary person bewails – fortune, reputation, family, or friends – are not losses of true goods, and the possession of such things is not under our control, as virtuous conduct is. The good person, one who acts correctly in every situation, will have no reason to regret either his conduct or its consequences, bearing the losses imposed by fortune with equanimity. Williams had little regard for this Stoical view, which resurfaces in Kant's ethics. The loss of the objects and states just cited is precisely what matters most to us, and regret over our past conduct, for harms perpetrated to others, either unwittingly or on account of our drives to satisfy our own desires, is inevitable in the life of any reasonably sensitive person. The future is not predictable, and what kind of person one will be in the future, or what one will feel about one's past, having done certain things and refrained from doing others, are not predictable either.

We can deliberate well and yet find that things turn out badly; for that matter, we can deliberate poorly and yet find that things turn out well. The experiences of regret, remorse, shame, guilt, and self-blame are at least somewhat independent of the rationality applied in decision making. Practical reason can help us foresee and avoid certain preventable evils, or to recuperate certain, though not all, losses, but to live with the aim of minimizing the quantity of what makes a life bad is to some extent impossible and to some extent possible but inadvisable. It is impossible to the extent that we often do not know what is bad for us until it actually happens, and to the extent that we are psychologically inclined radically to discount the future in view of its uncertainty. It is inadvisable to the extent that in adopting a policy of minimizing risk, we will miss out on much of what life has to offer.

How things happen to turn out, for reasons that are mostly beyond our control, Williams maintained, makes an episode morally reprehensible or not: a beautiful love story or a sordid episode may have exactly the same material and emotional antecedents. "It is an illusion to suppose that there had to be at the time of those episodes a particular kind of psychological event that occurred if things turned out in one of these ways, and not if they turned out in another" (*ML* 45). In this connection, Williams introduced the notion of "agent regret" to characterize an attitude that implies not just regret about what happened, but regret about one's own role in what happened or did not happen. Agent-regret came into play even if what happened was not the result of a deliberate plan on my part to make it happen, but just a situation in which I was involved. "One's history as an agent is a web," said Williams, referring to Sophocles' Oedipus, "in which anything that is the product of the will is surrounded and held up and partly formed by things that are not" (*ML* 28). The lorry-driver who runs over a child who suddenly darts into the street should not accept reassurances too soon. Although there is no way to assign him any precise degree of blameworthiness, and although the accident may have been in some sense unavoidable, it is right, Williams insisted, for the driver to feel that he is at fault.

In other cases, however, Williams suggested, there is no reason to feel regretful or guilty, even when some socially or philosophically approved duty has not been respected. To illustrate the problems of outdated promises, the importance of projects, and the psychological pallidity of duty, Williams discussed a hypothetical figure similar to the wayward painter Paul Gauguin (*ML* 20–39). "Gauguin," without submitting his proposed actions to Kantian or utilitarian tests for permissibility, follows his inclinations and abandons his wife and children to paint pictures in Tahiti. Things turn out reasonably well for those left behind, and "Gauguin" paints pictures of beauty and profundity that are a significant contribution to the history of art and to aesthetic experience, but "Gauguin's" actions might have brought about little except impoverishment, suicide, grief, and ruin. What Williams termed "agent-regret" would have been (in a normal person) the sequel, and the appropriateness of such regret was intended to be a substitute, in his scheme, for the attribution of objective wrongness. The possibility of agent-regret, not simply the possibility of falling foul of morality, is what makes certain decisions hazardous. As a result of his or her pursuing, or for that matter failing to pursue, some goal, "someone may have ruined his life, or if he will not let anything make such an absolute determination of it, at least he may have brought it to a state of dereliction from which large initiatives and a lot of luck would be needed to get it back to anything worth having" (*SN* 70).

5 Objectivity and Perspective in Ethics

The goal of some moral theorists is to enunciate a system of norms that is formally consistent and that violates as few strongly held moral intuitions of ordinary people as possible. Ethical inquiry, on this view, is largely concerned with resolving theoretical inconsistencies. Thus, if you claim to believe in the sanctity of human life, your principle apparently commits you, as a rational agent, to opposing both warfare and abortion. If you oppose one but not the other, you ought, according to Socratic criteria, to reformulate the terms in which you express your belief. Williams, like Wittgenstein, saw such technical criticism of beliefs as largely pointless. Must we aim at constructing logically consistent and broadly plausible moral belief sets – at acquiring a Cartesian "absolute conception" of moral reality?

Williams distinguished between *ethics*, the study of how to live, involving a sensitive, historically informed, analytical attention to questions of conduct and attitude that he tried to practice, and *morality*, which he intermittently stigmatized as a Kantian and post-Kantian "peculiar institution," organized around the concepts of ineluctable or overridable duties and immunity to luck and tragedy on the part of the truly moral agent. In *Ethics and the Limits of Philosophy*, he argued for a curb to the pretensions of contemporary moral theory to demonstrate the existence of obligations and permissions binding on everyone. Again, his interest in internal and external perspectives surfaced. He denied that any philosophical method could lead to such a result, considering in turn the problems raised by the amoralist option, by the existence of divergent cultural norms, and by individuality and projects. We cannot justify the norms that restrain unbridled egoism to someone who professes not to care, or show him why he must bring himself under any discipline, though, fortunately, few human beings really stand outside our ethical institutions and practices. Scientific opinion must and does converge at the limit of inquiry, and it employs methods that are themselves the subject of consensus; it is accordingly objective. But there is no analogy in morals; consensus is unlikely to occur without coercion, and even if it did occur, it would no more indicate the existence of objective moral norms than standardization of our clothes, one might say, would indicate the existence of objective dress codes. What one truly believes, Williams pointed out, must be consistent with what others truly believe, but it is false that properly conducted moral deliberation by me in situation X must be consistent with the results of properly conducted deliberation by others about what they or even I should do in situation X.

"Ethical knowledge" can refer either to judgments from within a way of life that control its practices, or it can refer to the judgments of people who are trying to evaluate their own or others' practices critically. Our moral discourse serves mainly to reaffirm and only occasionally to nudge or subvert particular beliefs of persons who already accept the idea of moral restraints and who will not lose them. The personal features of ethical decision-making are analogous to the local features of social institutions, and both imply the poverty of contractualism. Why must ethics posit rules that everyone can agree to, Williams wondered, rather than allowing for the coexistence of rival practices or a "non-aggression treaty"? As we move further away from our own culture to evaluate different practices, we have an ever-thinner basis for deciding what proposals for norms others could not reasonably reject, given the web of beliefs and practices in which any norm is embedded. Even within a culture, individual differences are such that people are unlikely to agree on much, except the wisdom of supplying the most basic and evident needs of nearby others and observing some elementary rules of reliable and peaceable interaction. At the same time, ethical conviction about what I ought to do or what ought to happen, Williams noted, is not a personal decision, or even a group-decision, because it is not a decision: "[E]thical conviction, like any other form of *being convinced*, must have some aspect of passivity to it, must in some sense come to you" (*EL* 169). But the strength of conviction is only one parameter relevant to the positing of valid ethical norms; consensus, dependent on "discussion, theorizing, and reflection," is another.

Williams's leaning to relativism had its limits. Relativism was not, according to his metaethical system, an assertible theory any more than universalism, and he did not doubt that the practices of some cultures, ancient and existing, were cruel and morally wrong. Critical theory, he thought, kept alive questions of ideology and justification; it brought different cultural practices into the space of critical comparison, and he did not dispute its value, so long as it was understood that demands for justification and criticism take place within a context in which there is a choice of which way the society is going to go.

Conflict and contradiction in scientific inquiry indicates a flaw in the theory at hand; the theory has to be fixed up or discarded in favor of a better theory. In moral inquiry too, conflict and contradiction indicate a flaw in the theory, but there is no reason to think the theory can be fixed or replaced by a better theory; the conflict may reflect a tension built into the nature of things, reflecting our inconsistent preferences. Not only can individual lives be full of unresolved moral conflict and inescapable regret, entire societies may be permeated with practical contradictions that cannot be completely ironed out. Social and sexual equality, for example, is an ideal we citizens of modern democracies hold that we make some effort to realize. However, it is incompatible with other ideals, such as efficiency through the division of labor. As a result, we endorse and participate in many institutions that erode equality and sustain its opposite (*PS* 230ff.). Many people believe both that more effort ought to be devoted to eradicating painful and pernicious social inequality, and, simultaneously, that people ought to be free to do the work they most enjoy doing and that they should be free to earn as much money as they can induce others to pay them on the basis of their talents and efforts. They want the security and stability of marriages contracted for life, but also the freedom to change their minds. Even if we could reduce such conflicts in social ideals, Williams insisted, we might not gain thereby: "You might perhaps bring about a society whose values were less conflicting, more clearly articulated, more efficient, and people once arrived in this state might have no sense of loss. But that would not mean there was no loss. It would mean that there was another loss, the loss of the sense of loss" (*ML* 80).

6 Conclusions

In view of the boldness of his thought, Williams's legacy in philosophy is necessarily mixed. His fluid view of personal identity, and his insistence that the fact that a project or an action will be or was "mine" gives it a significance that the project or action does not have, considered simply as anyone's, have found considerable favor amongst moral philosophers. So too has his point that people have personal interests – "desires for things for oneself, one's family and friends, including the basic necessities of life, and, in more relaxed circumstances, objects of taste . . . pursuits and interests of an intellectual, cultural or creative character" (CU 110). The utilitarian project to enhance all lives would have no grounding, were this not the case; at the same time, given those interests, the impersonal utilitarian calculus can only be a philosopher's artifice that can be worshipped as an idol but that cannot command the deep loyalty of anyone who is not a dangerous fanatic. Williams's criticisms of moral realism still merit close study and development.

Williams's rather tragic approach to political philosophy has been little emulated, however. Many contemporary philosophers are apt to find his pessimism overstated and his skepticism about moral theory and what he termed "the morality system" or, applying the term once used in connection with American slavery, "the peculiar institution," unwarranted. Concerned to break down dichotomies that he found artificial, between pathological and moral motivation, between responsibility and exemption from responsibility, Williams posited certain problematic dichotomies of his own. The contrast between the personal goals of the agent and the impartially considered "good order of the world" need not, for example, be posed so starkly; an impartial good ordering of the world involves agent-sparing and agent-freeing measures. Kantians, it might be observed, can accommodate agent-sparing or liberating policies, provided they do not reflect the privilege and excess power of a person or group, or impose unacceptable levels of suffering on victims. Williams recognized that the purpose of morality was to dampen egoism, to combat the assumption that "the comfort, excitement, self-esteem, power, or other advantage of the agent" could take priority over the needs of others (*EL* 11); and he was willing to apply this conclusion to real world affairs; the Royal Commission on Obscenity and Censorship, which he chaired, recommended that films that portrayed "actual physical harm" of a sadomasochistic variety be banned.

His metaethics made it difficult for him, however, to characterize moral achievement, or the conditions of moral progress, or to fit the justified criticism of historically or culturally "remote" practices into his scheme. (His work on the Royal Commission was arguably too laissez-faire in restricting only pedophilic and sadomasochistic films, leaving the pornography industry free to create and vend the remainder of its wares to any and all.) His claim that we gain a better appreciation of morality in attending to applications of "thick" ethical concepts – terms like "courageous," "generous," "duplicitous," in place of the "thin" concepts of the Kantian tradition: "right," "wrong," "permissible," "forbidden," and the like – has been observed to carry a certain conservative bias, since to understand a thick term is normally to concur in its current application. Finally, Williams's attempt to make his notion of "agent-regret" function in lieu of the notion of objective moral failure was problematic, for appropriate kinds and degrees of agent-regret can only be experienced by morally educated agents; Williams appeared tacitly to presuppose a notion of a good moral education, one that leads to feeling ashamed or guilty in situations in which one ought to, and not otherwise. Even if the details of such an education could have been spelled out without reference to the main schools of moral philosophy that he criticized, it might be said that Williams assumed, wrongly and uncharacteristically, that his own educational experiences were universal experiences.

In some contexts, Williams strongly emphasized the improvisatory aspects of life, the need to respond to opportunities by breaking bonds with the past. Elsewhere, he expressed his fascination with the ways in which the feeling of an internal "must" leads to the deployment of ethical policies, rigid ones, that are part of "character" in the ancient Greek sense, and perhaps one of the losses of modernity. He did not really bring these two opposing features of the moral life into a single frame, though if he had written an essay on rigidity and improvisation in moral theory, it would likely have been both insightful and disturbing. His understanding of and love for the archaic seemed to conflict with his view that remote folkways are in no sense real options for members of other societies. Did Williams's often divided mind – on the existence of identifiable "real interests," and the possibility of social equality, for example – reflect the theoretical undecidability and tragic conflict he often posited, or did he simply bring on these conclusions too soon? These questions, together with others arising from consideration of his writings, are likely to continue to occupy philosophers for some time.

References

"A Critique of Utilitarianism" [CU], in *Utilitarianism: For and Against*, ed. with J. J. C. Smart. Cambridge: Cambridge University Press, 1973, pp. 82–117.

Descartes: The Project of Pure Inquiry [D]. Brighton, Sussex: Harvester Press, 1978.

Ethics and the Limits of Philosophy [EL]. London: Fontana, 1985.

Moral Luck [ML]. Cambridge: Cambridge University Press, 1981.

Morality: An Introduction to Ethics. Cambridge: Cambridge University Press, 1993; orig. pub. New York: Harper and Row, 1972.

Problems of the Self [PS]. Cambridge: Cambridge University Press, 1973.

Shame and Necessity [SN]. Berkeley and Los Angeles: University of California Press, 1993.

Truth and Truthfulness: An Essay in Genealogy. Princeton, NJ: Princeton University Press, 2002.

5 RORTY

ALAN MALACHOWSKI

Rorty has an unsettling vision of philosophy, science, and culture, and it matters to what extent he is right.

Bernard Williams[1]

It is a sure sign, though not the only one, that a philosopher has become a "figure" when their work cannot easily be spoken of without breaking it up into different periods. If this turns out to be the case during a philosopher's own lifetime, and there is already some controversy as to the suitability of the periodization involved, then we can be fairly certain that the philosopher in question is a major figure. By that standard, Richard Rorty had been a major philosophical figure for quite some time before his unfortunate death on June 8, 2007.

Since at least as far back as the publication of his book *Contingency, Irony, and Solidarity* in 1989, Rorty's philosophical writings have commonly been divided into three categories: (1) those that contribute fairly straightforwardly to important debates in analytic philosophy; (2) those that seek to undermine the presuppositions and main concerns of analytic philosophy; and (3) those that expound, explore, and celebrate what is perhaps best called "post-analytic pragmatism." As befits a "figure," these categories match up with three successive time periods. Hence, (1) corresponds to "Early Rorty," someone who made solid, but also ingenious, contributions to analytic philosophy; (2) falls in with "Middle Rorty," a philosopher who issued a severe challenge to philosophy's traditional self-image, but who did not cut his own umbilical cord and hence remained attached to that image in various ways; and (3) covers "Late Rorty," a thinker who espoused "post-analytic pragmatism," but, for the most part, roamed free of conventional philosophical boundaries, setting his own agenda as he did so.

Controversy surrounds the philosophical value judgments attached to these different "periods" and, as part of this, the divisions marked out by the latter are themselves disputed. Those who are most hostile to Rorty tend to fall into two camps. These are divided by the opposing assessments they make of his work over the three periods. Members of the first camp, let's call them Traditionalists, begrudgingly admit that the "Early Rorty" notched up significant achievements in analytic philosophy. Here they refer mainly to his contributions to the philosophy of mind, and to his articles on "eliminative materialism" in particular. But occasionally, his work on "transcendental arguments" is also given a favorable mention. In this latter case, Rorty provided "revisions of and additions to" P. F. Strawson's "new and improved version of the central argument of the *Transcendental Deduction*" – where Kant argues that "the possibility of experience somehow involves the possibility of the experience of objects" (SOA 213).

However, having made this concession, such critics then claim that in his middle period, Rorty turned his back on his earlier achievements and set himself on a path that would prevent him from doing any work of further philosophical interest. Of the "Late Rorty," their view is simply that his writings confirm their verdict as to what happened after he lost his early enthusiasm for analytic philosophy: his mature writings are philosophically suspect, and can even be very harmful if taken seriously. For them, there are really only two Rortys. The first is "analytic Rorty," a thinker they admire and respect and would continue to do so if only he had kept on the straight and narrow. As for the second, the "rogue-pragmatist Rorty," they regard him as someone who went off the philosophical rails and unfortunately made quite a name for himself in doing so.

In the other camp, are philosophers who work outside the analytic tradition, but mainly with the European fold. We can call these the Continentals. They are annoyed with Rorty on diametrically opposed grounds. For them, "Early Rorty" was just one more example of an analytic philosopher who helped marginalize, or at best trivialize, a great tradition of serious thinking that runs from Hegel through Nietzsche and onwards to Heidegger and Derrida. It is "Middle" and "Late Rorty" to whom they fiercely object. Here, they do not accept the Traditionalists' view that Rorty betrayed analytic philosophy. It is rather they feel that Rorty betrayed *them*. They are suspicious of the very idea that Rorty rebelled against analytic philosophy. They do not accept that he ever broke free from it, and regard his writings on non-analytic thinkers, such as Heidegger and Derrida, as insidious attempts to re-establish the hegemony of the analytic approach. In their eyes, Rorty's brand of pragmatism with extra-analytical trimmings is something of a Trojan horse. Again, there are only two Rortys. Neither is valued, though the reasons for this differ. In the first case, it is simply a matter of indifference. Whereas, in the second, on the grounds, presumably, that an enemy who poses as your friend is the deadliest enemy of all, there is quite open hostility.

It is against this background of highly contentious disputes that Rorty's philosophical writings must currently be interpreted and assessed. But, before we say a bit more about the significance of such disputes and whether they are likely ever to be resolved, we should fill in some of the details regarding Rorty's personal history and the chronology of his major writings.

1　Radical Roots

At 12, I knew that the point of being human was to spend one's life fighting social injustice. ("Trotsky and the Wild Orchids," in PSH *6)*

Rorty was born on October 4, 1931 in New York City. He was raised within a politicized family that consorted with many of the key progressive thinkers of the day and encouraged leftist activism. No doubt this at least partly explains Rorty's lifelong interest in politics,[2] and perhaps also his ability to engage with social issues in a knowledgeable, clear-minded and accessible manner even though he opted to pursue a purely academic career after studying philosophy at the Universities of Chicago and Yale. That career turned out to be a distinguished one. In 1961, Rorty moved from his first main teaching post at Wellesley College to one of the most prominent departments of philosophy in the world at Princeton University, where he stayed for more than 20 years. He then transferred to the University of Virginia, spending another 15 extremely productive years there, before taking up his final appointment, still prolific as ever, in the Department of Comparative Literature at Stanford University. He was an Emeritus Professor of Stanford at the time of his death.

Rorty's first notable writings concerned, as we stated above, the philosophy of mind and transcendental arguments. In a series of intricate and influential articles,[3] he took up the cause of "materialism," advocating an "eliminative" or "disappearance" account of the relationship between sensations and brain processes. On this account, the language associated with the former, language that is supposed to designate or describe subjective experiences, is fated to "disappear" or be "eliminated" from discourse. It might linger on for some purposes of social interaction, but it will play no role in a proper philosophical explanation of the nature of the mind. To the obvious retort that it is absurd to imply, as his own account seems to, that words like "itch," "burn," and "pain" will be made redundant when they are replaced by other words that have a purely physical reference point, Rorty responded with the kind of insouciance about the possibility of a radical change in linguistic usage under the pressure of social convenience that his critics would later find provocative:

> [the] absurdity of saying "Nobody has ever felt a pain" is no greater than that of saying "Nobody has ever seen a demon" *if* we have a suitable answer to the question "What was I reporting when I said I felt a pain?" To this question, the science of the future may reply, "You were reporting the occurrence of a certain brain-process and it would make life simpler for us if you would in future *say* 'My C-fibres are firing' instead of saying 'I'm in pain.'" (M–BI: 30)

Rorty also published a number of articles on the general theme of "transcendental arguments," taking his cue, as we indicated earlier, from Strawson's attempt to reconstruct an improved version of Kant's anti-skeptical strategy. The major claim that Rorty was seeking to establish has been well summarized by Anthony Brueckner: "If one is a self-conscious being and therefore possesses the concept of an experience, then one also possesses the concept of a physical object."[4] If Rorty had published nothing other than the work we have referred to so far, he would still have warranted at least a footnote to any adequate account of the analytic chapter in philosophy's history. However, it was the next stage in his publishing career that catapulted him into a higher league and set the stage for his appearance as a more provocative and influential thinker.

2 Challenging the Tradition

The picture which holds traditional philosophy captive is that of the mind as a great mirror, containing various representations — some accurate, some not — and capable of being studied by non-empirical means. (PMN 12)

The work that apparently marked out this next stage was *Philosophy and the Mirror of Nature* (1980), a book that soon gained sufficient notoriety to match the scale of its ambition.[5] *PMN* was ambitious in the sense that it sought to free modern Western philosophy from its perennial problems, the kind of problems that had concerned it, in one way or another, since the Greeks. And what seemed so disreputable to opponents was the *way* in which *PMN* attempted to achieve this goal. For it did not seek to solve these problems, or even offer detailed arguments to show that they were not really serious problems at all. Instead, it wove a complex quasi-historical narrative within which the problems in question appeared to be entirely optional. Furthermore, it claimed to have detected an "internal dialectic" by means of which some of the key players in modern analytic philosophy marked out the first important steps toward the conclusion of this narrative.

In taking this approach, Rorty appeared to be doing philosophy itself a great disservice. He implied that its traditional subject-matter could be sidestepped with impunity, that it was no longer worth taking time out to try to answer the sort of questions the greatest philosophers had battled with down the ages. Many of Rorty's critics carried this further, regarding *PMN* as an attempt to kill off philosophy once and for all. And they resented Rorty's insinuation that when philosophy finally succumbed to his attacks, the hands of a number of important thinkers within the analytic tradition, including Wittgenstein, Sellars, Quine, and Davidson, would perhaps be more bloodstained than his own. For Rorty claimed that such thinkers had started a process of undermining analytic philosophy that he was merely carrying to its natural conclusion. Much ink was wasted in combating his supposed role as the would-be undertaker. This was a mistake, one that was encouraged by some of the rhetoric in the book, but a mistake nonetheless. As we shall see, Rorty's position on this can be captured by the following line of argument: (1) philosophy has no "core," (2) a fortiori it has no intellectual quintessence, and (3) therefore there is no point in trying to destroy it by intellectual means.

PMN opens with the statement: "Almost as soon as I began to study philosophy, I was impressed by the way in which philosophical problems appeared, disappeared, or changed shape as a result of new assumptions or vocabularies" (p. xiii). This is important. It paves the way for the fresh conception of the nature of philosophical problems that Rorty develops throughout the book as a whole. Under this conception, philosophy is "historical" through and through. It has no essential nature. This means that philosophy does not depend on any particular issues, methods, or general subject-matter. Philosophical problems can *seem* inescapable, but that is because the background assumptions that generate them, and the vocabularies in which they are described, have already been uncritically accepted. Dig those up for inspection, show how they are rooted in socio-historical circumstances, and the problems in question need no longer appear compelling. Rorty devotes a considerable portion of *PMN* to showing how philosophical issues concerning the nature of mind and the definition of knowledge arise out of such circumstances.

Rorty believes that these two sets of issues are vital to philosophy's self-image as the "master discipline." And he claims they are intimately connected. They are vital because once philosophy hijacks them and provides its own account of them, dominion over the rest of culture looks like the next natural step. If philosophers have special knowledge of mind or, more precisely, of what it is that makes minds special, namely consciousness, then they stand in a privileged position with regard to understanding the nature of human beings. Furthermore, when philosophers possess a unique understanding of knowledge, they are in a position to stand in judgment over all other disciplines. They can rank these according to whether they are able to yield genuine knowledge. Philosophy stands at the top of the tree of intellectual culture because only it is qualified to carry out the ranking, only it has the appropriate knowledge required to do this: knowledge of knowledge.

The linkage that we referred to is important because it is only on the general conception of mind that supposedly gives philosophers privileged access to its nature that issues relating to knowledge gain their importance. If consciousness is the key feature of the mind, and it is regarded as a private feature in the sense that its contents can only be properly known from the inside, as it were, then a gap opens up between the mind's "self-knowledge" and its "other-knowledge," its knowledge of all other things. Into this gap between mind and the world springs epistemology, the (philosophical) theory of knowledge. Of course, all this is very schematic, but in *PMN*, Rorty paints in enough historical detail to show how the age-old philosophical questions about mind and knowledge – "How are the mind and body related?" "How can skepticism about the very possibility of knowledge be overcome?" and so on – only become "problems" on the back of a wealth of historically contingent assumptions.

At times, Rorty writes as if the sheer fact of their "contingency," is enough to render traditional philosophical problems redundant. This is wrong. From the fact that something is optional, it does not follow that this thing is uninteresting or unimportant. If we mistakenly believe that chess is a game that we just *have to play* once we discover its existence, its status might well go down in our estimation when we discover that we are wrong about this, wrong to have ever believed that chess-playing is mandatory, but we need not then automatically regard it as trivial, a game we would do well to dispose of.

Nevertheless, there is something to what Rorty says. It counters the myth that the questions philosophers have tended to concern themselves with are questions that *must* arise as soon as we begin to reflect properly on the world and our relationship to it. And Rorty is right to suggest that here the notion of "reflecting properly" begs all the interesting questions, that philosophers have failed to show that *other* ways of thinking about the same thing, ways that do not throw up certain kinds of questions, are illegitimate. Furthermore, he has another, more practical, string to his bow.

Put the thought that certain philosophical problems are "contingent," in the sense we have just alluded to, together with the thought that the practical benefits of tackling these problems over the years have been meager at best, and then it seems perfectly reasonable to suggest that they be set aside. This is Rorty's own proposal in *PMN*. It is not that we should sideline such problems simply because *we can*, it is rather that, having seen they are no longer compelling (the "contingency" claim) and having noted that nothing much has been gained from treating them as if they *are* compelling (the "lack of practical results" claim), moving on from them would be a very sensible thing for our culture to do. However, Rorty's account of what moving on involves has also provoked controversy. Rorty himself is to blame for this. But his critics are also partly culpable for not reading him carefully enough.

Rorty is at fault because of a structural ambiguity that he has to a certain extent allowed to infect the composition of *PMN*. The book weaves a complex, meandering narrative, but it always appears to be moving in one climactic direction: to a place where, after abandoning their fruitless, traditional pursuits, philosophers are finally concerned with what they ought to be concerned with. In this place, or so readers might be deceived into thinking, philosophers spend all their time practicing what, towards the end of *PMN*, Rorty flags as "hermeneutics." But, if readers are so deceived, and clearly many have been, they will be puzzled as to what the term "hermeneutics" means. And they will be thwarted if they think that, having reached the final section of *PMN*, which is simply entitled "Philosophy," they will discover what philosophy should be all about when they crack the meaning of "hermeneutics." Earlier, in chapter 4, which he regards as central to the book, Rorty introduces another alternative to traditional epistemology. He calls this "epistemological behaviorism," and glosses it as "explaining rationality and epistemic authority by reference to what society lets us say, rather than the latter by the former" (p. 174). However, he never develops this far enough to obviate the thought that "hermeneutics" has a lot of work to do if it is to enable philosophy to survive in any recognisable and stable form.

To his credit, and to the detriment of those who allow themselves to be deceived in the way we have just indicated, Rorty makes a concerted effort to undermine any expectation that the final section of *PMN* will offer a straightforward alternative to traditional philosophy. With regard to "hermeneutics," he is quite explicit: "I want to make clear at the outset that I am *not* putting hermeneutics forward as a "successor subject" to epistemo- logy, as an activity which fills the cultural vacancy once filled by epistemo- logically centred philosophy" (p. 315). However, such efforts are insufficient. And, there are the two main reasons why.

First, Rorty cannot expect to create a structural momentum that seems to be leading to a particular sort of denouement and then, when the time comes, simply announce that what looks and sounds like "the final act," in which the key questions raised by the plot are resolved, is not a final act at all. This is a particularly bad move on Rorty's part, given that he has already described the miasmic effect that traditional philosophy has had on its practi- tioners who must surely be his target audience. The mistake is compounded, and this is our second reason, by the elusive way in which Rorty does explain the nature of hermeneutics:

> [It is not] the name for a discipline, nor for a method of achieving the sort of results which epistemology failed to achieve, nor for a program of research. On the contrary, hermeneutics is an expression of hope that the cultural space left by the demise of epistemology will not be filled — that our culture should become one in which the demand for constraint and confrontation is no longer felt. The notion that there is a permanent neutral framework whose "structure" philosophy can display is that notion that the objects to be confronted by the mind, or the rules which constrain inquiry are common to all discourse, or at least to every dis- course on a given topic. Hermeneutics is largely a struggle against this assumption. (*PMN* 315–16)

In addition to "epistemologial behaviorism" and "hermeneutics," Rorty invokes three philosophical heroes who are supposed to demonstrate how philosophy can be done outside the tradition that he criticizes in *PMN*. These are John Dewey, Martin Heidegger, and Ludwig Wittgenstein. At first blush they seem a very mixed, and historically incompatible, bunch. But Rorty displays remarkable powers of appropriation in managing to find something in the writings of each of them that chimes with what he is trying to do in *PMN*. Thus, Dewey is praised for his "conception of knowledge as what we are justified in believing," as someone who enables us to "see 'justification' as a social phenomenon rather than a transaction between 'the knowing subject' and 'reality'" (p. 9). Heidegger is co-opted as a thinker who found a way of retelling the history of philosophy that "lets us see the beginnings of Cartesian imagery in the Greeks and the metamorphoses of this imagery during the last three centuries." Rorty views him as someone who "thus lets us 'distance' ourselves from the tradition" (p. 12). And finally, Wittgenstein is called upon on account of his "flair for deconstructing captivating pictures" (ibid.). Rorty reads Wittgenstein's *Philosophical Investigations* as an attempt to break the spell cast by all previous ambitions to turn philosophy into a "master discipline." Although his discussion of these "heroes" touches on some intriguing possibilities for the future development of philosophy, their actual role is no more than emblematic. Much more needs to be said to head off the kind of concern raised so trenchantly by Bernard Williams:

> I doubt, in fact, whether Rorty has extracted from the ruins, as he sees it, of Philosophy any activity that will sustain a post-Philosophical culture of the kind that he sketches. It is not very realistic to suppose that we could for long sustain much of a culture, or indeed keep away boredom, by playfully abusing the texts of writers who believed in an activity which we now know to he helpless.[6]

Although Rorty's attempt to describe the transition from traditional philosophy to "philosophy as endorsed by the tenets of PMN" is unsatisfactory, this is not a flaw that lingers on to stain the whole of his career. For he later found that the perfect way to solve this problem was by simply philosophizing in the new mode without looking back over his shoulder to see how the tradition was reacting. And he did this with some aplomb in his next major publication *Contingency, Irony, and Solidarity* (1989).

3   The Liberal Ironist

In *Philosophy and the Mirror of Nature*, Rorty tried to show that "the notion of knowledge as the assemblage of accurate representations is optional" (p. 11). He then went on to generalize this endeavor by trying also to show that even the most recent advances in philosophy, for example in the philosophy of language and the philosophy of mind, have failed to escape the hypnotic effects of this "notion," that the philosophers concerned are still laboring under the illusion that they can construct a "permanent, neutral framework of inquiry, and thus for all culture" (p. 8). We pointed out that to show a philosophical problem to be "historically optional" is not, by itself, sufficient to show that it should be abandoned. In *Contingency, Irony, and Solidarity*, Rorty paints a much broader picture of "contingency." And, in this picture, philosophy loses its veneer of necessity, of dealing with issues we *must* confront, not just because the claims it makes and the methods it uses to support these claims are optional, but also because the very world in which philosophy has to find roots, and in some sense account for, is rife with "contingencies." Rorty's overall aim is to show us how to become friends with the idea, so inimical to the analytic tradition, that everything in our lives is the "product of time and chance."

He deploys three main strategies in *CIS* to foster and then enliven this kind of "friendship," one that he feels, for the reason just alluded to, will be especially difficult for many philosophers. First, in the opening three chapters, he redescribes large areas of our lives in ways that reveal the ubiquity of "time and chance." These areas involve our use of language, our sense of personal identity, and our conception of community. Rorty's second strategy is to show how relatively recent developments in our intellectual culture have prepared us for such a redescription. Whether or not we know it, the time is ripe for us to come to terms with the part that chance plays in human affairs. Finally, Rorty provides a handy vocabulary which we can use to talk to each other in terms that do not involve, and indeed celebrate our liberation from, ahistorical myths.

In working through these strategies, Rorty does something unusual, perhaps unique. He introduces a series of important themes, such as the nature of human identity, that resonate with traditional philosophical concerns, and he does this in a way that makes it clear that *CIS* definitely belongs in the "Philosophy" section of libraries – so, for example, the names of many philosophers are mentioned. However, in doing this, the book ushers readers into new territory, beyond the borders marked out by traditional philosophical writings. Moreover, Rorty spends very little time constructing arguments for particular theses, and when he tackles a theme that seems to emerge out of the long tradition stretching at least as far back as Plato, he puts a special spin on it that lifts it above the kind of philosophical concerns that were the life-blood of that tradition. He does this mainly by undercutting the dominant images and metaphors behind these concerns and then replacing them with new ones, ones that arise out of a more "literary" approach to philosophy. In *Philosophy and the Mirror of Nature*, Rorty tried to show that attempts to make language answerable to reality itself were bound to end in philosophical tears. This put different uses of language, for example scientific as opposed to fictional, on the same footing. It thus cleared the path for poets and novelists to make a more significant contribution to philosophy. For they are able to bend language into shapes that make life richer and more interesting and thus achieve philosophical goals which, for Rorty, make more sense than the traditional one of fidelity to the facts, or, more simply, "Truth."

Take the case of personal identity. Philosophical debates on this topic have been generated by a basic, "essentialist" assumption: there must be something that distinguishes a human being from other entities; there must be something that makes me who I am.[7] This assumption is culturally embedded, and many philosophers from Hume to Parfit have tried to refute it. The candidates for the special "something" here range from "the soul" to "reason," "consciousness," and, even, "social convention." Rorty does not attempt to enter the debate as to whether such candidates are either necessary or suitable. Instead, he jumps straight into a roving discussion of fresh issues concerning our sense of "self-hood." In this discussion, previous philosophical considerations fall naturally by the wayside. And, as these fresh issues grab our attention, it no longer seems important to answer the old questions about personal identity, questions such as "Does the self have a non-contingent core? And if it does what criteria can we use to identify it?"

Rorty kicks off the discussion independently of the thinkers whose work raises these "old questions" – thinkers such as Descartes and Locke. Instead, he starts with some reflections on the final sections of Philip Larkin's poem "Continuing to Live." He takes the main theme of the poem to be the fear of dying, where the poet's fundamental aim is to make the nature of this "fear" more explicit by reflecting on what it is that has to die, "what it is that will not be" (*CIS* 23). These reflections suggest to Rorty that there are ways of pursuing and then developing Larkin's line of interest that avoid traditional philosophical worries about the self being extinguished, worries such as whether, when death looms, some special, soul-like substance or entity, some "essence" of the person involved, is about to be preserved or erased. Apprehension about "what it is that will not be" need not be met with Socratic ploys, designed to tease out, or show the impossibility of, a final definition of "the self."

What Larkin fears most, according to Rorty, is the dissipation of "his idiosyncratic lading-list, his individual sense of what was possible and import-ant. That is what made him different from all the other I's" (ibid.):

> And once you have walked the length of your mind, what
> You command is as clear as a lading-list
> Anything else must not, for you, be thought
> To exist.[8]

This apprehension concerns what is unique in Larkin's body of work, what is special about the various poems he has created. The outcome he dreads is that his poetic creations will merely be seamlessly absorbed into the anonymity of mass culture, that, in the end, "nobody will find anything distinctive in them" (*CIS* 24). The moral Rorty draws here is that creative people may well worry that "The words (or shapes, or theorems, or models of physical nature) marshaled to one's command may seem merely stock items, rearranged in routine ways . . . [in which case] One will not have impressed one's mark on language but rather, will have spent one's life shoving about already coined pieces" (ibid.).

Such comments may seem to be leading us away from traditional philosophical issues, deep issues regarding "death" and "the self," and at the cost of having to entertain some rather mundane thoughts about "originality" in art and other forms of creativity. However, Rorty's next sentence cuts straight through such an impression: "so one would not really have had an I at all" (ibid.). For this contention shifts the whole discussion even further away from essentialist queries as to what constitutes "selfhood" to a more open-ended discussion concerning the possibilities of *creating* a self. In this discussion, worries about what is already "given" in the constitution of the self are no longer relevant. What matters is what has been "made." But we should not take it that Rorty is arguing for any thesis along the lines of "The self is nothing until it is created." He is not saying that the traditional approach is wrong because it failed to subscribe to such a thesis, but rather something like this: "Here is a potentially interesting way of talking about the self, one that does require the continuation of sterile traditional debates. Let's try it out!"

Having broken free from traditional philosophical worries about personal identity, Rorty branches out to anticipate the objection that his way of "talking about the self" is too specialized; that, although it might be fine for leading artistic figures, it ignores the ordinary person, the person not just lacking, but incapable of producing, creative output. Rorty counters the claim that his approach to "selfhood" only caters for history's chosen ones, the creative elite, by appealing to Nietzsche and Freud and, in the process, moves even further beyond the preoccupations of traditional philosophers. Nietzsche is piped on board because he identifies "the strong poet, the maker, as humanity's hero" and regards "self knowledge as self creation" (*CIS* 27). But it is only when Freud is invoked that it becomes clear how Rorty's approach can be generalized to include just about everyone. In Rorty's view, Freud democratizes Nietzsche by making it plausible to believe that the minutiae of *each life* is the stuff of poetry, the raw material for self-knowledge – a point anticipated in more lofty terms by Keats in *The Fall of Hyperion: A Dream*:

> Who alive can say,
> "Thou art no Poet — may'st not tell thy dreams"?
> Since every man whose soul is not a clod
> Hath visions, and would speak, if he had loved,
> And been well nurtured in his mother tongue.[9]

Rorty's Freud puts a mundane spin on this. All of us generate "creative output" simply by living:

> Freud's account of unconscious fantasy shows us how to see every human life as a poem — or more exactly, every human life not so racked by pain as to be unable to learn a language nor so immersed in toil as to have no leisure in which to generate a — self-description. He sees every life as an attempt to clothe itself in metaphors. (*CIS* 35–6)

Rorty develops this discussion further by making it clear that Freud should not be construed as someone who makes assertions in "the traditional philosophical reductionist way," but rather as someone who "just wants to give us one more redescription of things to be filed alongside all the others, one more vocabulary, one more set of metaphors which he thinks will have a chance of being used and thereby literalized" (p. 39).

To help make us comfortable with the notion that it is better for artists and intellectuals to throw creative linguistic possibilities at us rather than claims to authoritative knowledge of reality, Rorty invites us to become "liberal ironists." And, he prefaces this invitation with an outline of what he calls a "final vocabulary":

> All human beings carry about a set of words which they employ to justify their actions, their beliefs, and their lives. These are the words in which we formulate praise of our friends and contempt for our enemies, our long-term projects, our deepest self-doubts and our highest hopes. They are the words in which we tell, sometimes prospectively and sometimes retrospectively, the story of our lives. I shall call these words a person's 'final vocabulary.' (p. 141)

The philosophical tradition that Rorty wants us to escape from has its own vision as to what such a vocabulary should contain. It should contain those words that capture the nature of reality, words that can be used to settle, once and for all, any doubts about our relationship to that "reality." Naturally, Rorty has a different view. For him, a final vocabulary is "final" only in the sense that it is the vocabulary of last *practical resort*, final in the sense that "if doubt is cast upon the worth of these words, their user has no noncircular argumentative recourse" (ibid.). "Liberal ironists" are those who understand the contingent status of their own final vocabulary and have come to terms with it. In doing so, although Rorty does not spell this out, they have tamed "postmodernism." For such a person lives comfortably in a state of what, for a traditional philosopher, looks like radical instability:

1 She has radical and continuing doubts about the final vocabulary she currently uses, because she has been impressed by other vocabularies taken as final by people or books she has encountered.
2 She realizes that argument phrased in her present vocabulary can neither underwrite nor dissolve these doubts.
3 Insofar as she philosophizes about her situation, she does not think her vocabulary is closer to reality than others, that it is in touch with a power not herself. (p. 73)

Notice that in the liberal ironist's final vocabulary, philosophical words have no special standing. They are not banished from such a vocabulary. Some people will still find nothing better to wrap "the story of their lives" in than phrases such as "categorical imperatives," "necessary truths," and "causal conditionals." However, as "ironists" they will have realized that such language has no inherent advantage over other kinds of words, that it has to compete with such words on equal terms, having only its practical usefulness and metaphoric attractiveness to commend it. Rather than trying to dig down to philosophical bedrock, Rorty encourages us to reach out sideways, so to speak, to the work of other creative people in the culture around them who have founds innovative ways of living with contingency, people such as Proust:

Proust temporalized and finitized the authority figures he had met by seeing them as creatures of contingent circumstances. Like Nietzsche, he rid himself of the fear that there was an antecedent truth about himself, a real essence which others might have detected. But, Proust was able to do so without claiming to know a truth which was hidden from the authority figures of his earlier years. He managed to debunk authority without setting himself up as an authority, to debunk the ambitions of the powerful without sharing them. He finitized authority figures not by detecting what they "really" were but by watching them become different than they had been, and by seeing how they looked when redescribed in terms offered by still other authority figures, whom he played off against the first. The result of all this finitization was to make Proust unashamed of his own finitude. He mastered contingency by recognizing it, and thus freed himself from the fear that the contingencies he had encountered were more than just contingencies. He turned other people from his judges into his fellow sufferers, and thus succeeded in creating the taste by which he judged himself. (p. 103)

Contingency, Irony, and Solidarity provides a wealth of other material for creatively bolstering the liberal ironist's confidence without having recourse to standard philosophical forms of justification. The book also tries to show why "liberalism" and "irony" are made for one another. For this form of politics provides the individual with the personal space, the freedom, to develop their own vocabularies of self-creation and is, itself, ideally served by such a vocabulary because it requires no philosophical underpinning.

In this late phase of his writings, Rorty has gained the confidence to answer the big question left hanging at the end of *Philosophy and the Mirror of Nature*: how can philosophy continue if it breaks away from its ancestral roots and gives up on its traditional ambitions? He does so by simply exploring a number of themes, including personal identity, human solidarity, the nature of cruelty and the public/private distinction, without stopping to find out whether what he is doing is philosophically respectable. The criterion of success for this venture is whether these themes, and Rorty's way of dealing with them, catch on, whether they stimulate enough interest to supplant the concerns of the tradition derided in *Philosophy and the Mirror of Nature*.

4 Essays Against the Tradition

We can now see the shape of Rorty's career in broad outline, and we can see how it matches up with the "Early," "Middle," and "Late" characterizations of Rorty mentioned earlier. But to end the story there would be to miss out a vital element: the part played by *essays* in Rorty's philosophical development. These are important, not because of the sheer quantity involved (many of which are now collected in four separate volumes[10]), but rather on account of their strategic role. When his essays are taken into consideration, the career shape that we just referred to undergoes a significant deformation, to the extent that the very notion of "the three Rortys" is subverted. And this also has a bearing of the controversies we referred to at the start.

This "subversion" starts very early on, well before *Philosophy and the Mirror of Nature* was published. And it starts not with a volume of Rorty's own essays, but with his substantial, 39-page, editorial introduction to a collection of the writings of other philosophers that he gathered together under the title *The Linguistic Turn* (1967). For those who wish to understand Rorty's philosophical development in the round, this "introduction" is now an important text in his own right – all the more so, since Rorty himself seems to have overlooked its significance. In "Twenty-five Years After," a retrospective essay appended to a much later (1992) reprinting of *The Linguistic Turn*, Rorty is too busy taking himself to task for a few sentences that celebrated the triumph of "linguistic philosophy" to notice the disruptive framework he had constructed around those remarks. He says that these remarks now strike him:

> as merely the attempt of a thirty-three-year-old philosopher to convince himself that he had had the luck to be born at the right time – to persuade himself that the disciplinary matrix in which he happened to find himself (philosophy as taught in most English-speaking universities in the 1960s) was more than just one more philosophical school, one more tempest in an academic teapot. (*LT* 371)

However, this self-assessment needs to set against the backcloth of many of Rorty's other introductory remarks where he demonstrates that he has done some hard thinking about the potential weaknesses of the "linguistic" approach to philosophy. In these, he displays an acute sensitivity to the historical context of "philosophical problems," a lack of enthusiasm for the notion of a universal "philosophical method," an empathy with classic American pragmatism and a keen interest in meta-philosophical issues, all of which show him to be out of step with established conceptions of linguistic philosophy. Indeed, he starts off by doing something no exponent of this approach would normally be inclined to do: he provides an *historicist*, almost Hegelian, picture of how revolutions in philosophy take place. In this picture he identifies a general problem that makes it difficult for any philosopher to rest content that the method of doing philosophy that they have adopted is the right one:

> To know what method to adopt, one must already have arrived at some metaphysical and some epistemological conclusions. If one attempts to defend these conclusions by the use of one's chosen method, one is open to the charge of circularity. If one does not so defend them, maintaining that given these conclusions, the need to adopt the chosen method follows, one is open to the charge that the chosen method is inadequate, for it cannot be used to establish the crucial metaphysical and epistemological theses which are in dispute. Since philosophical method is in itself a philosophical topic (or, in other words, since different criteria for the satisfactory solution of a philosophical problem are adopted, and argued for, by different schools of philosophers), every philosophical revolutionary is open to the charge of circularity or to the charge of having begged the question. (*LT* 1–2)

It may well be the case that Rorty's early awareness of this "general problem" was one of the factors that made him, throughout his career and to the great annoyance of his critics, so reluctant to "justify" his own philosophical predilections.[11]

Finally, when reflecting in some detail on how the future of philosophy might unfold, although Rorty is not ungenerous towards linguistic philosophy, the options he describes have some striking affinities with his own later writings. These include: (1) linguistic philosophy is regarded "as having led to a dead end;" (2) philosophy "grows closer to poetry;" (3) philosophy is seen "as a cultural disease which has been cured;" and (4), most presciently, philosophers concern themselves with "the creation of new and fruitful ways of thinking about things in general." The latter option chimes perfectly with the "redescriptive" rhetoric of *Contingency, Irony, and Solidarity*.

The conclusion to draw here is that the Rorty who gained wider attention on account of the controversy surrounding the publication of *Philosophy and the Mirror of Nature* over a decade later was not some newborn rebel, someone who had only just defected from the analytic camp, but rather a much deeper thinker who, in that book, at last found a way of giving systematic voice to the kind of concerns and doubts he had since he became a professional philosopher. When the considerable number of Rorty's "early essays" are made more accessible,[12] more evidence will emerge, even from the heartland of his "analytic work," to support this assessment.

There is a second manner in which Rorty's essays tend to be "strategic," and in this case, too, the tripartite characterization of his publishing career comes under pressure. Consider, for example, the thought that *Philosophy and the Mirror of Nature* represents a dramatic turning point in Rorty's career. We have already adduced some evidence against this, but when we turn to essays that he wrote before and just after *PMN*, the bulk of which are collected together in *Consequences of Pragmatism* (1982), we find that they also undermine the notion that *PMN* was somehow treasonous, that it showed Rorty to be a turncoat. These essays flesh out some of the material in *PMN*, and to some extent prepare the ground for it. In his "Introduction," again a text that has assumed an importance in its own right, Rorty says a good deal about how pragmatists are able to bypass some of the traditional issues associated with "truth," a topic that receives scant attention in *PMN*. He also puts some meat on the skeleton accounts he gave of his three designated heroes: Dewey, Heidegger, and Wittgenstein. The impression gained from reading these essays, and indeed Rorty's other essays, is that his philosophical career progressed much more smoothly than the "tripartite" account suggests. If there is a break in the overall continuum, it comes when he gains the confidence we referred to above and starts to practice the relatively autonomous approach to philosophical discussion and inquiry found in *Contingency, Irony, and Solidarity*.

5 Pragmatism

"Pragmatism" is a vague, ambiguous, and overworked word. Nevertheless, it names the chief glory of our country's intellectual tradition. (CP 160)

Rorty is one of the key players in the recent revival of pragmatism. Hence, it may seem surprising that we have not yet discussed this. However, the explanation is quite straightforward, even though it has two strands to it. The first concerns the role that pragmatism actually plays in Rorty's major published works, leaving aside his essays. This role is minimal. In *Philosophy and the Mirror of Nature*, pragmatism has no more than an honorific presence, somewhat in line with that of Dewey, Heidegger, and Wittgenstein. A glance at the index will show, for example, that the philosopher Gilbert Ryle merits more attention than pragmatism. In *Contingency, Irony, and Solidarity*, pragmatism is almost invisible. Some essays pay more detailed attention to the topic, but they do not attempt to outline a unique pragmatist position.[13] Often, Rorty simply makes very general allusions to the writings of classic pragmatists, especially James and Dewey, without working that material up into hard-and-fast principles or theoretical claims. Here is a typical example: "For the pragmatists (among whom I number myself), the traditional questions of metaphysics and epistemology can be neglected because they have no social utility. It is not that they are devoid of meaning, nor that they rest on false premises; it is simply that the vocabulary of metaphysics and epistemology is of no practical use" (*WUT* 37–8). What are we to make of all this?

The answer comes in the shape of our second strand. This involves what we earlier flagged as "post-analytic pragmatism." Such pragmatism is "post-analytic" not in the sense that it comes *after* or *replaces* analytic philosophy, but rather in the sense that it defines its philosophical identity independently of that tradition. It is the kind of pragmatism that, unlike its progenitor, ceases to allow itself to be defined by the concerns of the analytic tradition. The classic pragmatists, especially William James and John Dewey, spent a great deal of their time arguing with their peers and deflecting the criticisms of philosophers such as Bertrand Russell and G. E. Moore. In many ways, this was a mistake, because it enabled the enemies of pragmatism to decide the terms of debate and to fight their battles with it on their own territory. Rorty identified this mistake, and resolved to avoid it. Hence, when he talks about "pragmatism," he is talking about something that derives from classic pragmatism to the extent that it tends to substitute plain conceptions of practical utility (which include "what helps us cope," "what assuages our pain," "what is of most interest to us," and "what we find it best to do in the circumstances") for the abstract, highly theoretical constructs that philosophy has generally preferred. This pragmatism – post-analytic pragmatism – has the courage to strike out on its own. It no longer holds itself answerable to the philosophical tradition from which it diverges.[14]

Hence, when Rorty is actually *doing* philosophy, much of the terminology of classic pragmatism – terminology that made the kind of references, deemed necessary at the time, to traditional philosophical topics such as "knowledge" and "truth" – falls by the wayside. Post-analytic pragmatism no longer needs to keep reminding itself that it is a form of "pragmatism;" it can just get on with the job of exploring issues of interest. It is for this reason, when he is not deploying a framework of ideas to make things safer for it, that Rorty often writes without explicitly invoking the name of pragmatism.

It is not easy to assess Rorty's accomplishments at this stage, because a large part of his project involves challenging the current standards for such assessments. We have shown that at least some of the controversy about Rorty will die down when his work is read more carefully. For then the sharp divisions in his work will be smoothed out. The more homogeneous Rorty that emerges from this process is still likely to enrage Traditionalists. But he will have triumphed on his own terms if he has persuaded history not to judge him according to their criteria. Whether he has surpassed Proust by creating the taste by which he is judged rather than simply that "by which he judges himself" is for history to decide. If that decision is favorable, history will take a practical view of Rorty's achievements, paying tribute to the way in which he has opened up philosophical discussion, encouraged philosophers to cross the analytic/continental philosophy divide, introduced new authors into the canon, and stimulated debate in diverse areas including law, feminism, literary theory, and even accountancy. On that score, he should be judged very kindly indeed.[15]

Notes

1 B. Williams, "Auto-da-fe: *Consequences of Pragmatism*," in Malachowski (ed.), *Reading Rorty*. Oxford: Blackwell, 1990, p. 33.
2 Useful evidence of this "interest" can be found in his *Against Bosses, Against Oligarchies*.
3 See, for example, "Mind–Body Identity, Privacy, and Categories."
4 A. L. Brueckner, "Transcendental Arguments I," *Nous* 17/1 (1983): 551–75.
5 For a more detailed overview of *Philosophy and the Mirror of Nature*, see A. Malachowski, "Richard Rorty: *Philosophy and the Mirror of Nature*," in J. Shand (ed.),

Central Works of Philosophy, vol. 5: *The Twentieth Century: Quine and After*. Chesham: Acumen, 2006, pp. 126–45.

6 "Auto-da-fe: *Consequences of Pragmatism*," p. 33.

7 These two formulations are not strictly equivalent. They raise different issues, but they can be equated here for brevity's sake.

8 P. Larkin, *Collected Poems*. London: Faber and Faber, 1988, p. 94.

9 *John Keats: Collected Poems*. London: Penguin, 1988, p. 435.

10 See Philosophical Papers, vols. I–IV: *Objectivity, Relativism, and Truth* (1991); *Essays on Heidegger and Others* (1991); *Truth and Progress* (1998); and *Cultural Politics* (2007).

11 This speculation is reinforced by Rorty's biographical remarks where he claims to have been concerned from the start that philosophers may never be able to furnish objective, non-circular justification of their views. See "Trotsky and the Wild Orchids."

12 Plans are afoot to publish them in collected format, though these are provisional and, as yet, no publication date is available.

13 For insightful attempts to make something more systematic of Rorty's approach to pragmatism, see G. Brodsky, "Rorty's Interpretation of Pragmatism," *Transactions of the Charles Pierce Society* XVII/4 (1982): 311–37; R. Kraut, "Varieties of Pragmatism," *Mind* 99 (April 1990): 157–83, repr. in A. Malachowski (ed.), *Richard Rorty*, vol. III. London: Sage Publications, 2004, pp. 260–84.

14 For some elaboration of this point, see A. Malachowski, "Pragmatism in its Own Right," in Malachowski, *Pragmatism*, 3 vols. London: Sage Publications.

15 I am grateful to the editors for useful comments on an earlier version of this article.

References

Achieving Our Country: Leftist Though in Twentieth-Century America. Cambridge MA: Harvard University Press: 1998.

Against Bosses, Against Oligarchies. Chicago: Prickly Paradigm Press, 2002.

Consequences of Pragmatism [*CP*]. Cambridge: Cambridge University Press, 1982.

Contingency, Irony, and Solidarity [*CIS*]. Cambridge: Cambridge University Press, 1989.

The Linguistic Turn (ed.), 2nd edn [*LT*]. Chicago: University of Chicago Press, 1992; orig. pub. 1976.

"Mind–Body Identity, Privacy, and Categories" [M–BI], *Review of Metaphysics* 19 (September 1965): 24–54.

Philosophical Papers I: *Objectivity, Relativism, and Truth*. Cambridge: Cambridge University Press, 1991.

Philosophical Papers II: *Essays on Heidegger and Others*. Cambridge: Cambridge University Press, 1991.

Philosophical Papers III: *Truth and Progress*. Cambridge: Cambridge University Press, 1998.

Philosophical Papers IV: *Cultural Politics*. Cambridge: Cambridge University Press, 2007.

Philosophy and the Mirror of Nature [PMN]. Oxford: Blackwell, 1980.

Philosophy and Social Hope [PSH]. Harmondsworth: Penguin, 2000.

"Strawson's Objectivity Argument" [SOA], *Review of Metaphysics* 24 (December 1970): 207–44.

"Trotsky and the Wild Orchids," in *Philosophy and Social Hope*.

What's the Use of Truth? [WUT]. New York: Columbia University Press, 2007.

A selection of other articles by Rorty (not published in Philosophical Papers I–IV)

"Davidson Between Wittgenstein and Tarski," *Critica: Revista hispaoamericana de Filsofia* 30/88 (April 1998): 49–71.

"In Defense of Eliminative Materialism," *Review of Metaphysics* 24 (September 1970): 112–21.

"Empiricism, Extensionalism, and Reductionism," *Mind* 72 (April 1963): 176–86.

"Incorrigibility as the Mark of the Mental," *Journal of Philosophy* 67 (June 1970): 399–429.

"Pragmatism, Categories, and Language," *Philosophical Review* 70 (April 1961): 197–223.

"Remarks on Deconstruction and Pragmatism," in C. Mouffe (ed.), *Deconstruction and Pragmatism*. London: Routledge, 1996, pp. 13–18.

"Thugs and Theorists: A Reply to Bernstein," *Political Theory* 15 (November 1987): 564–580.

"Transcendental Argument, Self–reference, and Pragmatism," in P. Bieri, R. P. Hortsman, and L. Kruger (eds.), *Transcendental Arguments and Science*. Dordrecht: Reidel, 1979, pp. 77–92.

"Truth and Freedom: A Reply to Thomas McCarthy," *Critical Inquiry* 16 (1990): 633–43.

"Verificationism and transcendental Arguments," *Nous* 5 (1971): 3–14.

"Wittgenstein, Privileged Access, and Incommunability," *American Philosophical Quarterly* 7 (July 1970): 192–205.

6 FODOR

JOSÉ LUIS BERMÚDEZ

While perhaps not itself an academic discipline in the traditional sense, cognitive science draws upon and integrates the resources of many disciplines. These include artificial intelligence, neuroscience, linguistics, cognitive psychology, and computer science. The relation of philosophy to cognitive science is at best ambiguous, however. Some philosophers repudiate cognitive science utterly, seeing it as a doomed attempt to bring the realm of reason, thought, and reflection under the mechanistic laws of the type that govern the unthinking and inanimate world. Others have gone to the other extreme, looking to cognitive science for answers to problems that have traditionally been thought of as philosophical, and hence not susceptible to an empirical solution. For a third group of philosophers, who take the middle ground between these extremes, the philosophy of mind has become very much a type of theoretical cognitive science, concerned with thinking through the basic principles and assumptions that both drive empirical work and determine how it is interpreted.

Jerry Fodor (1935–) is without question one of the leading exponents of this approach to the philosophy of mind (two other well-known figures are John Searle and Daniel Dennett). Fodor has made significant contributions at the interface between philosophy and cognitive science. Whereas many people who work at the boundaries between two academic fields succeed only in being ignored by both of them, Fodor is widely recognized as having set agendas that dominate much of contemporary debate. In what follows, I survey two of the ideas with which Fodor is most closely associated. The aim is both to introduce Fodor and to give a flavor of some of the central debates in this area.

The first section explains Fodor's "master argument" for what he calls the *language of thought hypothesis*. Many cognitive scientists take the digital computer as a model for understanding the mind. Minds are computers and thinking is a form of computation. Fodor interprets this in a distinctive way, to give what he calls the "representational theory of mind." According to Fodor, minds are computers that process sentences in the language of thought. He argues, most comprehensively in his book *Psychosemantics* (1987), that this way of thinking about the mind serves to legitimate our commonsense practices of explaining behavior in terms of beliefs, desires, and other instances of what philosophers call the *propositional attitudes*.[1] Thinking of the mind as a computer running on sentences in the language of thought is not, Fodor argues, an alternative to thinking of persons as having beliefs and desires. Rather, it gives us a way (perhaps the only way) of explaining how those beliefs and desires can produce behavior.

In the second section we consider Fodor's famous proposal for understanding the large-scale organization of the mind. We need to distinguish, he argues, between two fundamentally different types of cognition. On the one hand, there are highly specialized information-processing tasks, such as identifying the outlines of objects in the immediate environment, or working out where the gaps between words come in a stream of sound. These tasks are carried out automatically, and involve only a limited amount of information. In his influential book *The Modularity of Mind* (1983) Fodor argues that tasks of this first kind are carried out by dedicated cognitive systems that he called modules. These modules are *domain-specific* – that is, they are responsible only for tasks falling in particular domains. On the other hand, there are tasks, such as deciding where to have dinner or how to plant the front garden, that involve much more complex and wide-ranging inferences and to which an indefinite amount of background information is potentially relevant. The information processing involved in carrying out these tasks is *domain-general* (the opposite of domain-specific). On the basis of this analysis, Fodor develops a picture of the organization of the mind as involving both specialized modules and what he calls domain-general, non-modular cognition.

In the final section I look at the relation between these two claims. There is a definite tension between them that has come to the surface in some of

Fodor's more recent writings, particularly *The Mind Doesn't Work That Way* (2000). The features of the computer model of the mind that Fodor stresses in order to explain how it can validate commonsense psychology seem most applicable to the information processing involved in lower-level, modular cognition. However, reasoning and inference involving propositional attitudes are paradigm examples of higher-level, non-modular cognition, which he takes to function in a fundamentally different way. This has led him to a degree of pessimism about the prospects of cognitive science as a tool for understanding the mind. I suggest that it also creates a problem for his attempt to legitimate commonsense psychology.

1 From Commonsense Psychology to the Language of Thought

One of the two basic assumptions of cognitive science is that the mind is an information-processing machine. It is obvious that the mind *receives* information about its environment. Some of this information is carried by light waves arriving at the retina or sound waves hitting the eardrum. It is also obvious that what we do is not *determined* by the information that we receive. Different people, or the same person at different times, react differently to the same situation. There is no standard response to the pattern of sound waves associated (in English) with a cry of "Help" for example. How we behave depends upon what our minds do with the information that they receive – how they *process* that information. If I run to your assistance when you cry "Help," it is because my mind has somehow managed to decode your utterance as a word in English, worked out what you are trying to communicate, and then decided how to respond. This is all complex processing of the initial information that arrived at my eardrum.

But how does this information processing take place? How do vibrations on the eardrum lead to the muscle contractions involved when I save you from drowning? The information has to be carried by something. We know how the information is carried in the auditory system; we know that vibrations in the eardrum are transmitted by the ossicles to the inner ear, for example. What happens the further away the information travels from the eardrum is not so well understood, but another integral part of the general picture of the mind as an information processor is that there are physical structures that carry information and, by so doing, serve as *representations* of the immediate environment (or, of course, of things that are more abstract or remote). This is the second basic assumption of cognitive science. Information processing is, at bottom, a matter of transforming these representations in a way that finally yields the activity in the nervous system that "instructs" my limbs to jump into the water.

Here, then, are the two basic assumptions of cognitive science:

1   The mind is an information processor
2   Information processing involves transforming representations, which are physical structures that carry information.

Fodor is particularly interested in the representations that correspond to beliefs, desires, and comparable psychological states such as hopes and fears. These are called *propositional attitudes* by philosophers, because they can all be analyzed in terms of a thinker standing in different attitudes (e.g. belief, or hope) to particular propositions (such as the proposition that it is raining, or that the traffic will shortly start to move). He is convinced that there have to be internal representations corresponding to the propositional attitudes. We are, by and large, successful in explaining and predicting other people's behavior in terms of what they believe about the world and what they want to achieve. According to Fodor, this success can only be explained if beliefs and desires really are what cause our behavior. This means that beliefs and desires have to be internal items that can bring about the bodily movements that we are trying to explain. He calls this view *intentional realism*. It is a form of *realism* because it takes propositional attitudes to be really existing physical entities. And it is *intentional* because the propositional attitudes all have what philosophers call *intentionality* – that is, they represent the world as being a certain way.

What I am calling Fodor's "master argument" is his argument from intentional realism to his particular version of the computer model of the mind (which he calls the representational theory of mind). Intentional realism requires that we be able to think about beliefs and desires as the sorts of things that can cause behavior. But this is a special type of causation. There is a fundamental difference between my leg moving because I am trying to achieve something (perhaps the journey of 1,000 miles that starts with a single step) and my leg moving because a doctor has hit my knee with his hammer. In the first case, what causes my movement is what the desire is a desire for – namely, the beginning of the journey of 1,000 miles. This is what philosophers call the *content* of the desire. Had the content been different, the movement would have been different. Beliefs and desires cause behavior in virtue of how they represent the world – in virtue of their content. Any satisfactory account of intentional realism must explain how this type of *causation by content* is possible. In particular, it needs to do justice to the rational relations holding between belief and desires, on the one hand, and the behavior that they cause, on the other. Beliefs and desires cause behavior that makes sense in the light of them. Moving my leg is a rational thing to do if I desire to begin the journey of 1,000 miles and believe that I am pointing in the right direction.

Yet causation by content is deeply mysterious. In one sense, representations are simply objects like any other – they might be patterns of sound waves, populations of neurons, or pieces of paper. Thought of in this way there is no more difficulty in understanding how representations can cause behavior than there is in understanding how the doctor's hammer can make my leg move. But the representations that we are interested in (the propositional attitudes) are also things that bear a special *semantic* relation to the world – that is, they have meaning; they are *about* things such as one's mother or the planet Mars. The puzzle is not just how representations can have causal effects within the world, but, rather, how representations can have causal effects within the world as a function of what they mean, as a function of the relations in which they stand to other objects in the world (objects which may not in fact even be in existence).

The great advantage of the computer model of the mind, for Fodor, is that it solves the puzzle of causation by content. In order to see why we need to formulate the puzzle more precisely, Fodor, along with almost all cognitive scientists and the vast majority of philosophers, holds that the manipulations that the brain carries out on representations are purely physical and mechanical. Brains and the representations that they contain are physical entities and this means that they can only be sensitive to certain types of property in mental representations. My utterance of the word "cat" is ultimately no more than a particular pattern of sound waves. These sound waves have certain physical properties that can have certain effects on the brain. They have amplitude, wavelength, frequency, and so on. These are properties to which the brain is directly sensitive through the senses. But the fact that those sound waves represent cats for English-speakers is a very different type of property – and not one to which the brain can be directly sensitive (or at least, so the argument goes).

Let us call the physical properties that can be manipulated within brains *formal properties*. We call them this because they have to do with the physical *form* of the representation. And let us call the properties in virtue of which representations represent *semantic properties* – just as semantics is the branch of linguistics that deals with the meanings of words (how words represent). The fundamental source of the problem of causation by content is that semantic properties are not formal properties. It is easy to think of examples of pairs of representations that have identical formal properties, but very different semantic properties. Think of the following two inscriptions, for example:

1101   1101

It is easy to give a formal description of these two inscriptions. Each can be described, for example, as two "1"s followed by a "0" and then another "1." Or, more abstractly, we might describe them in terms of vertical strokes and circular strokes. Plainly, however, the formal description of the left-hand inscription will be exactly the same as the formal description of the right-hand inscription. It is perfectly possible, nonetheless, for these two formally identical inscriptions to have very different semantic properties. Imagine, for example, that the left-hand inscription represents the number 1,101 (one thousand, one hundred and one) in our ordinary decimal system, while the right-hand inscription represents the number 13 in the binary system. Here we have two representations identical in their formal/physical properties, but with very different semantic/meaning properties.

This makes very explicit the problem of causation by content. The brain is an information-processing machine that is sensitive only to the formal properties of representations. As far as direct inputs to the brain are concerned, there can be no difference between the left-hand and the right-hand inscriptions. And yet, there is all the difference in the world between 13 and 1101. Somehow our brains are sensitive to this difference. After all, we can distinguish between "1101" as a binary representation and "1101" as a decimal representation. We can see that the two inscriptions carry very different types of information – and we are capable of reacting very differently to the two inscriptions. The problem of causation by content is the problem of explaining how this is possible. How can the brain be an information-processing machine if it is blind to the semantic properties of representations? How can the brain be an information-processing machine if all it can process are the formal properties of representations?

There is an important analogy between brains and computers in this respect. Computers essentially manipulate strings of symbols, where we can think of a symbol as a representation that has a certain shape. A computer programmed in binary, for example, manipulates strings of 1s and 0s. The manipulations that the computer carries out are determined solely by the shape of those symbols. This string of 1s and 0s might represent a natural number, in the way that, in binary, 10 represents the number 2 and 11 represents the number 3. Or it might represent something completely different. It might represent whether or not the individual members of a long series of pixels are on or off, for example. In fact, with a suitable coding, a string of 1s and 0s can represent just about anything. As far as the computer is concerned, however, what the string of 1s and 0s represents is completely irrelevant. The semantic properties of the string are irrelevant. The computer simply manipulates the formal properties of the string of 1s and 0s.

Nonetheless, and this is the crucial point, the computer is programmed to manipulate strings of 1s and 0s in certain ways that yield the right result relative to the interpretation that is intended, even though the computer is blind to that interpretation. If the computer is a calculator, for example, and it is given two strings of 0s and 1s it will output a third string of 1s and 0s. If the first two strings represent the numbers 5 and 7 respectively, then the third string will be a binary representation of the number 12. But these semantic properties are irrelevant to the mechanics of what the computer actually does. All that the computer is doing is mechanically manipulating 1s and 0s, operating on their formal properties. But it is designed in such a way that these formal manipulations produce the desired effect at the semantic level. The pocket calculator manipulates 0s and 1s in such a way that it ends up performing (correct) arithmetical operations on the numbers represented by those strings of 0s and 1s.

So, computers manipulate symbols in a way that is sensitive only to their formal properties while respecting their semantic properties. And this, Fodor argues, is exactly what brains have to do. Brains are physical systems that can be sensitive only to the formal properties of mental representations. But nonetheless, as information-processing machines, they (like computers) have to respect the semantic properties of mental representations. We can understand Fodor's argument from intentional realism to the computer model of the mind as follows: since brains and computers have to solve the same problem, and we understand how computers solve it, the easiest way to understand how the brain solves it is to think of the brain as a kind of computer.

But how exactly does the analogy work? The following three claims summarize Fodor's distinctive way of working out the computer model of the mind.

1   Causation through content is ultimately a matter of causal interactions between physical states.
2   These physical states have the structure of sentences and their sentence-like structure determines how they are made up and how they interact with each other.
3   Causal transitions between sentences in the language of thought respect the rational relations between the contents of those sentences in the language of thought.

The second and third claims represent Fodor's characteristic contribution to the problem of causation by content. This is his influential view that the medium of cognition is what he calls the language of thought. According to Fodor, we think in sentences, but these are not sentences of a natural language such as English. The language of thought is much more like a formal language, such as the predicate calculus, which was devised by logicians to represent the logical structure of sentences and arguments in English. Like the languages in which computers are programmed (to which it is in fact very closely related), the predicate calculus is supposed to be free of the ambiguities and inaccuracies of English.

The analogy between the language of thought and formal languages such as computer languages and the predicate calculus is at the heart of Fodor's solution to the problem of causation by content. It is what lies behind claim (3). The basic fact about formal languages that Fodor exploits is the clear separation that they afford between formal properties and semantics. Viewed syntactically, a formal language such as the predicate calculus is simply a set of symbols of various types together with rules for manipulating those symbols according to their types. The symbols in the predicate calculus fall into different types. Some symbols, typically represented by lower case letters from the beginning of the alphabet (a, b, and so on), do the job of representing individual objects. Others, typically represented by upper case letters such as F, do the job of representing properties. Combining these symbols gives representations of states of affairs. So, for example, if "a" represents Jane and "F" represents the property of running, then the symbol "Fa" represents the state of affairs of Jane running. The predicate calculus contains symbols corresponding to various logical operations, such as "&" (for conjoining different symbols) and "¬" for negating symbols, as well as quantifiers "∃" and "∀" denoting "at least one" and "all" respectively.

The rules that govern how individual symbols can be combined to form sentences can be stated solely in terms of the formal properties of the individual symbols. An example would be the rule that the space after an upper case letter (e.g. the space in "F—") can only be filled with a lower case letter (e.g. "a"). This rule is a way of capturing at the syntactic level the intuitive thought that properties apply primarily to things, but it does this without adverting at all to the idea that upper-case letters serve as the names of properties while lower-case letters serve as the names of things. It is a matter purely of the *syntax* of the language. Applying the rule is a purely mechanical matter of exactly the type that computers excel in performing.

The connection between the formal system and what it is about, on the other hand, comes at the level of *semantics*. It is when we think about the semantics of a formal language that we assign objects to the individual constants, properties to the predicates, and logical operators to the connectives. To provide a semantics for a language is to give an interpretation to the symbols it contains – to turn it from a collection of meaningless symbols into a representational system.

Just as one can view the symbols of a formal system both syntactically and semantically, so too can one view the transitions between those symbols in either of these two ways. The rule of existential generalization in the predicate calculus, for example, can be viewed either syntactically or semantically. Viewed syntactically, the rule states that if on one line of a proof one has a formula of the form Fa, then on the next line of the proof one can write the formula $\exists x$ Fx. Viewed semantically, the rule states that if it is true that one particular thing is F, then it must be true that something is F (since the interpretation of "$\exists x$ Fx" is that at least one thing is F). All transitions in formal systems can be viewed in these two ways, either as rules for manipulating essentially meaningless symbols, or as rules determining relations between interpreted propositions.

Fodor's basic proposal, then, is that we use this model of the relation between syntax and semantics in a formal system to understand the relation between a sentence in the language of thought and its content (what it represents). The mind is a computer operating on sentences in the language of thought. These sentences can be viewed purely syntactically, as physical symbol structures composed of basic symbols concatenated according to certain rules of composition, or they can be viewed semantically in terms of how they represent the world (in which case they are being viewed as the vehicles of propositional attitudes). And so, by extension, transitions between sentences in the language of thought can be viewed either syntactically or semantically – either in terms of formal relations holding between physical symbol structures, or in terms of semantic relations holding between states that represent the world.

Let us go back to Fodor's claim (3). Information processing in the mind is ultimately a matter of causal transitions between sentences in the language of thought, just as information processing in a computer is ultimately a matter of causal transitions between sentences in the programming language. Suppose we think that the causal transitions holding between sentences in the language of thought are essentially formal, holding purely in virtue of the formal properties of the relevant symbols irrespective of what those symbols might refer to. Then what we are effectively asking is: What makes it the case that the formal relations holding between sentences in the language of thought should map onto the semantic relations holding between the propositional contents corresponding to those sentences? And, if we take seriously the idea that the language of thought is a formal system, then this question has a perfectly straightforward answer. Syntactic transitions between sentences in the language of thought will track semantic transitions between the contents of those sentences for precisely the same reason that syntax tracks semantics in any properly designed formal system.

Fodor can (and does) appeal to well-known results in metalogic (the study of the expressive capacities and formal structure of logical systems) establishing a significant degree of correspondence between syntactic derivability and semantic validity. So, for example, it is known that the first-order predicate calculus is sound and complete. That is to say, in every well-formed proof in the first-order predicate calculus the conclusion really is a logical consequence of the premises (*soundness*) and, conversely, for every argument in which the conclusion follows logically from the premises and both conclusion and premises are formulable in the first-order predicate calculus there is a well-formed proof (*completeness*). Put in the terms we have been employing, if a series of legitimate and formally definable inferential transitions leads one from formula A to a second formula B, then one can be sure that A cannot be true without B being true – and, conversely, if A entails B in a semantic sense, then one can be sure that there will be a series of formally definable inferential transitions leading from A to B.

In summary, then, beliefs and desires are realized by language-like physical structures (sentences in the language of thought), and practical reasoning and other forms of thinking are ultimately to be understood in terms of causal interactions between those structures. These causal interactions are sensitive only to the formal, syntactic properties of the physical structures. Yet, because the language of thought is a formal language with analogs of the formal properties of soundness and completeness, these purely syntactic transitions respect the semantic relations between the contents of the relevant beliefs and desires. This is how (Fodor claims) causation by content takes place in a purely physical system such as the human brain. And so, he argues, commonsense psychological explanation is vindicated by thinking of the mind as a computer processing sentences in the language of thought.

2   The Modularity of Mind

Philosophers have tended to be preoccupied with higher-level cognitive phenomena, such as practical reasoning, linguistic understanding, and conscious perceptual experience. Psychologists and cognitive scientists, in contrast, have tended to place much greater emphasis on lower-level cognitive tasks, such as extracting edges from patterns of light on the retina, or separate words from streams of sounds arriving at the ear. It is plain that the mind carries out both types of task very successfully, and an obvious question for a philosopher of mind interested in cognitive science is how the two types of task are related. Is there a single cognitive mechanism that carries out both types of task? Is the difference between high-level and low-level tasks a difference of kind, or simply one of degree?

At various stages in the history of psychology, the idea that there is a single mechanism underlying all cognition has had great currency. During the prehistory of psychology in the eighteenth century, for example, the philosophers known as the British empiricists proposed an associationist picture of the mind, according to which all thinking is grounded in the strength of associations between ideas. The stimulus-response psychology at the heart of psychological behaviorism is a recognizable descendant of this view and so too, some have argued, is the increasing popularity of appeals to artificial neural networks. One of Fodor's most significant contributions to thinking about what is sometimes called the architecture of cognition is the idea that any such monolithic view of cognition is fundamentally wrong-headed.[2]

In a characteristically provocative maneuver, Fodor presents his main thesis in *The Modularity of Mind* as a defense of the type of faculty psychology proposed by the phrenologist Franz Joseph Gall. Although Fodor is not proposing to rehabilitate Gall's completely discredited idea that character traits and propensities to criminality can be read off the shape of the skull, he argues that Gall was basically correct to think of the mind as made up of semi-autonomous cognitive faculties. Gall was wrong to think of these cognitive faculties as individuated in terms of their location in the brain, but (according to Fodor) he was quite right to argue that they are specialized for performing particular cognitive tasks.

Gall's faculty psychology is an alternative, Fodor argues, not just to the type of monolithic conception of cognitive architecture that we find in stimulus-response behaviorism, but also to what he calls the horizontal faculty psychology that is characteristic of much contemporary psychology and cognitive science. Although they tend not to use the language of faculties, psychologists and cognitive scientists often describe themselves as studying memory, for example, or attention. These are taken to be separate cognitive mechanisms that can be studied each on their own terms. And nor is it simply an artifact of disciplinary specialization that the experimental study of memory is independent of the experimental study of attention. The guiding assumption is that memory and attention are distinct cognitive mechanisms performing distinct cognitive tasks. In the case of memory, the task is (broadly speaking) the retention and recall of information, while in the case of attention the task is selecting what is particularly salient in some body of information. What makes this a version of *horizontal* faculty psychology, according to Fodor, is that these faculties are what he calls domain-general. There are no limits to the types of information that can be remembered, or to which attention can be applied. The faculties of attention and memory cut across cognitive domains.

What Fodor sees as Gall's great insight is the existence of what he terms *vertical* cognitive faculties. These are cognitive systems that are domain-specific. They perform determinate types of processing on fixed and circumscribed bodies of information. Moreover, they are *informationally encapsulated*. It is not just that they only process specific types of information. They can only call upon a very limited range of proprietary information in performing their task. These vertical cognitive faculties are what Fodor calls *cognitive modules*.

Building on this idea, Fodor makes a general distinction between modular and non-modular cognitive processes. This is, in essence, a distinction between high-level cognitive processes that are open-ended and that involve bringing a wide range of information to bear on very general problems, and lower-level cognitive processes that work quickly to provide rapid solutions to highly determinate problems. In more detail, modular processes are generally held to have most, if not all, of the following four characteristics.

1 *Domain-specificity*. Modules are highly specified mechanisms with a relatively circumscribed functional specification and field of application.
2 *Informational encapsulation*. Modular processing remains unaffected by what is going on elsewhere in the mind. Modular systems cannot be "infiltrated" by background knowledge and expectations.
3 *Mandatory application*. Cognitive modules respond automatically to stimuli of the appropriate kind, rather than being under any executive control. It is evidence that certain types of visual processing are modular that we cannot help but perceive visual illusions, even when we know them to be illusions.
4 *Fast*. Modular processing transforms input (e.g. patterns of intensity values picked up by photoreceptors in the retina) into output (e.g. representations of three-dimensional objects) quickly enough to be used in the on-line control of action.

In addition to these "canonical" characteristics of modular processes, Fodor draws attention to two further features that sometimes characterize modular processes.

5   *Fixed neural architecture.* It is sometimes possible to identify determinate regions of the brain associated with particular types of modular processing.
6   *Specific breakdown patterns.* Modular processing can fail in highly determinate ways. These breakdowns can provide clues as to the form and structure of that processing.

Fodor's reason for downplaying these last two characteristics is that he sees cognitive modules as functionally rather than physiologically individuated. A cognitive module has to perform a single, circumscribed, domain-specific task. But it is not necessary that it map on to a particular part of the brain. Some modules do seem to be localizable, but for others we have (as yet) no evidence either way. Certainly there does not seem to be any incoherence in the idea that the information processing involved in a cognitive module should be distributed across anatomical boundaries in the brain.

Cognitive modules form the first layer of cognitive processing. They are closely tied to perceptual systems. Here is Fodor on various candidate mechanisms that he thinks likely to count as cognitive modules:

> Candidates might include, in the case of vision, mechanisms for color perception, for the analysis of shape, and for the analysis of three-dimensional spatial relations. They might also include quite narrowly task-specific "higher level" systems concerned with the visual guidance of bodily motions or with the recognition of faces of conspecifics. Candidates in audition might include computational systems that assign grammatical descriptions to token utterances; or ones that detect the melodic or rhythmic structure of acoustic arrays; or, for that matter, ones that mediate the recognition of *voices* of conspecifics. (*MM*: 47)

Some of these candidate modules are close to the sensory periphery. That is to say, relatively little processing intervenes between information reaching the sense organs and it serving as inputs to the module. This is clearly the case for color perception. Others systems are much further "downstream". An example here would be the face-recognition system. Moreover, some cognitive modules can take the outputs of other modules as inputs. It is likely that information about the rhythmic structure of an acoustic array will be relevant to identifying the voice of a member of one's own species.

Not all cognition can be carried out by modular mechanisms, however. Fodor is emphatic that there have to be psychological processes that cut across cognitive domains. He stresses the distinction between what cognitive systems compute and what the organism believes. The representations that are processed within cognitive modules are very different from the propositional attitudes that were the focus of the last section. And nor can we identify beliefs and other propositional attitudes with the outputs of cognitive modules. The very features of cognitive modules that make them computationally powerful, such as their speed and informational encapsulation, mean that their outputs are not always a good guide to the layout of the perceived environment. Appearances can be deceptive! As Fodor puts it,

> Such representations want correction in light of background knowledge (e.g., information in memory) and of the simultaneous results of input analysis in other domains. Call the process of arriving at such corrected representations "the fixation of perceptual belief." To a first approximation we can assume that the mechanisms that effect this process work like this: They look simultaneously at the representations delivered by the various input systems and at the information currently in memory, and they arrive at a best (i.e. best available) hypothesis about how the world must be, given these various sorts of data. (*MM*: 102)

As he immediately points out, systems that can do all this cannot be either domain-general nor informationally encapsulated. So, there must be non-modular processing – or what Fodor and others often call central processing, to distinguish it from modular processing, which is peripheral.

Central processing, Fodor suggests, has two distinguishing features. It is *Quinean* and *isotropic*. What he means by describing central processing as Quinean (after the philosopher Willard Van Orman Quine, who famously proposed a holistic view of knowledge and confirmation) is that central processing aims at certain epistemic properties that are defined over the propositional attitude system as a whole. Fodor sees each organism's belief system as, in important respects, analogous to a scientific theory. It is, in fact, the organism's theory of the world. As such, it shares certain important properties with scientific theories. It is the belief system as a whole that is evaluated for consistency and coherence, for example. We cannot consider how accurate or well confirmed individual beliefs are in isolation, since how we evaluate individual beliefs cannot be divorced from how we think about other elements of the system in which they are embedded. The isotropic nature of central processing is in many ways a corollary of its Quinean property. To say that central processing is isotropic is, in essence, to say that it is *not* informationally encapsulated. In principle, any part of the belief system is relevant to confirming any other. We cannot draw boundaries within the belief system and hope to contain the process of confirmation within those boundaries.

The basic distinction that Fodor made in *The Modularity of Mind* between modular and non-modular processing has received far more attention than one of the morals that he drew from the distinction. The chapter of the book devoted to central processing contains what Fodor provocatively refers to as "Fodor's First Law of the Nonexistence of Cognitive Science." Basically, "the more global (i.e. the more isotropic) a cognitive process is, the less anybody understands it. *Very* global processes, like analogical reasoning, aren't understood at all" (*MM*: 107). In *The Modularity of Mind* this controversial claim is not backed up by argument. To the extent that it was backed up at all, Fodor justified it with some rather controversial claims about contemporary cognitive science – such as the claim that the traditional artificial intelligence project of developing a general model of intelligent problem-solving had come to a dead end and that relatively little serious work was any longer being done on building an intelligent machine. Unsurprisingly, enthusiasts for AI and cognitive science were not much moved by his polemical claims. In more recent work, however, Fodor has, in effect, provided an argument for his "First Law." In the next section we will look at this argument and consider how it bears upon the project that we looked at in the first section – the project of using the language of thought hypothesis to legitimate commonsense psychology.

3   Fodor on the Limits of Cognitive Science

In the two previous sections we have considered two fundamental claims that Fodor makes about the mind. The first claim is that the mind is a computational engine. Thoughts are represented by sentences of an internal language of thought whose syntactic structure matches the logical form of their content. Transitions between thoughts are a function solely of their syntactic properties. Only when understood in these terms, maintains Fodor, can thoughts be causally efficacious and intentional realism preserved. The second basic claim is the distinction between two fundamentally different types of mental processing. Some processing is modular, taking place in specialized systems that carry out a restricted set of operations on a limited type of input. The type of parsing of the visual array that takes place in the early visual system is a paradigm of modular processing. But the most interesting types of processing (at least from a philosophical point of view) are neither domain-specific nor informationally encapsulated. Modules such as the early visual system produce inputs for the non-modular processing underpinning belief fixation and practical deliberation.

Since the propositional attitude system is paradigmatically Quinean (with certain epistemic properties defined over the whole set of propositional attitudes) and isotropic (with any member being potentially relevant to the confirmation of any other), Fodor's "First Law of the Nonexistence of Cognitive Science" implies that the prospects for a computational explanation of practical reasoning and ordinary decision-making are vanishingly slender. And so it is quite consistent for Fodor to go on the attack against cognitive scientists who do claim that central processing can be computationally explained. His book *The Mind Doesn't Work That Way* (2000) is a concerted attack on what Fodor terms the New Synthesis.[3] This is a hybrid view that combines computational psychology and evolutionary theory in an overarching account of the mind. The key tenet of the New Synthesis is that the mind is massively modular. There is no such thing as central processing. The mind is composed entirely of dedicated and domain specific modules that evolved in the depths of human prehistory to solve problems faced by our early ancestors.

Fodor offers an elegant argument against the massive modularity hypothesis. The central feature of a modular system is that it takes only a limited range of inputs. But how are the relevant inputs selected? In particular, is any processing involved in the selection? For what we might term classical Fodorian modules, the answer is straightforward. Modules responsible for relatively low-level tasks such as early visual processing and syntactic parsing can plausibly be described as operating directly on sensory inputs and it is standard to postulate sensory systems (so-called transducers) that directly filter the relevant inputs. But, of course, if the massive modularity hypothesis is well-founded then the mind is composed of modules that are anything but low level. The famous Cheater Detection Module postulated by the evolutionary psychologists Cosmides and Tooby, for example, is alleged to have evolved to detect cheaters in social exchanges.[4] Its inputs are presumably representations of social exchanges. But only the most radical empiricist would claim that representations of social exchanges can be immediately identified in a way that would make it plausible to postulate social exchange transducers. In which case, some processing is required to generate the appropriate inputs for the cheater detection module. According to the massive modularity thesis, this processing must be modular – but, as Fodor points out, any module that can carry out this filtering process will be less domain-specific (i.e. will have a broader range of inputs) than the module for which it is doing the filtering. A similar line of reasoning will, Fodor maintains, be applicable to the filtering module itself, and so, he concludes, we end up with processing that can hardly be described as modular at all.

The massive modularity thesis collapses – and, with it, the project of an all-embracing computational psychology.

Fodor is quite happy to accept that there are no prospects for a computational psychology that extends to non-modular processing. What I want to focus on in the remainder of this section, however, are the implications that this negative thesis has for his attempt to legitimate commonsense psychology through the language of thought hypothesis.

As we saw in the first section, the key to the legitimating strategy is the idea that causal transitions determined by the syntactic properties of sentences in the language of thought can track the semantic properties of those syntactic items. The sentences in the language of thought are the physical structures that realize beliefs and other propositional attitudes. The semantic properties of those physical structures are the contents of those beliefs. The plausibility of this claim rests in turn upon viewing the syntactic properties of a sentence in the language of thought as intrinsic, physical properties of that physical structure. If this is not the case, then it is hard to see how syntactic properties could enter into causal interactions. The whole problem of causation by content stems from the basic assumption that semantic properties, unlike syntactic properties, are not intrinsic, physical properties of sentences in the language of thought. The basic idea behind Fodor's legitimation strategy is that the representational theory of mind is a way of ensuring that the intrinsic physical properties of sentences move in tandem with their non-intrinsic semantic properties – in an analogous way to how transformations of the physical shapes of symbols in a logical proof move in tandem with the interpretation of those symbols.

A natural question to ask at this point is how exactly "intrinsic" is to be understood. It seems plausible that the intrinsic properties of mental representations cannot be context-sensitive. That is to say, the intrinsic properties of a mental representation cannot vary with the cognitive processes in which it is involved and/or the other mental representations to which it is responsive. The analogy with logic is helpful once again. The interdependence of derivability and validity would be completely undermined if the shape of a logical symbol on one line of a proof varied according to what is going on in earlier or later lines of that proof.

Putting all this together, we can conclude that syntactic properties have to be context-insensitive. And this is the source of the difficulty for Fodor's attempt to legitimate commonsense psychology through the language of thought hypothesis. The basic problem is that context-insensitivity goes hand in hand with informational encapsulation. Saying that information processing is context-insensitive is really just another way of saying that it rests upon relatively little contextual and background information. Yet, the information processing associated with propositional attitude psychology is a paradigm example of processing that is not informationally encapsulated. According to Fodor, non-modular processing is Quinean and isotropic. But, because non-modular processing is Quinean and isotropic, it often ends up being context-sensitive.

Here is an example. Many of the beliefs that we form are instances of inference to the best explanation (also known as *abduction*). Beliefs reached by inference to the best explanation are not *entailed* by the evidence on which they are based. There is no way of *deducing* the belief from the evidence. It is simply that the belief does a better job of explaining the evidence than any of the alternatives. But what does "better" mean here? In many cases, an explanation is better because it is simpler than the alternatives. In other cases, an explanation is better because it explains other phenomena that the alternatives cannot explain. In still other cases, an explanation is better because it is more conservative (it requires the believer to make fewer adjustments to the other things that one believes). What all these considerations (of simplicity, explanatory power, and conservativeness) have in common is that they are dependent upon global properties of the belief system. But processing that is dependent upon global properties in this way is *ipso facto* context-sensitive.

We can now see the fundamental tension between the theory of the representational mind and the way that Fodor characterizes the distinction between modular and non-modular processing. The language of thought hypothesis at the heart of the theory of the representational mind requires that transitions between sentences in the language of thought be a function purely of the syntactic properties of those sentences. These syntactic properties must be context-insensitive. Yet, the characteristics of the propositional attitude system that Fodor highlights in drawing the distinction between modular and non-modular processing have the consequence that, when we are dealing with sentences in the language of thought corresponding to beliefs and other propositional attitudes, we have transitions between sentences in the language of thought that are context-sensitive. Because these transitions are context-sensitive, they cannot be purely syntactic. But if those properties are not purely syntactic, then Fodor's solution to the puzzle of causation by content breaks down.

In *The Mind Doesn't Work That Way* Fodor shows himself to be clearly aware of the problem. In effect, he acknowledges that only modular processing is syntactic in the traditional sense (see his chapter 5, for example) and expresses his confidence that non-modular processing will prove to be syntactic in a weaker sense. He has nothing to say, however, about how to understand that weaker sense, or about how it might be exploited to solve the puzzle of causation by content. Nonetheless, it is a testament to the power and originality of Fodor's thinking in these areas that these questions remain fundamental both to philosophy of mind and to cognitive science. The language of thought hypothesis and the distinction between modular and non-modular processing have been so influential that news of a tension between them is news indeed.

Notes

1 Besides beliefs and desires, the propositional attitudes include hopes, fears, and so on. I can believe that it is raining, desire that it rain, hope that it rain, or fear that it is raining. In each case there is a single proposition (the proposition that it is raining) to which I bear a different attitude (the attitude of belief, desire, and so on).
2 J. A. Fodor and Z. W. Pylyshyn, "Connectionism and Cognitive Architecture: A Critical Analysis," *Cognition* 28 (1988): 3–71.
3 See Stephen Pinker, *How the Mind Works*. New York: Norton, 1999.
4 Jerome H. Barkow, Leda Cosmides, and John Tooby (eds.), *The Adapted Mind: Evolutionary Psychology and the Generation of Culture*. Oxford: Oxford University Press, 1992.

References

The Mind Doesn't Work That Way: The Scope and Limits of Computational Psychology. Cambridge, MA: MIT Press, 2000.
The Modularity of Mind [MM]. Cambridge, MA: MIT Press, 1983.
Psychosemantics. Cambridge, MA: MIT Press, 1987.

NAGEL

SONIA SEDIVY

We are contained in the world, yet there is no single world. Thomas Nagel (1937–) offers a synoptic understanding of the age-old philosophical problems concerning our nature and our relationship to the world that traces them to this seemingly paradoxical situation. He champions our core intuition, the realist intuition that we are contained in the world, but shows how it entails, perhaps surprisingly, that there is no single world because of the multiplicity of subjective viewpoints that are part of what is real. The reality of such perspectives, together with our capacity to detach from our subjectivity for more objective or impersonal outlooks, not only sets us on the path of knowledge and opens us to the possibility of moral value, but also sets up irreconcilable tensions in both domains. This situation often leads us to give a distorting primacy to the deliverances of one type of viewpoint at the expense of the other.

Nagel's achievement lies in lucid argumentation that explains how this fundamental structure of subjective and objective viewpoints and facts, and the largely irreconcilable tensions that it creates, yields most of the perennial philosophical problems, indeed most of the problems that we confront as ordinary human beings striving to act in a world that we wish to understand. His contribution lies no less in his ability to argue that this inherently contradictory predicament is something that we must face without oversimplifying, without prioritizing either perspective at the cost of the other. And his focus is never only theoretical; his works address the ways in which we must face this predicament no less in order to live and to act in the world than to theorize.

Most of this work has been written while Nagel has been professor of philosophy and law at New York University, where he has taught since 1980. His professional work began at the University of California, Berkeley in 1963, and gathered momentum at Princeton University, where he taught from 1966 to 1980. Nagel wrote his doctoral dissertation under the supervision of John Rawls, receiving his PhD from Harvard University in 1963. The breadth of Nagel's work might be due in part to the range of his philosophical training, beginning in the 1950s at Cornell where the work of the later Wittgenstein was a heated concern, continuing at Oxford where he received a British perspective with his BPhil in 1960, and then coming together at Harvard through contact with some of the defining figures of mid-century analytic philosophy such as Quine, Goodman, and, of course, Rawls.

There is no question that Nagel stands out among his contemporaries along several dimensions. In the first place, his work is distinguished thematically by its opposition to the cultural and philosophical trends gaining momentum through the latter half of the twentieth century. His framework helps us understand the somewhat paradoxical tenor of late twentieth-century thought which errs with respect to both subjective and objective perspectives. Nagel casts the prevailing mood as one of idealism and subjectivism, which is manifest in the relativist tenor of the times and the reductive aims of most theories. This makes sense, since Nagel can show that even though reductive theories might privilege certain forms of scientific explanation, such theories are forms of idealism because they adopt an "epistemological criterion of reality – that only what can be understood in a certain way exists" (*VN* 15). Nagel offers staunchly anti-reductionist and anti-relativist alternatives across metaphysics, theory of mind and of knowledge. In ethics, he opposes the growing trend towards relativism, which holds that we are capable of only parochial outlooks in place of genuinely moral reasoning. But he also argues against moral theories that privilege the objective outlook to the extent of either denying values altogether or recognizing only highly impartial "agent-neutral" ones. Nagel himself describes his classic *The View From Nowhere* as "in some respects a deliberately reactionary work" and identifies his anti-relativist views of language and logic in *The Last Word* as "heretical."

The systematicity of Nagel's work is also distinctive. His philosophy offers a unified way to understand issues spanning from metaphysics through value theory; or more specifically, from metaphysical problems centering around our nature – problems of consciousness, personal identity and freedom – through theory of knowledge, to the key challenges confronting moral theory in both ethics and political theory. This is significant in an era of specialization, when few theorists offer synoptic outlooks.

Yet Nagel's views are also almost startling in the modesty of their counsel, which urges that in many domains we lack appropriate conceptual resources that would allow us to reconcile the fundamental tensions that result from our containment in a world consisting of subjective and objective facts, personal and impersonal values. This means that we must recognize that in some domains integration of subjective and objective viewpoints and resolution of their problematic clashes is not to be had.

Finally, Nagel stands out by the thoroughly non-technical nature of his argumentation and the pellucid quality of his writing. Though his arguments show mastery of arguments of contemporaries such as Saul Kripke or Donald Davidson that are grounded in modern symbolic logic and philosophy of language, his own treatment of their arguments involves no explicit technicality, while remaining responsible to their achievements and engaging with them. Perhaps this remarkable gift for philosophical writing explains in part the last feature which separates Nagel from most of his contemporaries, namely his engagement with contemporary societal issues and problems, beginning in the 1960s with issues raised by the Vietnam war, through to such problems as poverty and charity, privacy, assisted suicide and currently directed towards identity politics and evolutionary theory, among others. In both professional articles and countless book reviews for the public press – not to mention a non-technical yet conceptually innovative book reversing usual attitudes about taxation – Nagel has continuously addressed the difficult issues confronting his society. His work strives to contribute to public debate despite a cultural climate that seems to place no value on the concerns or methods of analytic philosophy.

Nagel is identified with the realist position of *The View from Nowhere* and the strong egalitarianism developed throughout his writings from *The Possibility of Altruism*, through *The View from Nowhere* to *Equality and Partiality*. Since the systematic range of his work precludes examining its entire scope, I will focus on his defining book, *The View from Nowhere*, along with two later texts, *Equality and Partiality* and *The Last Word*, in order to trace his reasoning across four pivotal junctures, considered in the same order as his classic argument in *The View from Nowhere*: mind and knowledge, value and ethics-politics.

1 Mind and Knowledge

The single problem with which Nagel is concerned in all its aspects arises from the fact of subjectivity. This is the incontrovertible fact that some creatures are not only sentient, but are also sufficiently complex to recognize their subjectivity. In other words, some sentient creatures – such as ourselves – can recognize that they perceive and think about the world from a perspective that is marked by their make-up as individual members of a species. From this follows another, perhaps not so evident, fact that Nagel brings out. Just as to recognize any thing or event is to recognize an instance of a kind, to recognize one's own subjectivity or the subjectivity of one's species is to recognize subjectivity as an instance of a type or kind. But to grasp that one's subjectivity belongs as an instance to a kind is to confront the possibility of other species of subjectivity, and this recognition is one and the same as the "objective impulse," the realization that it is possible to gain an understanding that is not limited – or is less limited – by the nature of one's own type of subjectivity (*VN* 18). Recognizing one's own subjectivity is *one and the same as* recognizing the possibility of detaching from it – from one's particularity as well as from one's type – in order to comprehend and transcend it in increasingly detached conceptions of the world.

But the distinctive nature of subjective outlooks must not be mistaken as a matter of privacy. Subjective perspectives are not private. Rather, the subjectivity of some aspects of our mental lives is a matter of their particularity. Nagel follows Wittgenstein in arguing for the intersubjective nature of concepts of experiences, thoughts, etc. which are public, though their public or intersubjective nature differs from that of concepts that apply to the physical world. This is important because the intersubjective nature of these concepts yields the seriousness of the problems we confront: "the subjective idea of experience, of action, and of the self are in some sense public or common property. That is why the problems of mind and body, free will, and personal identity are not just problems about one's own case" (SO 207).

Nagel traces these problems to our capacity to recognize our subjectivity, urging that increasingly controversial implications follow from this fact. First, he argues that the sheer generality of the concept of experience – the fact that there is such a concept at all – entails that the concept extends to cases where there are external signs of an experiential mental life even though that mental life seems so unlike our own that we cannot imaginatively extrapolate from our own first person grasp of what our experience is like. Nagel makes this fact vivid by asking us to imagine "What is it like to be a bat?" in a paper of that same title that immediately became a classic in theory of mind.[1] The paper, as well as the opening of *The View from Nowhere*, argues that we can meaningfully apply the concept of experience beyond conditions that make it applicable in our own case.

Even more contentious is the further step Nagel takes in this line of argument. Once we acknowledge the sort of case that bats exemplify, he argues that we also need to countenance cases where there might be a mental life without any external signs that we could identify. This key move attempts to establish that we have concepts some of whose conditions of application we cannot conceive, but which are bona fide concepts nonetheless. The controversial issue is whether "on the basis of examples of reality with which (one) is acquainted" one might have "a general concept which applies beyond everything with which (one) and (one's) like could conceivably be acquainted?" (*VN* 96). Nagel argues that the fact that our concepts have complements extends to examples such as " 'all the things we can't describe', 'all the things we can't conceive of', and finally, 'all the things humans are constitutionally incapable of ever conceiving' " (*VN* 98).

This is the pivotal moment in Nagel's approach. It is a contention that goes against the still current tendency to argue from limitations on meaningful application of our concepts to what can be conceived, what can be known, and ultimately to what there is. And it yields the basic structure that Nagel believes configures our relationship – as agents, thinkers, theorists – to the world.

That structure is realism rather than idealism. Realism and idealism are theories about the nature of reality and our place in reality. To argue that we have general concepts of experience, mind, and reality that extend or transcend the conditions in which we might apply them – the set of implications we just traversed – is to argue for realism. More specifically, Nagel suggests that recognizing our subjectivity as an instance of a general phenomenon shows that our relationship to the world is one of sheer containment, where we are parts of the world that do not stand to it in any more specific relation. The idea of containment is the core or "pure idea of realism" (*VN* 70):

Creatures who recognize both their limited nature and their containment in the world must recognize both that reality may extend beyond our conceptual reach and that there may be concepts that we could not understand. The condition is met by a general concept of reality under which one's actual conception, as well as the possible extensions of that conception, falls as an instance. This concept

> seems to me adequately explained through the idea of a hierarchical set of conceptions, extending from those much more limited than one's own but contained in it to those larger than one's own but containing it – of which some are reachable by discoveries one might make but others, larger still, are not. (*VN* 98)

But this realism includes the paradoxical twist that there is no one way that things are, no single reality that could be encompassed by an objective viewpoint detached from the particulars of subjective viewpoints, because the multiplicity of subjective viewpoints and the facts evident from those viewpoints are all part of reality. This is the cost of the realism Nagel offers. It is the hallmark of his approach since it undercuts the ambitions of objective and reductive theories to offer complete explanations of what is real. Precisely because increasingly objective explanations that detach from our specific ways of experiencing the world leave behind those experiences and the "appearances" evident to those experiences, such explanations – despite their explanatory successes – cannot claim to be exhaustive. We must not forget the distinction, Nagel counsels, between objectivity, which is a mode of explanation, and reality. "[T]he fundamental impulse behind the objective impulse is that the world is not our world. This idea can be betrayed if we turn objective comprehensibility into a new standard of reality" (*VN* 18).

In theory of mind, physicalism is the objectifying mode of explanation against whose seduction we must guard. Physicalism holds that all reality is physical and hence requires explanations that show how our thoughts and experiences are physical despite their qualitative, subjective, and conscious nature. Physicalism requires some form of reduction – "behaviorist, causal or functionalist" – that shows that the identity conditions of mental states are and can be specified in terms that can ultimately be identified with physical conditions. Physicalism in theory of mind is an example of the sort of overextension or betrayal of the objective impulse against which Nagel warns:

> Physicalism, though unacceptable, has behind it the broader impulse to which it gives distorted and ultimately self-defeating expression. That is the impulse to find a way of thinking about the world as it is, so that everything in it, not just atoms and planets, can be regarded as real in the same way: not just an aspect of the world as it appears to us, but something that is *really there*. (*VN* 16)

But if physicalism distorts the fundamental need to show that subjective viewpoints are part of reality, how might the need be met? If we reject any form of psycho-physical reduction (any explanatory mapping of psychological facts to physical ones) what alternative is there? This is one of the key junctures where Nagel's approach takes a distinctively modest turn. He argues that we do not yet have the conceptual resources to grasp how reality could be fundamentally dual in nature – both mental and physical. Our physical and metaphysical understanding at present is not even in the right ballpark for understanding the nature of minds. What we need would be a dual aspect theory that explains how the fundamental constituents of reality have both physical and mental (or proto-mental) properties so that combinations of them can yield systems that have physical or mental properties, or both. But this is a gesture to an area of conceptual space that we have no idea how to fill, given our current physical understanding of the universe.

Yet it is also physics that should alert us to the need for openness to radical conceptual change. Just as electricity and magnetism required the development of new conceptual tools that changed our understanding of the universe from the mechanical framework of Newton, so we need new concepts to account for subjectivity. But this requires that we undertake the first step, which seems antithetical at present, namely to recognize that minds cannot be explained in any terms compatible with extant physical theory – just as explaining electricity and magnetism required recognizing the need for new distinctive conceptual resources before it was possible to frame a new unifying physical theory:

> The strange truth seems to be that certain complex, biologically generated physical systems, of which each of us is an example, have rich nonphysical properties. An integrated theory of reality must account for this, and I believe that if and when it arrives, probably not for centuries, it will alter our conception of the universe as radically as anything has to date. (*VN* 51)

What does this realist framework indicate concerning our capacity for knowledge in general, rather than, as in the particular case just considered, our ability to explain minds? Nagel divides theories of knowledge into three categories: skeptical, reductive, and heroic (or quixotic, depending on one's realist or idealist outlook). One of the defining tendencies in twentieth-century analytic philosophy is to deflate skeptical challenges by showing that they transgress conditions for the use, meaning, or reference of our concepts. Such conditions can be conceived in a variety of ways – as verification conditions, conditions of use, conditions of interpretability, or causal conditions of reference. But the upshot is argued to be the same, namely to deny that we can articulate the skeptical possibility that the world might be unimaginably different from how we take it to be. Such linguistically based objections keep company with more epistemically grounded considerations against the possibility of wholesale justification that would require a standpoint independent of, or external to, any we can actually occupy – a standpoint from which we could question the validity of all of our conceptual resource while needing to use those resources to articulate the requirement. In direct opposition, Nagel argues that skeptical challenges can be meaningfully posed and inevitably attend our "natural" realist outlook. His view that we have general concepts of mind and reality that extend beyond their causal conditions or conditions in which we apply such concepts contradicts theories that tie our use of concepts to the conditions in which we might verify them or apply them interpretively. So where does the burden of proof lie in this stark opposition of views? Nagel strives to turn the force of anti-skeptical arguments against themselves. Rather than showing that skeptical possibilities cannot be meaningfully articulated, the inability of recent theories of language to explain how we can frame skeptical possibilities displays their failure to be adequate to all of our capacities, conceptual and linguistic. Indeed, Nagel charges that recent anti-skeptical arguments vitiate the views of language on which they depend.

The upshot is that we can (and should) strive for knowledge without restricting what we believe there is to what we can conceive. We can expand our objective understanding – with the proviso that we avoid false objectification and reduction where objective and reductive explanation is not appropriate. Attempts to increase our understanding need to proceed under the recognition that such attempts may be more or less limited, just as the skeptical outlook warns. Objective knowledge and skepticism come together as "products of one capacity," the capacity that lies in the objective impulse, the "pure idea of realism" to detach from our own viewpoints to form conceptions of the world in which we are contained (*VN* 71).

Yet, despite the persuasive clarity with which Nagel draws out these implications of recognizing the sheer fact of complex sentience, one might feel discomfort with his suggestion that the "pure idea of realism" is one of containment. Yes, one might agree that much contemporary philosophy turns on misguided objectification, accepting epistemic criteria for what is real in just the ways that Nagel diagnoses: mistaking one mode of understanding what is real with reality itself. But is there no alternative between accepting what we can conceive as what there is, and Nagel's view that recognizing our subjectivity and hence our containment in a reality consisting of both subjective and objective facts "implies nothing specific about the relation between the appearances and reality, except that we and our inner lives are part of reality" (*VN* 70)? What is in question is Nagel's reliance on imagery of containment. The alternative would be to argue that we are integral parts of reality, so that understanding that relationship would be more informative about both ourselves and the world. The question is whether it might be possible to argue for such a view *without* employing an epistemically obtained criterion of what is real and our relation to it.

This pressure point in Nagel's framework might explain his abiding fascination with the later philosophy of Wittgenstein. *The View from Nowhere* singles out Wittgenstein as "one of the most important sources of contemporary idealism" (*VN* 105) Yet Nagel also has a growing sense that the idealism increasingly attributed to Wittgenstein since the 1980s, the view that meaning is grounded in nothing more than our forms of life, "yields such a radical and obviously false view of truth in various domains that I think it can't be correct as an interpretation, even though I don't have an alternative" (*OT* 45: introduction to reprinting of "Wittgenstein: The Egocentric Predicament"). Nagel's conflicted attitude to Wittgenstein is telling, especially in light of the fact that at roughly the same time, contemporary philosophers such as Cora Diamond, John McDowell, and Hilary Putnam were arguing that, far from idealism, Wittgenstein's later work offered "realism with a human face." This view would be an example of an alternative realism that tries to show how our conceptual and rational capacities – characterized by a normative dimension and a reach that transcend their actual application – depend on and emerge from contingent practices. If tenable, it would figure between the forms of idealism prevailing in the twentieth century and the stark realism of "sheer containment" Nagel advocates.

Indeed, Nagel devotes a recent book to this issue, focusing on the justification and explanation of our rational and conceptual capacities. *The Last Word* asks just what is the last word or ground of our ability to conceptualize and reason across diverse domains from mathematics to morals. He considers Cora Diamond's work, while arguing against Saul Kripke's influential anti-realist understanding of Wittgenstein's considerations of rule-following, which set the tone of most debate since its publication in 1982. Nagel agrees with the realist interpretation that Wittgenstein's aim is to resist explaining our concepts and thoughts from the outside – in any way that presents non-normative facts as constitutive for capacities that are normative, involving a right and a wrong way of being carried out such as an incorrect application of a concept. But he does not go so far as to find an alternative realism in Wittgenstein's work. It is telling that Nagel is uncomfortable with Wittgenstein's argumentation because it encourages the relativist misreading that all there is to meaning and rationality is to be found in our local practices – even though it is true and important that those practices can only be examined and justified from within rather than from without.

Perhaps there is no deeper understanding of the reach of meaning than that involved in our ordinary understanding of the expressions themselves. But then that understanding is not adequately represented by the sort of facial description of our practices that Wittgenstein recommends as an instrument of demystification. I would prefer to say that the infinite reach of mathematical language can be understood only from inside it, by engaging in that form of life. That means that we cannot understand even the form of life by describing its practices from outside. The order of explanation is the reverse of that in the common (mis)interpretation of Wittgenstein: The rule-following practices of our linguistic community can be understood only through the substantive content of our thoughts – for example, the arithmetical ones. Otherwise they are impotent rituals. We cannot make sense of them viewing them as items of natural history. (*LW* 52–3)

This nuanced interpretation of Wittgenstein illustrates the development in Nagel's own thinking. It shows his growing emphasis that the need to avoid reductive explanation requires understanding and argumentation "from within" our contingent practices – while maintaining his strong metaphysical realism. Nevertheless, Nagel's own framework raises the question whether his metaphysical realism is too stark, by offering a non-metaphysical normative realism concerning value that might stand as a model for metaphysical realism as well.

2 Value and Ethics-Politics

Nagel argues for a normative realism by emphasizing the difference between realism about values and realism about facts. This is a distinction he maintains as the critical underpinning of his moral theory from *The View from Nowhere* through to *The Last Word*:

Normative realism is the view that propositions about what gives us reasons for action can be true and false independently of how things appear to us, and that we can hope to discover the truth by transcending appearances and subjecting them to critical assessment. What we aim to discover by this method is not a new aspect of the external world, called value, but rather just the truth about what we and others should do and want. . . .

The picture I associate with normative realism is not that of an extra set of properties of things and events in the world, but of a series of possible steps in the development of human motivation which would improve the way we lead our lives, whether or not we will actually take them. We begin with a partial and inaccurate view, but by stepping outside of ourselves and constructing and comparing alternatives we can reach a new motivational condition at a higher level of objectivity. (*VN* 139–40)

Before examining Nagel's normative realism in its own right, it is important to consider the contrast it poses to his metaphysical realism about facts. His transition from metaphysical realism to normative non-metaphysical realism about value is a key junction that gives his synoptic framework its distinctive shape. Distinguishing normative realism from metaphysical realism, as Nagel does, raises the question whether realism about facts should be structurally similar to normative realism about value, rather than the alternative that Nagel rejects, that realism about value should be analogous to metaphysical realism about facts. Why isn't realism unified by the method and defining possibility that he reserves for normative realism: the possibility of steps in the development of concepts and of beliefs, not only of motivations, which would improve our capacities to understand the world as well as to lead our lives, whether or not we will actually take them – since given their possibility, they are "there" to be taken, whether we do so or not. (This is arguably the sort of alternative realism in question above.)

To raise this challenge is to question the way Nagel connects the objective impulse with two distinct types of realism: a "stark" realism about facts and a "weaker" or non-metaphysical normative realism; but not to question his fundamental point, that our capacity for forming a more detached objective view underlies both our capacities to understand the world and to be ethical. Indeed, the fundamental bifurcation of viewpoints is responsible for the fact that we are ethical beings at all – since it is the objective impulse that makes us consider what matters to us not only from the viewpoint of our own desires and motivations, but also from a viewpoint that includes ourselves as one among many agents who need to act in the world, a perspective from which one can't claim that what is important to oneself matters more than what is important to others. While the objective impulse opens us up to value, it also makes it difficult to act from the reasons that become available. Ethics begins from taking a more detached or impersonal viewpoint and attempting to solve the conflicts that arise not simply between the values and reasons that are evident at an impartial viewpoint and the desires and motives that are distinct to our own particular outlook, but among the variety of impersonal values that become evident as one adopts an impartial outlook. Theoretically, Nagel argues that a strongly egalitarian resolution that is Kantian in form could in principle ease at least some key tensions. But his modesty is chilling, since he also highlights many obstacles, some seemingly insuperable, standing in the way. It is in drawing out the implications of our bifurcated viewpoint for moral and political theory that Nagel is at his most empathetic and eloquent.

In the first place, moral theory needs to avoid the erroneous tendencies towards over-objectification and reduction that accompany the objective outlook. Objectification, reduction, and skepticism configure the theoretical options, but they do so differently from the way they structure the domain of metaphysical and epistemic theories. Unlike realism about facts, which is accompanied by skeptical doubt concerning our capacity to grasp such facts, normative realism is opposed by skepticism, which insists that there are no genuine values. One key difference between values and facts is that the object-ive viewpoint threatens to make values disappear, so that all that seems to remain from an objective viewpoint are subjective facts about the desires and inclinations of individual agents. This is the broadly Humean predicament in moral theory. Nagel's diagnosis should be predictable: a Humean outlook over-objectifies by taking a certain mode of knowledge – for example, causal knowledge, as in a naturalistic psychology – to be criterial of what there is. The way to avoid over-objectification and reduction is distinct to the moral domain because of the non-metaphysical nature of reasons and values. Because Nagel argues that, unlike subjective and objective facts, motivations arising from our particular viewpoints and values available from impartial viewpoints are not "parts" of reality, he can also hold that they are not irreducibly distinct. Rather, the issue is to find the appropriate form that impersonal reasons might take, so that we can embrace and act on them. But even if we admit that values are real – without being "parts" or extra-ingredients of reality – and that they have their own objectivity – an objectivity of form – the tend-ency to over-objectification recurs, now as the belief that we need to find "the most objective possible account of all reasons for action: the account which engages us from a maximally neutral standpoint." This tendency is expressed in consequentialism. Nagel discusses both consequentialist and deontological ethics, to argue against the former and to explain the puzzling nature of the latter – an explanation that has proved to be most important for ongoing debate. Both discussions feed into his larger purpose, which is to explore the important differences among reasons that can be given a general form – reasons that stay in view or come into view at an impersonal perspective – so that we can reconcile tensions and develop our motivations.

Perhaps the most important respect in which reasons that can take a general form differ turns on whether that general form does or does not include an essential reference to the agent. Such reasons are agent-relative and agent-neutral respectively, and one might speak of the corresponding values as personal and impersonal. Nagel develops this distinction in terms of two correlative distinctions that are also generated by our dual viewpoints: the distinction between what we *do* and what *happens* and that between choosing *actions* as opposed to choosing *states of the world*. Reasons that are *relative* to the agent are "specified by universal principles which nevertheless refer incliminably to features or circumstances of the agent for whom they are reasons." Reasons that are *neutral* with respect to the agent "depend on what everyone ought to value, independently of its relation to himself" (*EP* 40). As agents, we act on *agent-relative* reasons because even though actions affect what happens in the world, in the first instance one's choice is necessarily between one's own actions. However, each of us is also an objective self that views the world detached from one's particular perspective. Consequently, the objective self chooses between different possible states of the world and its choice is based on *agent-neutral* reasons. This yields a way of explaining moral conflict, as due to the fact that "(e)very choice is two choices," every choice is at once a choice between actions and between states of the world. Moral conflict arises when the agent's choice concerning what to *do* conflicts with the objective self's choice concerning what should *happen*. This framework allows Nagel to explain that consequentialism gives primacy to the agent-neutral values on the basis of which the objective self chooses between world-states; while, in contrast, deontological theories give primacy to certain agent-relative reasons that restrict agents from acting in certain ways.

> We are faced with a choice. For the purposes of ethics should we identify with the detached, impersonal will that chooses total outcomes, and act on reasons that are determined accordingly? Or is this a denial of what we are really doing and an avoidance of the full range of reasons that apply to creatures like us? This is a true philosophical dilemma; it arises out of our nature, which includes different point of view on the world. . . . I believe the human duality of perspectives is too deep for us reasonably to hope to overcome it. (*VN* 185)

But the dilemma does not block us from making at least some headway, setting aside some positions along the way. In this vein, Nagel argues forcefully against consequentialism on the ground that it is a form of over-objectification. Not all values are impersonal – though some are – and there is no "completely general impersonal value of the satisfaction of desires and preferences." Objectivity in ethics does not require us to "eliminate perspective from the domain of real value to the greatest possible extent" (*VN* 173). He also explains deontological restrictions in terms of the fact that our actions are directed towards aims, so that it makes sense that in general, any particular agent is prohibited from directing their actions towards bad or evil aims, regardless of the impersonally viewable outcomes of those actions. But he also cautions that our understanding of specific deontological restrictions is still in progress, and that there may be conflicts with the impersonal viewpoint that might require us to alter some of the restrictions on human action we currently consider fixed.

His view of ethics parallels his view of metaphysics:

> It is clear that we are at a primitive stage of moral development. Even the most civilized human beings have only a haphazard understanding of how to live, how to treat others, how to organize societies. The idea that the basic principles of morality are *known*, and that the problems all come in their interpretation and application, is one of the most fantastic conceits to which our conceited species has been drawn. (*VN* 187)

This brings us to the inseparability of ethics from politics, and to Nagel's arguments for a Kantian and egalitarian resolution to the conflicts arising from our dual perspectives. These are the focus of his *Equality and Partiality*. Although political theory is typically understood as dealing with the relationship of the individual and society, Nagel holds that it deals with the relation of each individual to him- or herself since each one of us occupies both a particular individual viewpoint and the detached standpoint of the collectivity. The conflict between "the standpoint of the collectivity and the standpoint of the individual" has to be resolved by each individual, who needs to reconcile for herself the competing claims of the collectivity that she can appreciate from the impartial viewpoint, and the values that arise from her own unique character and commitments. That is why any social arrangement must in the first instance enable each one to settle these fundamental conflicts within ourselves, if that social arrangement is to allow us to live together harmoniously.

Nagel's fundamental point, that reconciling the values of the collectivity and the individual is a problem of uniting the two standpoints that each of us occupies, leads him to argue that the resolution would have a Kantian form. As he makes clear, subjective motivations and the fact that our objective impulse reveals both agent-relative and agent-neutral values, require us to go beyond the question "What can we all agree would be best, impersonally conceived?" to ask "What, if anything, can we all agree that we should do, given that our motives are not merely impersonal?" (*EP* 15). But the latter is already the form that Kant suggests our moral reasoning needs to take. Nagel's framework allows us to appreciate that the Kantian form of moral reasoning is akin to a perspective, one that develops the impartial viewpoint that is inherent to us in a way that does not discount the importance of personal values and commitments. Such reasoning is important because it "attempts to see things simultaneously from each individual's point of view and to arrive at a form of motivation which they can all share, instead of simply replacing the individual perspectives by an impersonal one reached by stepping outside them all – as happens in the attitude of pure impartial benevolence" (*EP* 15–16). That is why the Kantian outlook offers at least the possibility of reconciliation, insofar as it requires "what I can affirm that anyone ought to do in my place, and what therefore everyone ought to agree that it is right for me to do as things are" (*EP* 17).

But what such reconciliations would find more substantively is a matter of dispute even among contemporary Kantians, and Nagel does not offer any easy answers. Instead, as we might expect, he is cautious about what, if anything, we might argue more specifically:

> [T]here are, I suspect, no general principles governing both agent-relative, personal reasons, and their combination, which are acceptable from all points of view in light of their consequences under all realistically possible conditions. Under some conditions – including those of the actual world – any standards of individual conduct which try to accommodate both sorts of reasons will be either too demanding in terms of the first or not demanding enough in terms of the second. (*EP* 49)

He is pessimistic about the possibility that given our starting point at this time – the "sickening" disparities among us – we might devise political institutions that would allow us to develop motivations and values or "a form of rationality that leads to collective harmony." But this underscores the importance of public institutions and forms of life. Nagel's point throughout is that it is not a question of taking our inclinations, motives, and reasoning as they stand and finding a moral resolution to conflicting impersonal and personal values. Rather, what is at issue is to find a way to "re-order our minds" so that each of us can find a way to balance our inherent impartial standpoint with our personal values. It is institutions and practices that enable – or impede – such development. The Kantian form of our moral reasoning suggests that social arrangements or political institutions are legitimate only if they are unanimously supported by individuals – though not by individuals as they actually are, but as they would be insofar as they found themselves within institutions that allow them to transform some of their values and motives.

Unanimity is a strong condition on political legitimacy indeed. But Nagel charges that what is utopian is to insist on transforming our motivations in one direction only – the impersonal – since this would require us to forsake or transcend our personal motives. It is not utopian to transform our societies for a result – such as abolition of slavery, of a caste system, or of the subjugations of women – "which generates its own support by calling forth new possibilities of mutual respect and recognition of moral equality through adherence to cooperative institutions" (*EP* 26, 27).

Nagel gives qualified support to the well-explored liberal proposal that political institutions can allow us to transform our own motivations through a "division of moral labor." His framework gives us a deeper understanding of the idea that resolution lies in finding "the design of institutions which penetrate and in part reconstruct their individual members, by producing differentiation within the self between public and private roles" (*EP* 53) According to such a division, the social institutions in which we participate would allow us to act on our impartial, egalitarian motives, thereby freeing us to act on our personal motives outside our social roles. However, this is only the form of a solution, outlining the conditions that would make actual proposal minimally adequate. As such it is important. But Nagel also cautions that it is not specific, and that it might not be sufficiently transformative. What is important, he urges, is that a solution of this type would not simply separate our existing personal and impersonal motives into distinct spheres of action, but would need to transform and develop those motives through their separation. Even so, he worries that solutions of this kind might not be sufficiently transformative.

Liberal societies are one way, though presumably not the only way, to strive for such division of labor. But because of the wide disparities among the conditions of our lives – some of which are due to other aspects of liberal societies – the conflicts between our values remain severe. As Nagel puts it, even where we have institutions that enable us as individuals to externalize, to act on our impartial values, if the conditions are very inequitable – as they are – we will inevitably continue, despite best intentions, to find ourselves in conflicts that "approach the case of the last life-jacket as opposed to the last éclair" (*EP* 61).

That is why we need more transformative institutions and practices that individuals "could come to find natural" that allow us not merely to act on our impersonal reasons as occupants of various social roles – such as citizen, voter, taxpayer at one level, and as teacher, doctor, judge, etc. at another – but that "take us further toward an accommodation of the two standpoints." Such institutions and practices would give us "Rousseau's image of the social contract returning to each of us a reconstructed self" at a fine grain of resolution (*EP* 60–2). But of such institutions and practices, Nagel can offer no sketch.

Yet of one thing he is quite sure. Everyone is equal not only in the sense that no one's life matters any more than anyone else's, but in the sense that it is more important to improve the lives of the worse off than to add to the advantages of the better off. This egalitarian view is both strong – in substance – and general in scope, since it applies across the spectrum of human lives in economically stratified societies rather than only to those at the very lowest level of need. Nagel argues controversially that impartiality is in itself egalitarian. This means that egalitarian solutions to problems of inequality are not simply ones we might find – from an impartial viewpoint – as a consequence of additional facts that structure circumstances. One example of such an extrinsic fact that recommends an egalitarian outlook is diminishing marginal utility, which dictates that, "transferable resources will usually benefit a person with less more than they will benefit a person with significantly more" (*EP* 65).

Instead, Nagel tries to find ways to show that the concern for others inherent in the impartial outlook involves priority to those who are worse off. First, because what is at issue concerns the "prospective quality" of entire individual lives and prospects at birth are so different in unequal societies such as ours, it seems "intuitively right" to ameliorate those less well off, since such amelioration will have great impact even in the case of people who are not utterly abject. Second, the "best theoretical interpretation" of impartiality concerns all individuals, not only the most needy. Concern for everyone is concern for all individuals. But particular concern that considers each individual cannot simply be conglomerated or aggregated. This suggests that questions of equality need to be addressed by means of "non-aggregative, pairwise comparison." Such pairwise comparisons extend the range of egalitarian measures from the most abject to all those who stand in some significant way worse off than others. This method would indicate ameliorating many standing in the lower position in such pairwise contrasts, and not only those occupying the very lowest level in a descending series of contrasts.

> This is a direct consequence of . . . the proper form of imaginative identification with the points of view of others, when we recognize their importance from the impersonal standpoint. Instead of combining all their experiences into an undifferentiated whole, or choosing as if we had an equal chance of being any of them, we must try to think about it as if we were each of them separately – as if each of their lives were our only life. Even though this is a tall order and does not describe a logical possibility, I believe it means something imaginatively and morally: It belongs to the same moral outlook that requires unanimity as a condition of legitimacy. (*EP* 68)

Many problems – arising from issues of responsibility, consistency, and motivation – attend any attempt to put such egalitarian principles into political practice. *Equality and Partiality* addresses these problems in detail always directed to our bifurcated individual perspectives. That detail goes well beyond our scope here. But it should be clear that Nagel's moral and political outlook goes against current objectifying tendencies that typically stretch at most to an egalitarianism limited to those in greatest need rather than towards a more encompassing egalitarianism that considers the full spectrum of human lives in their full complexity. His approach also evidently opposes the broader relativist cultural climate, which undercuts the idea that we are capable of moral *reasoning*. Nagel's extended counter-argument to this ethos is in *The Last Word*. His defense of moral reasoning parallels his arguments about language, logic, and mathematics, considered above. Moral reasons are not even comprehensible as such, except from a moral standpoint. And it is only from a perspective that is internal to moral reasoning that we can challenge outlooks that claim to be moral – in order to defend, develop, or perhaps find no recourse but to abandon them.

In sum, Nagel's work takes the egalitarian substance of Rawls's theory of social justice and strives to give it a broader ethical significance. But he cannot share Rawls's "psychological expectations," and characteristically qualifies his proposal with doubts that we could arrive at "Kantian unanimity" on this issue. This qualification is not a small side-note since it opposes his arguments that such unanimity is required for political legitimacy. "We can get closer [to Kantian unanimity about egalitarianism] through political institutions, but a gap remains which can be closed only by a human transformation that seems, at the moment, utopian, or by institutional invention beyond anything that is at present imaginable" (*EP* 63).

3 Conclusion

The influence of Nagel's cautionary metaphysical and normative realism is hard to gauge. The importance of his sustained attack against reductive thinking in all its forms cannot be overstated. Yet it is not at all clear that those arguments are heeded rather than discounted in the rush to form theoretical accounts of mind, language, and knowledge. For this reason, Nagel's work seems to stand alone in these areas, almost in a category of its own, as a constraint that many theorists would rather not address. In contrast, his views are integral to ongoing debate in moral and political theory where they simply cannot be overlooked. His essays, often for the public press, continue to offer deeply reasoned yet accessible contributions on difficult issues – such as the changing nature of *privacy* in the United States with its far-reaching political consequences.

Without a doubt, Thomas Nagel's work stands as a unique contribution to twentieth-century philosophy in its acute sensitivity to the complexity of what it is like to be human –philosophy that uniquely balances and unifies the human side of this complexity with its theoretical dimensions and repercussions.

Note

1   "What Is It Like to Be a Bat?" repr. in *Mortal Questions*.

References

Equality and Partiality [*EP*]. Oxford: Oxford University Press, 1991.

The Last Word [*LW*]. Oxford: Oxford University Press, 1997.

Mortal Questions. Cambridge: Cambridge University Press, 1979.

Other Minds: Critical Essays, 1969–1994 [*OT*]. Oxford: Oxford University Press, 1995.

The Possibility of Altruism. Oxford University Press, 1970; repr. Princeton: Princeton University Press, 1978.

The View from Nowhere [*VN*]. Oxford: Oxford University Press, 1986.

A selection of other works by Nagel

Concealment and Exposure and Other Essays. Oxford: Oxford University Press, 2002.

The Myth of Ownership: Taxes and Justice (with Liam Murphy). Oxford: Oxford University Press, 2002.

What Does It All Mean? A Very Short Introduction to Philosophy. Oxford: Oxford University Press, 1987.

8 KRIPKE

ALEXANDER BIRD

1 Introduction

Saul Kripke, born in 1940, was a child prodigy. He published his first paper, on the semantics of modal logic, at 16, and went on to study mathematics at Harvard. Much of his work since then has also been of a technical, mathematical nature. But Kripke has matched this work in formal logic with a philosophical oeuvre that is both accessible and widely influential. The latter has played a central role in rehabilitating metaphysics in the latter part of the twentieth century and setting the agenda for philosophical logic since. Kripke was a professor at Princeton University, having taught previously at Rockefeller University and Cornell; he is now at the City University of New York Graduate Center.

The historical significance of Kripke's work must be understood against a particular background. Early and mid-twentieth century "analytic" philosophy was dominated by a combination of empiricism, logical positivism in particular, and the linguistic turn in philosophy, especially the work of Ludwig Wittgenstein. To appreciate Kripke's importance not all the details of these lines of thought need to be understood, although some will be explained below. For now, I shall mention two important features of the prevailing philosophical climate. First of all, *metaphysics* was rejected as an important field of philosophical knowledge. Since Plato and Aristotle (and before), philosophers had been asking questions about the essential natures of things, and about the very general kinds of thing there are, and about which facts are *necessary* (must be so) and which are *contingent* (could have been otherwise). The growth of empiricism in the eighteenth century was antithetical to metaphysics, since empiricism's emphasis on all genuine knowledge coming from the senses leaves little room for substantive philosophical knowledge in the form of metaphysics. In the nineteenth century, positivism actively rejected metaphysics; positivists regarded metaphysics as an intermediate stage of intellectual development coming after theology and before finally reaching a scientific, purely empirical mode of enquiry (i.e. theorizing about the world purely on the basis of experiment and observation). As a component of logical positivism, this rejection of metaphysics predominated for most of the half-century following the First World War.

Logical positivism was also deeply influenced by what has been called the "linguistic turn" in philosophy. Very roughly, the linguistic turn can be characterized as the widespread conviction that the problems of philosophy must be addressed through the analysis of language. Many such problems were held to arise from the vagaries of everyday natural language. Expressions of a natural language may be ambiguous. Or two sentences may seem to have the same grammatical structure yet have different logical implications: for example, "Bill doesn't swim" and "Father Christmas doesn't exist" are grammatically alike, but the truth of the first implies that Bill exists, whereas the truth of the second implies that Father Christmas does *not* exist. Following Gottlob Frege and Bertrand Russell, the logical positivists held that the replacement, for scientific and philosophical purposes at least, of natural languages by an artificial, formal language would lead to the elimination of many of the traditional problems of philosophy. While Wittgenstein, in his later work especially, was far from being a positivist, he too held that the traditional propositions of metaphysics were either the result of grammatical confusion, or, in the case of acceptable assertions, merely reflections of rules of grammar.

2 Necessity and Essence

A central concern of traditional metaphysics has been with *modality*. Modality deals with *necessity* – what must be the case; *possibility* – what could be the case; and *contingency* – what could be the case under some circumstances but could also fail to be the case under other circumstances. Thus, medieval philosophers asked whether God is a necessary being and whether God possesses certain properties, such as benevolence, necessarily: must God exist (or might He not have existed) and must God desire what is good (or could He desire what is bad)? Furthermore, the claims of metaphysics (and indeed other branches of philosophy) are themselves held to be necessary. For example, not only is it true that identical entities possess all their properties in common, but this is also necessarily the case. The deflation of metaphysics prevalent in twentieth-century philosophy entailed a corresponding deflation of the concept of necessity. The necessary propositions, it was held, are just those that are knowable a priori. A proposition is known a priori if it is known by pure reflection alone and without recourse to experience of the world, e.g. observation and experiment. The known propositions of logic and mathematics, for example, are known a priori. So what had been a distinctive metaphysical category was assimilated to an epistemic category, a category concerning knowledge. Furthermore, the a priori knowability of such propositions was explained by their being *analytic* – propositions that are true in virtue of their meaning. A standard example of an analytic proposition is "all vixens are foxes." Since "vixen" just means "female fox," that proposition asserts that all female foxes are foxes, which is a logical truth. And so a common line of thought asserted that the necessity of *any* necessary proposition (e.g. "the internal angles of an Euclidean triangle sum to two right angles") is just a matter of it being possible to know that proposition by pure reflection. And the latter is possible because once the meanings of its terms were understood, it could be seen to be equivalent to a logical truth. (It was often added that the basic logical truths provide implicit definitions of key logical terms such as "all.")

Kripke's work played an important part in the rehabilitation of modal metaphysics. In his formal work Kripke developed an elegant model or semantics for modality based on Leibniz's idea of a *possible world* – a way the world might have been. In the simplest case, what is possible is true in some possible world; what is necessary is true in all possible worlds. A proposition is true but contingently so, if it is true in the actual world but false in some other possible world (i.e. a proposition that is one that is actually true but possibly false). In a series of lectures, published as the book *Naming and Necessity*, Kripke makes a corresponding philosophical case for rejecting several central tenets of the anti-metaphysical, linguistically inclined philosophy of the twentieth century. Foremost among the rejected claims was the identification of necessity with a priori knowability (and with analyticity). Kripke argued that there are necessary propositions that are not knowable a priori but which are known only a posteriori, which is to say that they are known only with the aid of some experience of the world, for example they are known only thanks to observational evidence. Conversely, there are some propositions whose truth we can know a priori and which are not necessary but contingent, i.e. which could have been false.

To persuade us that a proposition can be necessarily true but not known a priori, Kripke asks us to consider Goldbach's conjecture that every even number can be expressed as the sum of two prime numbers. This conjecture has never been proven, but neither has anyone come up with a counterexample (an even number that is not the sum of two primes) or any other kind of disproof. Along with all mathematical propositions, Goldbach's conjecture is, if true, necessarily true. Likewise, if it is false, its negation is necessary. So either Goldbach's conjecture is a necessary truth, or its negation is. But neither is in fact known a priori. Perhaps there is a proof of the conjecture (or its negation) which would allow us to know it a priori, just as a proof was eventually found for Fermat's long-conjectured "last theorem." There is, however, no guarantee that any given true mathematical proposition has a proof. Kripke points out that Gödel's first incompleteness theorem shows that for any well-behaved set of axioms, there are infinitely many arithmetical truths that cannot be proved from that set. This makes it extremely implausible that every arithmetical truth can be proved from a set of axioms themselves knowable a priori. If that is right, infinitely many arithmetical propositions are necessary, but not knowable a priori.

Kripke provides other examples of propositions that are necessary but are known only thanks to worldly experience, and so are a posteriori and not a priori. He uses the example introduced by the logician Gottlob Frege, "Hesperus is Phosphorus." The early Greeks used "Hesperus" to name the planet that is also known as the evening star, the first planet to appear on the horizon at dusk; likewise, "Phosphorus" named the morning star, the last planet to remain visible on the horizon at dawn. The Greeks were eventually persuaded by the Babylonians that these were not two planets but one and the same planet; they thus came to know the truth of "Hesperus is Phosphorus." This knowledge is clearly a posteriori, not a priori – it had to be learned with the aid of the careful astronomical observations of the Babylonians, plus a bit of astronomical theorizing. However, argues Kripke, since Hesperus just is Phosphorus, this proposition that Hesperus is Phosphorus simply asserts of something that it is identical to itself and so is a necessary truth. Many similar examples arise with people who have pseudonyms, such as authors writing under a *nom de plume*. Thus the propositions "George Eliot is Mary Ann Evans" and "Mark Twain is Samuel

Clemens" cannot be known a priori, but are necessary, since in both cases they assert the identity of a person with themselves.

Kripke does acknowledge that we could imagine making a discovery that it would be natural to describe as the discovery that Hesperus is not Phosphorus, and indeed this is one reason why some philosophers, such as Frege, have thought that the identity of Hesperus and Phosphorus is contingent. But that would not be to imagine a genuine possible world where Hesperus is not Phosphorus. At best it would be to imagine a world where some planet is seen at dawn and a distinct planet appears at dusk. We might give the names "Hesperus" and "Phosphorus" to those planets, but that would not make them identical to the planet that is Heperus/Phosphorus. Kripke's claims about necessity thus lead to the rejection (or major modification) of Hume's idea that we can tell whether something is possible by imagining it.

Further examples of a posteriori necessities proposed by Kripke have proven to be more contentious. These concern the constitution, natures, and origin of kinds of thing and of individual things. Kripke starts from a discussion by Timothy Sprigge, in which he asks (in effect) whether the Queen, Elizabeth II, could have had different (biological) parents. Kripke acknowledges that it could be discovered that her parents are not the people we thought them to be (George VI and Elizabeth Bowes-Lyon). This shows that the proposition that Elizabeth II is the child of George VI and Elizabeth Bowes-Lyon, is a posteriori and not something we can know a priori. But, asks Kripke, given that Elizabeth II is indeed the child of George VI and Elizabeth Bowes-Lyon, could she in some other possible world have different parents, e.g. Mr and Mrs Truman? No, he says, they could have had a child with many of the same qualitative properties as Elizabeth II. But that child would not be *this* woman, Elizabeth II. It is impossible for a person to have originated from a different sperm and a different egg from the ones she did originate from.

In a similar vein, Kripke asks of a particular wooden table, could this very table have been made from a different hunk of wood, or even from water from the Thames frozen and made to look like wood. We might have to look carefully to check whether those things are true, which shows the relevant propositions to be a posteriori. Even so, given that the table *is* in fact made from some specific hunk of wood, it is impossible, says Kripke, that it could have been made from a different hunk of wood or from ice. A similar-looking table may be so constructed, but it would not be *this* very table.

These two examples suggest the principle that if a material object has its origin in a particular hunk of matter, it could not have had its origin in any other hunk of matter. If this principle is true, then we have another general source of propositions that are necessary but which can be known only a posteriori. An a posteriori investigation such as a paternity test, may be needed for us to come to know that Fred is Bill's father, but if Fred is indeed Bill's father, then Bill could not have had any other father.

Kripke then proceeds to discuss theoretical identities and the properties of substances and natural kinds of thing. Theoretical identities are cases where science tells us what something *is*. The examples Kripke uses are: light is a stream of photons; water is H_2O; lightning is an electrical discharge; gold is the element with atomic number 79.

Starting with the example of gold, let us consider an alternative view: that gold is defined in terms of its apparent observable properties, so that it is a priori that gold is a yellow metal (a view to be found in Kant). Kripke asks us to imagine that the yellowness of samples of gold is just an optical illusion. Would that mean that there is no gold? No, it just means that we were wrong all along in thinking that gold is yellow. Similarly, could the meaning of "tiger" be "a large carnivorous quadrupedal animal, tawny yellow in color with blackish transverse stripes and white belly"? No; once again it might be that all tigers are three-legged but that an optical illusion makes us think otherwise. At the same time, would anything that does satisfy this description thereby necessarily be a tiger? Let us suppose that we discover some hitherto hidden population of animals meeting this description but which, on investigation, turn out to be reptiles. Would they also be tigers? No, they would not be tigers, despite having the superficial appearance of tigers. Returning to gold, would some substance that had the superficial yellow, shiny appearance of gold be gold? Not necessarily – it would not be gold if its atomic structure were different from that of gold. Kripke discusses the other theoretical identities in a similar way. The natures of the kinds in question are not given by their superficial or observable qualities. A substance that had a completely different atomic structure from H_2O, however much it resembled water it its appearance, taste and so forth, would not be water – it would be "fool's water" (by analogy with "fool's gold" – iron pyrites, which can look like gold in its natural state). While light is known to us primarily though its effects on our vision, that is not the nature of light. A world where all humans are blind is not a world without light.

If the natures of tigers, water, gold, light, and so forth are not given by their superficial, observable characteristics, what does determine their natures? Kripke makes it clear that, in most cases at least, it is certain key *microstructural* properties that determine the nature of these natural kinds. This is explicit in his endorsement of the identities "water is H_2O," "gold is the element with atomic number 79," "light is a stream of photons," where the identity is between a kind in a familiar, everyday guise (water, gold, light) and a kind characterized by its inner or microstructure (H_2O, element with atomic number 79, stream of photons).

In such cases, the microstructure gives the *essence* of the kind. Kripke uses "essence" to mean a property that something has necessarily. That is necessarily, water is H_2O, since, as we discussed, a substance that is not H_2O would not be water, however much it superficially seemed like water. Likewise a compound or an element with an atomic number other than 79 would not be gold, even if it had a convincing appearance of gold. These kinds have a microstructural essence.

It is not only kinds that have essences, nor are all essences microstructural. We saw above that Kripke argues that Queen Elizabeth II could not have had parents other than George VI and Elizabeth Bowes-Lyon. Thus having those parents is an essential property of the Queen. In this case it is an individual who has an essence, and her essence concerns her origin, not her microstructure. Similarly, we saw Kripke argue that necessarily a certain table could not have originated from a different hunk of matter; a table made from a different hunk might be qualitatively identical but it would not be *that* table. And so such objects, Kripke thinks, as well as other material objects, all have their original matter essentially.

Interestingly, while Kripke takes these propositions asserting identities to be true, he takes correspondences between sensations and states of the brain to be contingent, and so not identities at all. For example, let the sensation of pain be correlated with the brain state that is the firing of C-fibers. Could the pain sensation *be* the firing of the C-fibers? No, says Kripke, because it is possible to have the firing of the C-fibers without there being any pain: there are possible worlds where brains have the firing of C-fibers but the persons with those brains feel no pain. So the relationship between pain and C-fibers firing is contingent and thus not an identity. Why cannot we treat this like this case of light, which could exist, even though it brought about no visual sensations? Kripke's reason is that our intuitions tell us that in such a case, the stream of photons would still be light. On the other hand, something that was not painful, that was not felt as pain, would not *be* a pain. In the case of light the relationship with the corresponding microstructure (stream of photons) is necessary, whereas its relationship with the sensations it causes (visual experiences, warmth) is contingent. For pain things are the other way around. The relationship between pain and the sensation of pain is necessary, while the relationship with the corresponding microstructure is contingent.

3 Naming and Reference

Kripke's metaphysical views were a radical departure from the orthodoxy that prevailed during the central part of the twentieth century. Although they are still the subject of much debate, those views, and in particular the claim that identity statements such as "Hesperus is Phosphorus" are necessary, seem to many today to be just plain obvious. "Hesperus is Phosphorus" just states of one thing that it is itself: surely that is necessary if anything is. So why should Kripke's claim be so revolutionary?

The principal reason is to be found in a philosophy of language, and in particular a theory of *reference*, which was taken for granted and which leads to a contrary view about the modal status (i.e. status as necessary or contingent) of identity statements. Kripke, of course, held that this philosophy language was mistaken and much of *Naming and Necessity* is devoted to correcting the picture of reference that is part of it. If Kripke is right, then what had been a deep-set view of meaning, which pervaded much of twentieth century philosophy, was deeply in error.

Not all identity statements, even on Kripke's metaphysics, are necessary. For example, "Benjamin Franklin is the inventor of bifocals" is true but contingent. That is because this statement contains a *definite description*: "the inventor of bifocals" (other definite descriptions include "the first Postmaster General of the United States," "the man who discovered that lightning is electrical"). A definite description is not a genuine name. In modal terms, the expression "the inventor of bifocals" denotes different entities in different possible worlds. In this world, it denotes Benjamin Franklin; in many other worlds it denotes some other person (e.g. it might denote Spinoza, if Spinoza had been the first person to make bifocals), or it might denote no one at all if bifocals were never invented or invented simultaneously by two or more people. In some of these other possible worlds Franklin still exists. So we may say that an identity statement containing a definite description such as this will be contingent, not necessary.

A definite description denotes some object in virtue of that object satisfying the description uniquely. "The F" denotes x precisely when x is F and is the only F. As remarked, different objects may be the unique F in different worlds. Now let us return to names. How do names denote what they do? This where the dispute between Kripke and his predecessors lies. We will come to Kripke's answer in due course. For now, we note that his view is that however names do get their meaning, a genuine name denotes one and the same object at all possible worlds where that object exists. That is, with respect to any world where the man Benjamin Franklin exists "Benjamin Franklin" denotes precisely that man. Terms that do this, denoting the same entity in all possible worlds (if any entity is denoted) are called *rigid designators*. Since "Benjamin Franklin" is a rigid designator and "the inventor of bifocals" is not a rigid designator, we can see that in some worlds "Benjamin Franklin is the inventor of bifocals" will be false. On the other hand "Hesperus is Phosphorus" is a statement of identity with two names, and so, on Kripke's view, with two rigid designators. Since "Hesperus" and "Phosphorus" are rigid designators, if they denote the same object in any world, they designate the same object in every world (if they designate at all). Hence "Hesperus is Phosphorus" is necessarily true or necessarily false. (Note that none of this suggests that Franklin's parents could not have called him "Fred" or that no one else was called "Benjamin Franklin." Those suppositions concern how certain words might have been used differently in other possible worlds. What we have been discussing is a different question: what do *our* words (i.e. the same words continuing to be used in the same way) denote when *we* (in this world) consider non-actual ways things might have been?)

There is, however, an alternative view about names, which takes names themselves to be disguised definite descriptions. Imagine that this were correct – then Kripke's claims would be false. Definite descriptions are not rigid designators and so names would also not be rigid designators. Identity statements involving two names would thus not, in general, be necessary but would typically be contingent, because they are really statements employing two definite descriptions. Russell held the view that names as we find them in everyday language ("Benjamin Franklin," "Mark Twain," "Hesperus") are not genuine names ("logically proper names") but are equivalent to definite descriptions. A related view may also be attributed to Frege. Frege did not regard ordinary names as logically equivalent to definite descriptions; nonetheless he did hold that every name has an associated *sense*, which we may take to be something like a definite description, and this sense fixes the denotation of the name. Thus Russell might have held that "Hesperus" *means* "the first planet to appear on the horizon at dusk" whereas Frege would have said that "Hesperus" has a sense that may be expressed by "the first planet to appear on the horizon at dusk." In both cases "Hesperus" denotes whichever planet it is that is the first to appear on the horizon at dusk.

Kripke advances a series of arguments against the description view of names. The first set of arguments against the description view of names is *modal* in nature, which is to say they are concerned with whether certain propositions are necessary or contingent. The description view renders "Hesperus is Phosphorus" contingent, which is an advantage, according to the traditional view that says that propositions that are known a posteriori are contingent. But, as Kripke points out, the view also has a very severe *disadvantage* in terms of modality. Let us imagine that the correct description associated with Moses is "the (unique) person who led the Israelites out of captivity in Egypt." If so, the proposition "Moses is the (unique) person who led the Israelites out of captivity in Egypt" is (a) necessary, (b) analytic, and (c) a priori. But clearly that proposition is none of those. Had Moses decided otherwise, he could have led a quiet and pleasant life in the courts of Egypt; it is a *contingent* fact that he embarked on leading the Israelites out of Egypt. Likewise, prominent candidates for the definite description equivalent to "Aristotle" might be "the last great philosopher of antiquity" or the "teacher of Alexander." If one or other *were* the correct description that is equivalent to "Aristotle," then it would be necessary that Aristotle was a philosopher or teacher. And that is not correct, for Aristotle might not have taken up a philosophical or pedagogic career (Aristotle would not have taught philosophy if he had not been sent to Athens by his guardian or if he had been killed when the Persians overran his home in Mysia); or he might have had an ever more philosophically illustrious pupil (had Alexander been as good at philosophy as at commanding an army and lived a little longer, Aristotle would not have been the *last* great philosopher of antiquity).

Kripke's modal criticism of the description view depends to some extent on his choice of putative descriptions to associate with the names "Aristotle" and "Moses." Would a different choice of descriptions have saved the description view from Kripke's arguments? Kripke does not deny that some descriptions may hold necessarily of a person, and indeed the essentialism we discussed above shows that he thinks that there are many necessary truths about individuals, and these may even suffice to identify them uniquely. Kripke takes it as part of the description view that the descriptions in question must be *analytically* equivalent to the associated definite description. That is to say, the definite description gives the *meaning* of the name. That being so, the relevant descriptions must be ones that a user of the name must, in principle at least, be able to associate with that name. Since pretty well all that we know about Moses comes from the Bible, any description equivalent to "Moses" must be one of (or some combination of) those found in the Bible. Likewise it is appropriate that Kripke choose as candidate descriptions to be equivalent to "Aristotle" those facts about Aristotle that are best known.

We can easily see that this aspect of the description view also leads rapidly to trouble. For we often use a name and succeed in referring to the bearer of the name even though we do not have sufficient knowledge of the bearer to identify them uniquely. Kripke uses the example of the name of the physicist Richard Feynman. He claims, almost certainly correctly, that many people can use "Feynman" to refer to Feynman, even though they may know nothing more about Feynman that the fact that he was a famous physicist. But that fact does not stop them referring to Feynman, and not, say, to Murray Gell-Mann, another famous physicist. (Imagine the following conversation. A: "Can you name any famous physicists?" B: "Yes, Feynman, he is a physicist." A: "Do you know anything else about Feynman, for example, what his theories are about?" B: "No, I only know that he is a physicist." B was indeed referring to Feynman, though B may also know of Gell-Mann that he too is a physicist, and only that.)

Those problems arise because we may know too few facts about someone to be able to associate a unique description to their name. Related problems will arise when what we do believe about someone is false. Many of us believe that Kurt Gödel was the first man to prove the incompleteness of arithmetic, and if that is all we believe about him, that should be the description that picks out the referent of "Gödel." Kripke now asks us to imagine that in fact some obscure Viennese called Schmidt, whose body was found in mysterious circumstances, was the first to prove the incompleteness of arithmetic and that Gödel somehow got hold of his manuscript. Now let us ask, to whom does the name "Gödel" refer? According to the description theory, that name refers to the unique person who first proved the incompleteness of arithmetic. And that person is Schmidt.

So, for many people, they will not be referring to the person who in fact was baptized "Kurt Friedrich Gödel" by his parents, who stole Schmidt's manuscript, who became famous for publishing it, and who became a friend of Einstein's at Princeton; rather they will be referring to the obscure and unfortunate Schmidt. Clearly, that is wrong. If the story about Schmidt's manuscript were true, it is natural and correct to think that people who believe of Gödel only that he was the first man to prove the incompleteness of arithmetic, have a false belief about the Princeton logician, not a true belief about Schmidt.

It looks then as if the definite description account of names has many and severe disadvantages. But the description view has at least this advantage: if names are just equivalent to definite descriptions, then we have a clear account of how the denotations of names are fixed. What is Kripke's alternative view of the denotation of names? He does not give a fully worked-out theory of naming, but he does present a more general picture of how naming works. Here is the simplest case. A name is given to a person or object in a naming ceremony, such as a baptism – a baby is given the name "Ichabod," for example. Jane was present at the baptism, which enables her to use the name to refer to that baby. She then talks about the baby to John who was not at the baptism. John now uses the name "Ichabod"; he intends to use it to refer to the baby to whom Jane was referring. So John's use of "Ichabod" is not dependent on his possessing some description of the baby in mind, but rather on the fact that he acquired the use of that name from someone who was present at the baptism. John can likewise pass on the use of the name to someone else, maintaining the same intended reference. Thus when someone says "Napoleon was the Emperor of the French," their use of "Napoleon" refers to Napoleon because there is a chain of reference preserving links going back to the baptism of Napoleon by his parents. This chain is a causal chain, since later use of the name is causally dependent on earlier use. Consequently the simple theory is often known as the "causal theory of reference." In the case of "Napoleon" the causal chain takes us back to Napoleon himself. But the chain of reference preservation need not do that in every case (it is the chain of preservation between speakers that is causal, not the link to the object named). In some cases a description may be used to identify some object as the intended recipient of the name, for example extrasolar planets are known to exist on the basis of theoretical inference rather than through observation; they can nonetheless be given names without those names being equivalent to the theoretical descriptions. In such cases there will be a causal connection between the object named and the process of naming it, but in other cases a definite description can introduce the name of an abstract object, e.g. "the ratio of the circumference of a circle to its diameter" for π, in which case there is no causal link to the object named.

As we saw above, Kripke extended his metaphysical views concerning identity and essence from individual to natural kinds and quantities. Likewise he extended his account of naming and reference to terms referring to such things. Thus terms such as "tiger," "water," and "gold" function like names, naming kinds of thing or substance rather than individuals. These "common names," like names of individuals, are rigid designators. In many cases their references are fixed by something akin to an initial baptism with samples: "Gold is the substance instantiated by the items over there." In other cases (heat, electricity) the reference is fixed via certain experiences or experimental effects. The kind (species, substance, quantity) terms may be associated with certain characteristic properties that are commonly used to identify members of the kind (e.g. yellow, shiny, malleable for gold). But those properties do not provide an analytic definition of the kind term, for it could be that genuine members of the kind lack those properties. Typically it is scientific investigation that reveals the properties that do fix kind membership, the properties that characterize the nature or essence of the kind.

The view of the meaning of names that Kripke's view promotes is not without its problems, as Kripke recognizes. It suggests that there is no more to the meaning of a name than the object it names. If so, two names that denote the same object have the same meaning. In which case it ought to make no difference to the meaning of a sentence which of two names one uses, so long as they denote the same thing. This name-swapping principle, however, leads to problems. Jane believes that Cicero was a great Roman orator who was bald. Not knowing that Cicero is Tully, she believes that Tully was a stoic philosopher who was not bald. So "Jane believes that Cicero was bald" and "Jane believes that Tully was not bald" are both true. Given the principle that we can swap names that denote the same object, the second of these sentences is equivalent to "Jane believes that Cicero was not bald." So we have the conclusion that Jane both believes that Cicero was bald and that Cicero was not bald. So it seems that we must find Jane is guilty of contradictory beliefs. Things may be even worse. Jane's active denial that Tully is bald would surely be taken as enough to show that she does not believe that Tully is bald. So "Jane does not believe that Tully is bald" is true and so also, thanks to our name-swapping principle, is "Jane does not believe that Cicero is bald." But we already agreed that Jane's beliefs about Cicero mean that "Jane believes that Cicero was bald" is true. So now *we* (not just Jane) are committed to a contradiction. A critic of Kripke's views of naming, perhaps a defender of the description account, would point to the name-swapping principle as the culprit.

Kripke raises this problem in an article "A puzzle about belief" and aims to defend the name-swapping principle by showing that similar problems arise when dealing with statements about belief even *without* using that principle. In which case, one might conclude that the name-swapping principle is not to blame; rather, there is some more general problem in dealing with statements concerning beliefs and their contents. Here is Kripke's example showing how we get a contradiction even without using the name-swapping principle. Pierre is a young Frenchman who asserts with full conviction the sentence (a) "Londres est jolie." He moves to an unattractive part of London, where he learns English by immersion, including the information that the city in which he is now living is named "London." Given his experience of London he asserts (b) "London is not pretty." But not knowing that "Londres" and "London" name the same city, he is still willing to assert (a). How should we English speakers express what Pierre believes when he asserts (a)? Clearly we should say (A) "Pierre believes that London is pretty" since "London is pretty" is a direct translation of "Londres est jolie." However, in virtue of his asserting the English (b) we must also say (B) "Pierre believes that London is not pretty"; indeed we presumably ought to commit ourselves also to (C) "Pierre does believe that London is pretty." (B) and (A) commit Pierre to a contradiction, and (C) and (A) commit *us* to a contradiction. So the position we are in with respect to Pierre is precisely that in which we were with respect to Jane, except that we have not, it appears, employed the name-swapping principle.

4   Rules and Meaning

The work of Kripke as discussed above is a reaction against a set of philosophical pictures and predilections that were part of the linguistic turn in philosophy. A major contributor to the latter was the Cambridge philosopher Ludwig Wittgenstein. It comes therefore as something of a surprise to find Kripke articulating and building on a skeptical paradox and a "skeptical solution" to it that he finds in Wittgenstein's *Philosophical Investigations* and which he takes "to be the central thread of Wittgenstein's later work on the philosophy of language and the philosophy of mathematics" (*WRPL* vii). According to Kripke, the paradox is central to Wittgenstein's "private language argument," which, in his view, is to be explicated in terms of the problem of "following a rule." While there is considerable debate as to whether Kripke's interpretation is at all true to Wittgenstein's intentions, for us the important thing is to understand Kripke's discussion in its own right.

Kripke asks us to imagine the following scenario. I am competent with ordinary arithmetic and I am asked to perform a straightforward addition sum. It is a sum that I have not computed before, and involves numbers larger than those in any calculation I have performed previously. Nonetheless, it is still well within my mathematical abilities. Let us say, for sake of argument, that the sum I have been asked to perform is "68 + 57." I am of course confident that the answer is "125." However a bizarre skeptic raises the following possibility. Consider, he says, the following function, which we will call "quus" and which we symbolize by "$\oplus$":

$$x \oplus y = x + y, \text{ if } x, y < 57$$
$$= 5 \text{ otherwise}$$

Perhaps, he suggests, in the past, when I used the word "plus" and the symbol "+" I did not mean the function plus (i.e. addition, the function yielding "125" as the correct answer) but rather I meant the function quus ("quaddition"). In which case, in giving the answer "125," I am mistaken – I should have answered "5." The mistake, Kripke emphasizes, would not be in arithmetic but is instead a mistake about my previous intentions and meanings. And of course, one can sometimes be mistaken about one's previous intentions (failure of memory, influence of drugs, etc.).

Although the possibility of a mistake has been raised, I am of course sure that there is no mistake. Since error and correctness make sense here, there must be, so it would seem, some fact of the matter about which I am correct, a fact of the matter that makes it the case that the skeptical suggestion is not only bizarre but indeed false. For example, imagine that I had performed this particular calculation many times before. The fact that I have on previous occasions given the answer "125" to "68 + 57" would show that I did not then intend quus by "+." However, we set the example up on the assumption that I had not performed this particular calculation before, and in any case there will always be some calculation that is a little bigger than any other I have performed before, and for *that* calculation we can construct a quus-like function concerning which we can pose the skeptical question. So my previous behavior – what I have said and done in the past – will be enough to rule out many skeptical hypotheses about my intentions. But that behavior will also be consistent with many other (indeed infinitely many other) skeptical hypotheses.

So one possible proposal for facts that determine that I meant plus not quus – my past behavior – is inadequate. The reason is that my past behavior has nothing to say about cases that differ from those I have come across before. Surely, one might think, *something* links my past behavior and my current answer and explains both. This would be my tendency or *disposition* to behave in one way rather than another. The answers I have given in the past and the one I give now are all manifestations of the same disposition, and it is this disposition that determines that I mean plus not quus and thus that "125" is the correct answer. Dispositions look like a good answer to the skeptical problem because dispositions can concern possible circumstances that have not yet arisen or indeed may never arise. Some vases (such as the Portland vase) are struck and their fragility is shown by their breaking; but an equally fragile, identical vase may be sufficiently well protected that it never exhibits its fragility; such a vase is still fragile. Here is another example: the elasticity of a rubber band will determine how might it stretches in response to varying degrees of force. It may never have been subjected to a force of 3.6 N, but its disposition, the degree of elasticity of the band, determines that it *would* stretch by 4 cm (and *not* by 5 cm). Likewise, my disposition might determine that in the past I *would* have answered "125" has I been given the question "68 + 57." So that fact determines that I didn't mean quus by "+," and more generally, my underlying disposition fixes it that I did mean plus.

Kripke has two principal objections to this dispositional answer to the skeptical challenge. The first is that even if my dispositions extend beyond my actual behavior, they are still not infinite in the way required to fix it that I mean plus rather than some quaddition-like function that starts to diverge from addition for very large numbers. For addition specifies a specific answer for *any* pair of numbers, however large. But some such numbers are so large that I cannot even *think* them, let alone attempt to add them together. So I do not have a disposition to give the sum, the output of the plus function, in answer to an addition question concerning such large numbers. Such cases show that my disposition does not fix on precisely addition rather than some other function.

Kripke's second objection focuses on the fact that meaning is a *normative* relation while my dispositions are purely causal and are not normative. That is to say, what I mean fixes what I *should* say, not what I do say nor what I *would* say. But as we all know, what we ought to do and what we are disposed to do can be quite different things. If I intend to play chess and so to play by the rules of that game, I *ought* to move my king only two squares when castling. If I inadvertently move the king three squares when castling on the queen's side, then that shows that I failed to do what I intended to do. It does not show that I did instead intend to play some other game that is a variant on chess. But what was I disposed to do when I moved my king three squares? It looks as if I was disposed to move the king three squares – after all that is what I did do, and the reasons for so doing all came from within me (it is not as if something else forced my hand to move the king three squares). So my disposition, argues Kripke, differs from my intention: I intended to castle according to the rules, but I was disposed to do something different. If we insist that my disposition does show what I intended, then we must conclude that after all I did intend to play by a rule other than the standard rule for castling. Either way, it cannot be true *both* that the rule I intended is the same as the pattern corresponding to my disposition *and* that I can err, failing to follow the rule I intend to follow.

So how should we respond to the rule-following paradox? Kripke distinguishes *straight* solutions from *skeptical* solutions. A straight solution would aim to show that there really is no paradox and that the paradoxer has made some error in arguing that there is a paradox. The dispositional solution is an attempted straight solution. If it were correct then it would show that there is a definitive answer ("my dispositions") to the question: what shows that I was following the plus rule rather than the quus rule? A skeptical solution, on the other hand, does not attempt to get rid of the paradox but instead seeks to explain why it does not have quite the negative impact one might at first suppose it to have. In this case Kripke's Wittgenstein proposes just such a skeptical solution. The conclusion of the paradox must be accepted. No fact about me makes it the case that I meant plus not quus.

If there is no fact that makes it the case that someone means plus, then surely it would never be reasonable to say the perfectly ordinary things we do say, such as "so-and-so means addition by '+'." This is where the skeptical solution comes in. According to Kripke, Wittgenstein denies this inference. Wittgenstein was concerned to reject a conception of meaning that dominates his own early *Tractatus Logico-Philosophicus*. According to this conception, sentences get their meanings by picturing or corresponding to some fact in the world. This is known as the "picture theory of meaning" and exemplifies a more general philosophy of meaning according to which the meaning of a sentence is given by specifying the conditions under which the sentence is true. Applying this "truth-conditional" approach to the case in hand, the meaning of "Jones means addition by '+'" is to be identified with some possible fact that would make this sentence true. But the rule-following paradox tells us that there is no such fact. Hence "Jones means addition by '+'" has no meaning. Note, however, that the rule-following paradox leads to the conclusion that assertions concerning meaning are themselves meaningless only because it has been combined with the truth-conditional approach to meaning. If we drop our adherence to the latter, then we are no longer committed to denying the meaningfulness of statements about meaning.

If we reject the truth-conditional approach to meaning, what replaces it? The answer is *assertion* or *justification* conditions. That is to say, the meaning the sentence "Jones means addition by '+'" is given by the conditions under which an assertion of that sentence is justified. What are those conditions? According to Kripke's understanding of Wittgenstein, they are the conditions under which the other members of my language community would concur with my assertion. I can justifiably assert a sentence when the other members of my community would agree with my assertion.

It is important to see that Kripke is *not* saying that a sentence is *true* just when my community would say that it is true. That would be to give another kind of "straight" answer to the paradox. Earlier we looked at the view that what makes it the case that I mean addition by "+" is my dispositions. The view now being considered, that what makes my assertion true is what my community would say, holds in effect that that what makes this the case is not *my* disposition but is rather *my community's* disposition. But as a straight answer, the community disposition answer suffers from entirely analogous problems to the individual disposition answer. Just as I don't have the appropriate disposition when it comes to enormously large numbers, neither does my community. Nor does my community's being disposed to say that something is right make it right. Even communities can err, in which case there can be a mismatch between what rule a community intends to follow and what it is disposed to do. So the Kripke–Wittgenstein community response is importantly different from the community disposition answer, and that is because the community's disposition makes my assertion justified but does not make it true; what the assertion means is given by the former, not the latter.

When we say that someone means something by the use of a word, it is very tempting to see this as asserting something about a hidden inner mental life. And so one might think that when someone uses the word "yellow" to describe a marigold that is because some inner process is going on: they recognize their visual experience as being of the kind that that have decided to call "yellow;" likewise, "pain" names a different kind of experience, and what I mean by "pain" is given by my associating it with that experience, as if, at some young age I connected that word with an inner experience of that sort, my first toothache for example. If my words were to get their meaning in that way, that would be what Wittgenstein calls a "private language." Wittgenstein regarded the possibility of a private language as an implicit but central part of the conception of the mind we have been working with ever since René Descartes in the seventeenth century. Wittgenstein's "private language argument" was intended to undermine that conception of the mind by showing that a private language is impossible. According to Kripke, the rule-following paradox is the key component of Wittgenstein's private language argument. Let us say that I do attempt to define a symbol "s" by reference to some inner experience or sensation; I am in effect giving myself a rule: the rule that some subsequent experience is to be called "s" if and only if it is like the original defining experience. It *seems* as if my act of inner definition is sufficient to fix that rule as the rule I intend and so fix the meaning of "s." But if the rule-following paradox is right, then nothing *I* can do will in fact achieve that.

Since the paradox and its skeptical solution are presented by Kripke as "Wittgenstein's argument as it struck Kripke, as it presented a problem for him" it is difficult to know quite which philosophical views to attribute to Kripke on the basis of this book. Presumably Kripke does think that the paradox is a genuine and interesting philosophical problem. And one might infer that Kripke does not think that there is any obvious straight solution – if there were, he would surely have mentioned it; and he would not have found the paradox so interesting in the first place. One might conjecture that Kripke at least thinks that the skeptical solution is worth considering, even if it is not a view we can attribute to him. On the other hand, clearly much of it takes us in a direction that is quite different from Kripke's work on modality and the philosophy of language. The latter is quite antithetical to Wittgenstein's later philosophy. There is one point of contact, however. We have seen that Kripke's account of reference is an "externalist" account – the reference of a name I use is not fixed solely by facts about me, rather it is fixed by certain external facts – the initial baptism plus the chain of communication between that baptism and my current use of the name – facts about which I may be completely ignorant. The rule-following paradox endorses a similar conclusion about meaning in general. Facts about me do not fix the meaning of my words and symbols, including "+." But the similarities stop here. Most significantly, the causal theory of names implicitly endorses a truth-conditional account of meaning. The meaning of "Mark Twain" is the man Mark Twain because it is that man who makes a contribution to the truth-conditions of sentences involving the name "Mark Twain" – for example, the meaning of "Mark Twain was a Mississippi riverboat pilot" is given by conditions under which the sentence is true, viz. its being the case that *that* man, Mark Twain, was a Mississippi riverboat pilot. But, as we have seen, the skeptical solution to the rule-following paradox rejects the idea of truth-conditions altogether.

5 Conclusion

Kripke's book on the rule-following paradox stands apart from the rest of his work. Even so, the fact that this paradox has generated so much discussion is further testament to the enormous fertility of Kripke's thought. We have not had the opportunity to look at Kripke's formal work, on account of its technical nature. Nonetheless, it is worth concluding with a few remarks on *why* it is so important. Some formal logic is best conceived straightforwardly as a branch of mathematics, generating most of its problems internally. Other areas of formal logic bear a closer relationship to philosophy, and their problems originate with philosophical problems. Sometimes the problems of philosophy are sufficiently subtle or complex that the relatively informal "prose" techniques of philosophy are insufficient to express or resolve them. In many such cases, representing the problem using a formal, mathematical symbolism will clarify the problem and the subsequent application of formal or mathematical techniques will provide answers to the problems thus clarified. Kripke's own formal work is a contribution to this kind of formal logic, and is exemplified by his semantics for modal logic and by his work on the theory of truth. Although formal logic was pursued actively throughout the twentieth century, there is an increasing, if as yet incomplete, readiness of philosophers to accept its relevance to "ordinary" philosophical problems. This also represents a further departure from the linguistic turn, and from the view of Wittgenstein and of the so-called "ordinary language" philosophers that a careful attention to the ways in which terms are used in everyday contexts will suffice to dissolve the problems of philosophy. Kripke's work was a major factor in determining these directions in contemporary philosophy.

Metaphysics is one of the most active areas of philosophy today. The linguistic turn caused it to be moribund for several decades in the middle part of the twentieth century. This rehabilitation of metaphysics and in particular an interest in essentialism owes much to Kripke. A key component of this achievement was his forceful arguments that the a priori and the necessary can be divorced. But this truth was obscured by a philosophy of language that took names to be equivalent to definite descriptions (or clusters of them). So a crucial step in the rehabilitation of essentialist metaphysics was the reformation of the theory of reference. Many philosophers have taken essentialism to be a direct consequence of Kripke's views about reference. This isn't quite correct and somewhat undervalues his achievement, by suggesting that the metaphysics and the theory of reference are two sides of the same coin. Kripke's account of reference *permits* essentialism, but does not require it. So his rehabilitation of metaphysics and his giving a new direction to the philosophy of language are two distinct if parallel contributions to philosophy whose significance can hardly be overstated.

References

Naming and Necessity. Oxford: Blackwell, 1980.
Wittgenstein on Rules and Private Language [*WRPL*]. Oxford: Blackwell, 1982.

9 NOZICK

A. R. LACEY

1 Introduction: Methodology

Robert Nozick was born in Brooklyn in 1938 of Russian Jewish parents He studied philosophy at Columbia as an undergraduate under Sidney Morgenbesser and at Princeton as a graduate under Carl Hempel, and acknowledged a great debt to these two philosophers of science. Most of his professional life he spent at Harvard. He died in January 2002.

As well as a fair number of articles, Nozick produced seven books. *Anarchy, State, and Utopia* (1974) was his main contribution to ethics and politics; *Philosophical Explanations* (1981) was a very long and uneven work containing, among other things, his main contributions to epistemology and philosophy of mind, as well as some further thoughts on ethics; *The Examined Life* (1989) was a collection of essays on various topics, often going beyond conventional philosophy and generally in a rather relaxed style; *The Normative Theory of Individual Choice* (1990) was simply a reprint of his technical 1963 PhD thesis on decision theory. *The Nature of Rationality* (1993) returned (after *The Examined Life*) to a more rigorous treatment of various topics relevant to its title; *Socratic Puzzles* (1997) was a set of reprints including his most important articles together with a variety of more general and popular pieces; finally

Invariances (2001) was a full-scale densely argued treatment of relativism, objectivity, necessity, consciousness, and the genealogy of ethics.

The hallmark of most of Nozick's philosophy is an approach which is rather at odds with the traditional analytical philosophy of the Anglophone world in the early and middle twentieth century. However, he began in the analytical tradition. His early mentors Morgenbesser and Hempel were thoroughly in that tradition, and his earliest interest was in philosophy of science, which became modified into an interest in the technicalities of decision theory in his 1963 PhD thesis. But his first published book, though still firmly anchored in the analytical tradition, is in the quite different area of moral and political philosophy. After his work on decision theory he had devoted some attention to free will, but got nowhere and so turned to social and political questions, which he had previously had some interest in, and decided to develop the libertarian views he felt instinctively drawn to. This can be seen as a kind of political version of the approach he will develop to philosophical discussion in general.

The kernel of the new approach is to replace proof with explanation and understanding as the aim of philosophical discussion, hoping that explanation will lead to understanding. He contrasts them because explanation "locates something in actuality" while understanding "locates it in a network of possibility" (*PE* 12) (roughly, contrast "What caused this?" with "Why this rather than other possibilities?"). More important, however, is the contrast between proof and explanation as our aim. Trying to convince people by knockdown proof, Nozick regards as coercive. Though he says quite a bit about coercion, and devotes a long article to it (reprinted in *SP*) it is not clear that his application of it to philosophical discussion is a very happy one. He points to the insecurity of a deductive argument, which will collapse if a single one of its premises is refuted. This is indeed true. Sometimes complicated deductive arguments are constructed and then applied to yield substantive philosophical conclusions. Usually such arguments are valid at every step, but they are only as strong as their weakest step, including tacit presuppositions. But what follows? To be coerced is, roughly, to be made to do something against one's will. We often talk of being compelled by an argument to come to an unwelcome conclusion. But we cannot be coerced into doing so, as against pretending to do so, or simply considering the argument or taking it seriously. We could be brainwashed into accepting it, but then our reason is being bypassed, not coerced. Perhaps, as Simon Hailwood has suggested, what Nozick is really objecting to is any aggressive attempt to browbeat others into accepting one's views instead of inspiring them to think for themselves. This may be partly true; but he seems to go beyond this in concentrating his fire on the use of deductive arguments rather than simply on a manner of conducting his arguments, and much of his later work embodies a genuinely different approach to philosophical procedure.

Of course, Nozick uses many deductive arguments himself, but his main aim is to stimulate the search for explanations. As he says: "[M]y desire is to explain how knowledge is possible, how free will is possible, how there can be ethical truths, how life can have meaning" (*PE* 21). He insists that he aims at truth, but this claim looks a bit problematic when he introduces a philosophical pluralism and talks of allowing a "basketful" of views – a libertarian approach indeed. Does this lead him into relativism? No, he answers, because the contents of the basket are ranked, but there is no privileged outside position to do the ranking; it must simply be done in terms of that position which one ranks first oneself. Sometimes he seems almost to attack rationality itself by saying that we cannot go on for ever giving reasons for accepting reasons, which suggests that we must stop at some arbitrary point. He would not accept that it was arbitrary, but he would do better, perhaps, to explain that we should stop at that point beyond which we find that we cannot think coherently – and that means that we cannot think at all – without accepting some principle like the law of non-contradiction. So it seems that we can only tentatively say that he establishes that the search for truth is his aim – but perhaps he could not complain at this in view of his insistence on the tentative nature of proper philosophical claims.

This approach is taken further in *The Examined Life*, which was designed to be "even less coercive" than *Philosophical Explanations*: "I wasn't asking the readers to accept what I was saying as the truth about those topics, but as a vehicle that could help them to think more deeply about those questions" as he puts it in Borradori's *The American Philosopher*.[1] He goes on to acknowledge Socrates as his "great master" and also the influence on him of Oriental, especially Indian, philosophy, which emphasized the subject's "expressive" side. Borradori brings out the irony of the fact that it was his beloved mentor Hempel, an archpriest of analytical philosophy, who turned his attention to the importance of the key notion of his later outlook, explanation.[2] *The Nature of Rationality* returns to a more rigorous approach in discussing various questions about strategies that should govern our rational thinking and we will return to it shortly.

2   Ethics

Anarchy, State, and Utopia is by far the most famous (some might say infamous) of Nozick's writings, a situation he later deplored, saying rightly that he was very far from being simply a "political philosopher." Nevertheless, ethics and politics do form an important slice of his writings, mainly but not exclusively early, and so do demand a fair amount of attention. *ASU* was particularly influential in the public sphere in instigating the rightward shift to the values of a free-market economy that has occurred on both sides of the Atlantic in the last quarter-century or so.

Two major strands in ethics are deontology, emphasizing the priority of "right," and teleology, emphasizing that of "good." Three years before *Anarchy, State, and Utopia*, deontology (and ethical and political philosophy generally) were reinvigorated by Rawls's *A Theory of Justice*.[3] This based justice on a hypothetical contract between people about to enter the world but completely ignorant of where or under what conditions. So far as it bases right action on a contract, this approach is deontological; but it is also teleological in that the contractors are seeking those rules which would maximize their own welfare, and being equally ignorant they agree on these rules, so that in effect (and omitting some complications) the system is designed to maximize the welfare of random people, or just people in general.

Nozick is more wholeheartedly deontological and devotes some 50 pages to critical discussion of Rawls. He rejects any attempt to justify a social system in terms of end states (like the greatest happiness of the greatest number) or patterned states (like distribution by merit, or egalitarianism, which anyway is likely to become unstable as soon as we start using our equal resources). The hallmark of his approach is individualism. He takes an atomistic view of individuals; we each have certain rights, and basically our obligations are limited to respecting the rights of others. Critics, and Nozick himself (*ASU* xiv, 9), have said that he never provides a proper basis for his moral philosophy, though one might ask just what such a basis could consist of; something must be taken for granted, on pain of defying Hume's ban on deriving an "ought" from an "is." He does give some basis for his individualism by insisting that it is individuals and not societies etc. that are the bearers of feelings and experiences and that are responsible for how they use their rights and for what happens to them as a result. But the rights we have are those of liberty, and the only rights we have against others are those of noninterference and the fulfillment of contracts; we cannot (as of right) call on them for aid, however needy we may be, and in particular we cannot be compulsorily taxed to help them (he compares taxation to forced labor, though admitting there are differences). This gives a very harsh tone to his philosophy, as he admits. He first found this disturbing, though he ceased to be disturbed on concluding that his proposals were derived by rational means and were rationally unavoidable. None of this of course stops Nozick saying, as he does, that we have a *moral* duty to help others through charity, etc. (he was himself a member of Amnesty, for instance). The point is simply that we should not be compelled to do so.

Humans are not only experiencers for Nozick, but also agents who must actively *live* their lives. Hence he thinks we would reject the notion of an "experience machine" where, by pushing a button, we can present ourselves with any experiences we like, and also with the results of any achievements we fancy, though without our having to *do* anything to achieve them. He implicitly rejects the view of Mill and, especially, Sidgwick, the main nineteenth-century utilitarians, that the only ultimately valuable things are certain experiences. To put it in contemporary terms, virtual reality would remain merely virtual. Animals occupy a sort of halfway house. They experience, but are not rational. They do not have rights, but there are things we may not do to them (hunting for fun is wrong: *ASU* 37). Criminals have a right to be treated with the respect due to a rational creature.

Nozick's theory of justice is an "entitlement" one. Its slogan is: "Whatever arises from a just situation by just steps is itself just" (*ASU* 51). This raises three topics: justice in acquisition, justice in transfer, and justice by the rectification of previous injustices. The discussion of justice in acquisition is complicated by Nozick's acceptance of Locke's proviso that, in taking from virgin resources (and not by transfer from a previous owner), I must leave "enough and as good . . . in common for others;" I cannot grab for myself the only well in the desert. Nozick devotes most of his discussion to justice in transfer, where his opposition to "patterned" theories (egalitarianism, etc.) becomes relevant, and the question arises whether his theory really does promote liberty more than rival theories do. Rectification of previous injustices involves issues about proper compensation, and also raises considerable difficulty in applying the theory to the real world because of the massive historical injustices that have led to the present distribution of resources. Finally, critics have seen all three topics as forcing him to blur the line between deontology and teleology and introduce elements of the latter.

In fact, in his later writings, Nozick considerably modifies his *Anarchy, State, and Utopia* position. (Mrs Thatcher and Mr Reagan, for good or for ill, seem not to have read these later works.) He now moves explicitly towards an intermediate position between deontology and teleology, though still admitting his "obvious leaning toward deontology" (*PE* 498). Even in *Anarchy, State, and Utopia* there is a rather casual footnote deflecting the question whether we can violate side-constraints to avoid "catastrophic moral horrors" (*ASU* 30n). He now asks how we are to be motivated to act morally. He thinks there is something "deeply correct" in Plato's view that it is really better for us to be moral than not, but adds that we cannot plausibly link morality always with self-interest or happiness. Instead *Philosophical Explanations* brings in and makes much of the notion of value, to which the appropriate attitude is one of approving, persevering, focusing, etc., which he sums up by the term "V-ing." That values should be V-ed is itself valuable and one who does V them is a valuable person. He then insists that to be a valuable person is better for one (intrinsically, and not just because "honesty is the best policy") than not to be so, even if one does not realize this fact; even if one does not value being a valuable person as things are, "value would inspire and motivate us under valuable conditions" (*PE* 438).

Nozick next turns his attention to what value is, and borrows G. E. Moore's notion of organic unity, which Moore defines as arising when a whole has a value which is greater than the sum of the values of its parts. We can avoid potential circularity by appealing to a definition Nozick gives in another context, where "[s]omething is a unity . . . if its identity over time is not equivalent to the sum of the identities over time of proper parts it may have" (*PE* 100). Organic unity is often a fertile source of value, especially in aesthetics, but he does not simply identify them, as there are too many obvious exceptions (the value often attaching to simple things or unique things as such, for instance), and the notion has been criticized for vagueness because he does not say how the two criteria for organic unity, unity induced and diversity of material, fit together.

In *Philosophical Explanations*, and implicitly in *Anarchy, State, and Utopia*, Nozick tells us, he thinks in terms of pushes and pulls, pushes being constraints on me in terms of what I am and pulls being constraints on me emanating from you, as a value-seeker, and ethical theory must show among other things that the push is at least as great as the pull (*PE* 401). The above discussion of motivation and value belongs to the sphere of the push, but Nozick then turns to the pull and back to deontology and teleology, whose competing claims are now represented by the intuitive pulls of pursuing the best acting and pursuing the best outcome, in each case involving a maximization strategy, something outlawed in *Anarchy, State, and Utopia*; but in accordance with the new approach, this represents not a proof of the superiority of either side, "but an explanation or understanding of why (or where) one holds while the other does not" (*PE* 498). The implications of all this for the political claims must wait until we have introduced those, but before we leave ethics let us briefly turn to a rather different question that occupies the last chapter of *Invariances*.

Here Nozick seeks the genealogy and the function of ethics. As so often, he appeals to evolution, which gives ethics its function of ensuring material cooperation, and he recommends as the "core principle" of ethics one that "makes mandatory the widest voluntary cooperation to mutual benefit" (*I* 259), banning, in general, interactions that are not to mutual benefit, unless they are voluntary for all parties or are intended to punish or prevent violations of the core principle. His discussion ranges far more widely of course, but he has been criticized for not further defining the core principle, and not discussing when ethical changes (like widening the social group to include outsiders) do or do not constitute progress.

3 Politics

Along with *A Theory of Justice*, *Anarchy, State, and Utopia* represents a major revival of political philosophy, which logical positivism and linguistic philosophy had left rather in the doldrums. The book aims to steer a middle course between a complete absence of government, or anarchism, and what Nozick might have called a nanny state, starting from the former by asking how far this could be improved upon without taking any morally impermissible steps and violating rights. *ASU* belongs in, and indeed largely constitutes, Nozick's early deontological and methodologically rigorous period, but already there are some tensions. He starts from a "state of nature," a notion derived from Hobbes and Locke, but he takes it for granted that people in it (who are assumed to be socialized and to have language, etc., but no kind of government) will be much like ourselves, in that usually – but not always – they will act morally without needing sanctions. Justifying a step involves showing, *inter alia*, that it leads to an improvement, even if only by increasing justice, which introduces a teleological element, though without departing significantly from his deontological stand – obviously any step aims to improve things or it would be pointless. More serious is that it is not always clear whether Nozick is concerned to justify, or simply to explain, the resulting situation. This is because of a certain ambiguity between whether the steps are those which *could* arise from a state of nature (which would let him select morally acceptable ones – but it has been objected that almost anything *could* arise) or ones which *would* arise, which suggest explanation as the target. The latter seems more plausible, but Nozick may think that explaining a situation is at least relevant to justifying it.

What happens is that people voluntarily set up, and pay for, insurance agencies which protect their clients against rights violations, whether by other clients or by outsiders. When competition reduces such agencies to one for a given region we have the "ultraminimal" state, which becomes the "minimal" (or "nightwatchman") state when non-clients are brought into the fold, apparently by (properly compensated) force if necessary, the state having become a monopoly covering them from rights violations, breaches of contract, and external aggression.

Obviously we have omitted many complications, but objections have been raised, from the anarchist side especially, both practical (mainly concerning the rise of the ultraminimal state) and principled (mainly concerning the transition to the minimal state, as well as the need for a firmer basis for rights). Welfarist criticisms have focused mainly on whether Nozick has too narrow a conception in limiting rights to those to liberty and fulfillment of contracts, and ignoring rights to receive at least enough of available resources to let one "lead a life" in the way he emphasizes – though this may amount to replacing his deontology by a more teleological approach. These latter criticisms apply especially to Part II, which argues that any development beyond the minimal state is illegitimate for reasons we have in effect considered in the ethics section above.

Anarchy, State, and Utopia ends with a proposal about utopias. Any group of like-minded people can set up their own utopia, as libertarian or authoritarian internally as they like provided they do not aggress against each other, while there is a libertarian framework (in effect the minimal state in a new guise) to oversee relations between utopias and protect certain rights of their members, such as that of emigrating to any utopia that will receive them. Hailwood and others have raised many objections, both practical and principled: who will run and who will control the framework and what happens if it dies through lack of support? Can the neutralism implied by the system be reconciled with the libertarianism implied by the framework? How do the choosers get to be as they are? Must parents in authoritarian utopias let their children know that libertarian utopias exist nearby? Can emigrants take their property with them and leave their debts behind? Nozick does not consider such objections, and the whole section is much shorter than the other sections of the book. But this should surely not detract from its value as an original idea thrown out for discussion. Hailwood compares the system to "a rerun of the history of the United States, but without the more unfortunate aspects."[4]

Like ethics, politics undergoes something of a sea-change in Nozick's later work, largely through the influences of symbolic utility, which barely appears in *Philosophical Explanations* (see p. 428), but is important in *The Examined Life* and is treated at some length in *The Nature of Rationality*. It appears most obviously in Freudian explanations or in sentimental value, but Nozick gives it a social as well as a personal role, and lets it supplement the new emphasis on values and responsiveness to value-seekers. "A large part of the richness of our lives consists in symbolic meanings and their expression, the symbolic meanings our culture attributes to things or the ones we ourselves bestow," and a theory of rationality need not exclude them (*NR* 30). The libertarianism of *Anarchy, State, and Utopia* was "seriously inadequate" because "it neglected the symbolic importance of an official political concern with issues or problems," and was one area where the theory in *Anarchy, State, and Utopia* "went wrong" – private charity is not enough. Taxation and a ban on discriminating against certain minorities are now brought in (*EL* 291), and also a modification of the inheritance laws (*EL* 30–2). Yet in *Invariances* (pp. 281–2), Nozick somewhat moderates his enthusiasm, if no more, by saying: "All that any society should (coercively) demand is adherence to the ethics of respect," in particular the "core principle" of cooperation; he calls this an "additional component" of his *Anarchy, State, and Utopia* position, but we must leave open the question of whether it involves any backsliding.

4 Epistemology

Philosophical Explanations had a mixed reception. R. Myers describes it as "far and away Nozick's greatest work," while M. F. Burnyeat calls its last three chapters "vapid, tedious, embarrassingly pretentious."[5] But everyone, Burnyeat included, agrees that chapter 3, on "Knowledge and Skepticism," is the best thing in it and an important (and much discussed) contribution, even though the main ideas were, as Nozick fully admits, anticipated by Fred Dretske.

Traditionally, it has been assumed that to know p, p must be true, I must believe it, and my belief must be in some sense justified. Some make this justification "internal" to myself: I must have adequate reasons. Others make it "external," applying to the belief itself, which must be likely to be true in the circumstances (or produced by a method which reliably leads to truth: reliabilism). Nozick is an externalist (perhaps a reliabilist: he is a bit unclear on this) with occasional internalist hankerings. But his main contribution is to use two basic notions. The first is that of "tracking" the truth. To know p, my true belief must satisfy two further conditions, which we can call Variation (that normally were p false I would not believe it) and Adherence (that were p true in somewhat different conditions I would still believe it); my belief must be sensitive to the truth. An initial complication concerns necessary truths, where Variation becomes irrelevant because we cannot coherently suppose them false, but adherence still applies; I may truly believe that Fermat's last theorem has been proved but do not know it if I would abandon my belief were someone to tell me (falsely) that the proof was flawed. Variation and Adherence contain subjunctive conditionals. To assess these, consider as an example: "Had I stepped off the sidewalk then I would have died." Now take various scenarios (usually called "possible worlds") where I do step off, like "I step off and a bus squashes me flat," "I step off and a terrorist bomb destroys the bus just before it reaches me," "I step off and a benevolent eagle snatches me up." Now decide (somehow) which of these is nearest to the actual world, where I do not step off and the bus passes peacefully by. Presumably in this example the first is nearest, so we say that it is true that had I stepped off I would have died. Roughly, Variation is satisfied if I drop the belief that p in the *nearest* possible worlds where p is false, and Adherence is satisfied if I keep the belief in the *nearest* possible worlds (not counting the actual world itself) where p is true (hence the vague "normally" and "somewhat" in my statements of Variation and Adherence).

The second basic notion I mentioned brings us to where commentators have said that Nozick "take[s] the most devastating objection to his view and embrace[s] it as one of its advantages" or "tries to turn critical weakness into spectacular strength."[6] The issue is skepticism, the perpetual bugbear of epistemology, and Nozick aims, in keeping with his new approach, not to refute the skeptic but to show how knowledge is possible despite what the skeptic says. One feature of Nozick's theory is that it involves denying Closure (as we can call it for short), i.e. that if I know p and know that p entails q, then I know q. Nonclosure (the denial of Closure) seems very implausible (though it has its defenders), but Nozick uses it to answer the skeptic, in the form of the brain-in-a-vat scenario. Some neuroscientists take a brain from its body, wipe it clean electronically of any memories, etc., and feed it with the sort of stimuli it would normally get from its afferent nerves, thus producing illusory experiences (and also experiences as of itself acting in response). How can I know I am not such a brain-in-a-vat? Nozick agrees with the skeptic that I cannot know this, but uses Nonclosure to argue that I can nevertheless know that I am at home (say), and that if I am at home I am not a brain-in-a-vat. This is because all Variation demands, if I am to know p, is that I cease to believe p in the nearest possible worlds where it is false. But in the *nearest* possible worlds where I am not at home, I am out shopping, etc; my being a brain-in-a-vat is a very distant world. So far so good, but Nozick has to (and does) swallow some unfortunate consequences, such as that I can sometimes know a conjunction without knowing each of its conjuncts.

Many other criticisms have been made of Nozick's analysis, some raising cases it will not cover, and others claiming that his results can be achieved without Nonclosure. But the notion of tracking has entered the philosophical armory, and has been used by both Nozick himself and others in contexts outside that of knowledge. He thought of it in seeking a parallel between action and knowledge (*PE* 169–71), and talks, e.g., of tracking value or "bestness" (*PE* 317–26).

5 Personal Identity

Nozick's second main contribution to philosophy, again not quite original (as he acknowledges), but substantially developed by him, concerns identity – a topic which primarily belongs to metaphysics, but its most important application, for Nozick and for most of us, is to personal identity.

On one intuitive view, identity should be intrinsic; i.e. whether a is identical to b (say, the morning star to the evening star) should not depend on whether some third thing c exists. But Nozick thinks that it can so depend, and that identity is extrinsic.

The usual example is Hobbes's "ship of Theseus," but let us go straight to personal identity. Nozick's theory applies to both.

Funny things can happen to people, in science fiction and increasingly in science fact. Crudely put, the brain has two lobes which can become separated, taking over each other's functions, whether in the same or, with suitable transplants, different bodies, so that there are now two persons instead of one. In teletransportation, the contents of the brain would be "read" electronically and transmitted to another brain cleared of its own contents and kept in a duplicate of the original brain's body, the resulting consciousness being subjectively indistinguishable from the original one. Which of the resulting duplicates in each case is the original person? Nozick's answer is that identity is carried by the closest continuer, provided it is close enough. Two marks of closeness are similarity and causation, but neither is without problems. If a is teletransported to produce b and survives the operation, then obviously he continues to be himself and b is a separate person. But if a perishes, then b will be his closest continuer, both as resembling a and as partly caused by a (plus the relevant engineers, etc.), and so now will *be a*, who has survived in this way. The idea of closeness is rather vague. If I die but an exact replica of me happens by some freakish chance to come to be elsewhere, will that be me continuing? Presumably not, despite the exact similarity, even if we add in some causation (my body's dissolution freed enough atoms to constitute the replica). And what if the replica came to be before I died? This is the problem of overlap, which Nozick thinks will indeed affect any claims for the identity of things larger than "atomic-point instants." Here he does point to a real difficulty for identity, which may underlie both neurological essentialism (the view that objects do not survive any replacement of parts) and some form of Buddhism. The extrinsic view that whether a equals b may depend on whether there is a closer continuer c makes identity a contingent relation, which Nozick seems to accept. He even allows that for ships, etc., identity may involve decision, but not for persons, for we care for our and our family's future and do not think we can decide what counts as the object of our caring. However, he does not clearly distinguish two kinds of caring. Fearing that our family will suffer pain is quite different from fearing that we will, and it is this latter that is really relevant in the present discussion.

All the above has been much discussed and criticized, but much less attention has been given to Nozick's obscure discussion of what a person or self is. Here he produces a typically Nozickian notion, which he himself calls "bizarre," of self-synthesis. The idea seems to be that in saying "I," I refer to myself as that which is constituted (partly?) by being the utterer of that very word "I." But I can synthesize myself as having various other properties too (despite what we said just above about not deciding what is to count as the object of our care). Nozick sees no circularity here, and "no special problem about something A that refers to itself in virtue of a property it bestows on itself" (*PE* 93).

6 Rationality

Newcomb's Problem troubled Nozick for most of his life and he had three shots at it. He first treated it in his dissertation, but he only published it to the world in an article in 1969; let us call these treatments A and B respectively. Finally, he returns to it in *The Nature of Rationality*; call this C.

The problem is this. Someone with an excellent track record for predicting human choices offers you two boxes, one transparent and containing £1,000 and the other opaque. You may take either the opaque box alone or both boxes. If this person has predicted that you will take only the opaque box, he puts £1,000,000 in it; if he has predicted that you will take both boxes (or will randomize your choice by tossing a coin) he leaves the opaque box empty. You know this, and that all or nearly all one-boxers have received

£1,000,000, while all or nearly all two-boxers have received only £1,000. What should you do?

Nozick first sketches two approaches: the "dominance" approach says that whether the opaque box is full or empty, taking both boxes "dominates," i.e. will give you more than taking the opaque box alone; the "expected utility" approach tells you to maximize the product of the utility of a result should it occur and the probability that it will occur. *A* takes the expected utility approach because the dominance approach should only be taken if the outcomes are probabilistically independent of our choices, i.e. our choice of a box has no bearing on the probability of its containing what it does, but the predictor's success rate shows they are not probabilistically independent here. *B*, however, takes the dominance approach, because *A* did not properly distinguish probabilistic and causal independence; given my choice, you may be able to infer the probability of a certain outcome, but this does not imply that my choice causally influenced it. *C* is more complex and follows commentators in thinking the issue is not between dominance and expected utility, but between two forms (evidential and causal) of expected utility. Nozick now combines these as weighted elements in "decision value," along with symbolic utility, though that is more relevant in his treatment of the Prisoner's Dilemma, a problem whose relation to Newcomb's Problem is disputed, but which we must pass over.

The Nature of Rationality contains Nozick's main treatment of rationality and it begins with a discussion of principles (scientific, legal, and moral) which he treats as "transmission devices for probability and for utility" (*NR* 35), and uses to discuss the rationality of our time preferences (preferring smaller imminent goods to larger deferred ones), and also of our attitude to what economists call sunk costs, where symbolic utility becomes relevant again. He does not, however, discuss the related questions of the rationality of egoism versus altruism and the honoring of sunk costs incurred by others. But he treats moral principles as having a teleological function, which shows the distance of *The Nature of Rationality* from *Anarchy, State, and Utopia*.

The Nature of Rationality also introduces Nozick's appeal to evolution to explain our intuitions or apparent intuitions, a topic which returns in *Invariances*. It is here that he claims to reverse Kant's "Copernican revolution," which says that "objects must conform to our knowledge, to the constitution of the faculty of our intuition" (*NR* 111), whereas for Nozick, "it is *reason* that is the dependent variable, shaped by the facts, and its dependence upon the facts explains the correlation and correspondence between them" (*NR* 112). Critics have not unnaturally asked how, in that case, we can trust our reason. We will return to this topic shortly.

7 Miscellaneous

At least three other topics are treated at some length in *Philosophical Explanations*. Here we will look very briefly at these.

Why is there something rather than nothing? This has troubled philosophers intermittently – though it is not always clear what the alternative is: No material objects? No space or time? No universals? No mathematical facts? Nozick brings to it two notions. First, a "fecundity assumption" that all possibilities are realized, which he distinguishes in ways that need not concern us from the "principle of plenitude" derived from Aristotle and Hobbes, and which he later limits in a way which also need not concern us; and second, and more important, a typical Nozickian notion which he will use in several other contexts, namely "self-subsumption." The idea here is that if we can find a true principle saying that all principles with characteristic C are true, then, if this principle itself has C, we can infer that it is true. This will not prove it of course, because we had to assume it, but Nozick thinks it might explain it, *if* it is true, and explanation not proof is what he is seeking. The hope is thus to apply this to the fecundity assumption. There are many complications, and criticisms, that we are ignoring, but I will end by just pointing to an interesting criticism of the principle of sufficient reason, interpreted as saying every truth has an explanation (at *PE* 140–1).

The free will problem troubled Nozick from his earliest years as a writer when he turned from it in despair to write *Anarchy, State, and Utopia*. He offered a solution in *Philosophical Explanations*, but himself described it as "rather cloudy" (*PE* 307). Let us simply note that he applies his notion of tracking, only now what we are to track is not truth but "bestness" (overall, not necessarily moral) or rightness (covering the permissible and the mandatory). The associated notion of retribution he first distinguishes from revenge and thinks that what merits it is flouting, or being "anti-linked" to, correct values, a notion which of course needs and receives elaboration; retribution's purpose is to connect the offender to those values, where he thinks nonteleological and teleological views of punishment are "intertwined" (*PE* 379).

The last chapter of *Philosophical Explanations* mainly treats the meaning of life, which rather few modern philosophers discuss.[7] Nozick's treatment is abstruse and has not been popular. Starting from the idea that something can only be given meaningfulness by something beyond it, he arrives at the all-inclusive infinity, which he calls by a Hebrew name, Ein Sof, whose own meaningfulness he tries to deal with by appeal to self-subsumption and his "closest continuer" theory of identity. After this, he distinguishes meaning and value, rather fancifully associating them with romanticism and classicism, and finally comes right down to earth with a general discussion of philosophy among the arts and sciences, including an attack on reductionism.

8 Nozick's Last Book

It is in his last book that Nozick gives us a far more elaborate and explicit discussion of some of the ideas that underlie his new approach, while still to some extent exemplifying the approach itself. *Invariances* is an impressive book by any account, but even more so when one realizes that throughout the seven years or so of its production Nozick was fighting an ultimately losing battle with stomach cancer, which he faced with an equanimity that must be the envy of us all. It consists of 300 dense pages with another 100, equally dense, of notes, plunging cheerfully into the technicalities of quantum mechanics and mathematical physics upon occasion and supported by detailed page references to a mass of relevant literature from a wide variety of sciences. This makes *Invariances* a forbidding read. Yet throughout, Nozick is concerned not to prove things but to broaden our philosophical horizons by raising and elaborating possibilities, defending them *as* possibilities. We have occasionally mentioned the later chapters already, but here we are concerned with the first three chapters, on relativism, objectivity, and necessity.

Chapter 1 starts by asking whether truth is relative. Nozick first defends the *coherence* (as against truth) of relativism by arguing that whatever claim the absolutist may make, the relativist can always reply: "That may be true for you, but it is not true for me." This may indeed hold for some cases; there are trivial cases where relativism is not only coherent but true (whether it is raining is relative to the time and place in question). But Nozick offers two reasons for defending as at least plausible a more substantive version of relativism. First, he thinks of truth as whatever property it is that accounts for the success of beliefs that have it (allowing that occasionally false beliefs may lead to success). This "truth property" may differ for different groups, being perhaps correspondence to facts for one group but something else (coherence, etc.) for another. It is implausible, he thinks, that it differs for cultures, genders, social classes, etc., but his aim to raise possibilities for discussion lets him speculate that truth itself might be "local" in that evolution might in some contexts use functional substitutes for beliefs and representations, and hence for truth, as guides for action towards success and survival (*I* 67). Second, he appeals to certain features of quantum mechanics, which makes it hard for most of us (certainly for me) to discuss; let me say only that he relies largely on distinguishing being true at a place or time and being determinate at that place or time. To return to the start of this paragraph, he does discuss at some length whether relativism undercuts itself, but seems to leave it unclear whether the relativist can really *maintain*, i.e. present as (absolutely) true, anything at all.

The second chapter is rather less controversial, despite being the central chapter in that it introduces the notion of invariance that gives the book its at first sight rather opaque title. The basic notion of the chapter is that of objectivity, for which he first mentions three strands or marks: accessibility by different people at different times, etc., the possibility of intersubjective agreement, and independence from our beliefs, desires, measuring techniques, etc. These, however, come in degrees, and should not be seen as individually necessary and jointly sufficient, and he goes on to mention a fourth mark, which is both more basic than and underlies the other three: invariance under certain transformations (as the speed of light is invariant under transformation of inertial reference frame) – but not just any old transformations, only "admissible" ones. For which these are, we must look to science, starting from a provisional and revisable list of objective facts, bringing our lists of objective facts and admissible transformations into "reflective equilibrium" (see especially *I* 79–80). The rest of the chapter develops and complicates these ideas and then goes on to a useful discussion of various scientific methodologies, such as Popper's view of scientific hypotheses as imaginative constructions set up as aunt sallies to be refuted, and Kuhn's view of science as proceeding by jumps from one paradigm to another.

In chapter 3, on necessity, we return to more controversial grounds. Nozick starts by expressing a general skepticism about necessities, though he wants not so much to refute them as to sketch an alternative approach and show how it might be true. He first asks how we know about metaphysical necessities (a ragbag term which usually seems to apply to those not more specifically classifiable as logical, mathematical, scientific, etc.), and suggests that we cannot think of any alternatives to them. But perhaps this just means our imaginations are not good enough: "Lack of invention is the mother of necessity" (*I* 136). At this point he brings in evolution again. It would help to avoid debates in this area, he thinks, if we had a "faculty of reason that could directly assess the possibility of general statements and of their denials" (*I* 122), but we have no such faculty, and the reason is that such a faculty would have been of no practical use to our ancestors and so was not selected for. Another example is our apparent "intuition" of the truth of Euclidean geometry. We do not "intuit" the truth of the non-Euclidean geometry we now accept, because it would be useful for Euclidean geometry to have seemed self-evident to our ancestors, but of no use for the more strictly accurate non-Euclidean geometry to have seemed so, when greater complexity would have, for instance, slowed our inferential processes. He admits that this evolutionary account may be only plausible rather than true, and also that such "intuitions" "might not have been within reach of what random mutation (in the absence of stepwise selective pressures) could produce from the generic endowment that existed" among our ancestors (*I* 124) – a rare example of something he pays too little attention to, namely how and on what materials selection is supposed to work. He has admittedly just said the process might comprise sudden jumps rather than small steps, but we might wonder if that is enough.

As well as listing various examples, like that of Euclidean geometry, of alleged necessary truths which turned out not to be so, Nozick attacks the Kripke–Putnam argument that "Water is H_2O" is necessarily true in the sense of being true in all possible worlds by distinguishing between "imported" and "indigenous" truths, where truth is imported into a world if it is true there only because it is true in some other world; otherwise it is indigenously true there. He then says "Water is H_2O" is true in the other possible worlds only because it is true in our world, and insists that a truth is only necessary if at each possible world it is indigenously true then. The point seems to be that Kripke, like Leibniz, gives no adequate reason for thinking that "Water is H_2O" *is* true in all the other possible worlds.

Even logical and mathematical necessity does not escape the axe. Apart from mentioning alternatives like intuitionism, paraconsistency, and the implications of quantum mechanics, Nozick conjectures that "logic functions as a filter to weed out data that can safely be ignored" (*I* 144), though without discussing in any depth things like whether the law of non-contradiction can be dispensed with.

9 Conclusion

So where does Nozick fit into the philosophical scheme of things? He was brought up in the analytical tradition and his early work remained firmly there, but then he changed his aim to that of promoting the search for explanation and understanding rather than seeking rigorous proof, and his later work suggests many possibilities for philosophers to consider, and also experiments for scientists to make. His first published book (at age 36 and after much work elsewhere in philosophy) was in ethics and politics and, as he later complained, provided the hallmark of his reputation. It was firmly deontological in tone, and was very influential, especially on practical politics, though later he modified its tone in a teleological direction, appealing *inter alia* to his notion of symbolic utility. Among philosophers, his great and lasting influence has been on the theory of knowledge and on personal identity, despite being strictly original in neither area. He also introduced Newcomb's Problem to the wider world and judged a *Scientific American* competition on it, and explored topics more popular with the public than with philosophers, such as why there is something rather than nothing and the meaning of life, though with results that are uneven in merit and have not proved very influential. Finally, he produced on his deathbed a major book, tightly integrated but often difficult and technical, both describing and illustrating his later methodology, but so far of minor influence only, though it is early days.

Notes

1 G. Borradori, *The American Philosopher*. Chicago: University of Chicago Press, 1994, p. 74.
2 Ibid., p. 84.
3 J. Rawls, *A Theory of Justice*. Oxford: Oxford University Press, 1971.
4 S. A. Hailwood, *Exploring Nozick: Beyond Anarchy, State, and Utopia*. Aldershot: Avebury, 1996, p. 88.
5 R. Myers, review of *Invariances*, in *Philosophy of the Social Sciences* 32/4 (December 2003): 514–18; M. F. Burnyeat, review of *Philosophical Explanations*, in *TLS* (October 15, 1983).
6 R. A. Fumerton and E. Sosa, "Nozick's Epistemology," in S. Luper-Foy (ed.), *The Possibility of Knowledge*. Totowa, NL: Rowman and Littlefield, 1987.
7 *The Examined Life*, chs. 15–17 also contain material relevant to this topic

References

Anarchy, State, and Utopia [*ASU*]. New York: Basic Books, 1974.
Philosophical Explanations [*PE*]. Cambridge, MA: Harvard University Press, 1981.
The Examined Life [*EL*]. New York: Simon and Schuster, 1989.
The Normative Theory of Individual Choice [*NTIC*]. New York: Garland Press, 1990; repr. of 1963 PhD thesis.
The Nature of Rationality [*NR*]. Princeton: Princeton University Press, 1993.
Socratic Puzzles [*SP*]. Cambridge, MA: Harvard University Press, 1997.
Invariances [*I*]. Cambridge, MA: Harvard University Press, 2001.

A selection of articles by Nozick (other than those reprinted in *Socratic Puzzles*)

"Escaping the Good Samaritan Paradox" (with R. Routley), *Mind* 71 (1962): 377–82.

"Simplicity as Fall-out," in L. Cauman, I. Levi, C. Parsons, and R. Schwartz (eds.), *How Many Questions? Essays in Honor of Sydney Morgenbesser*. Indianapolis, IN: Hackett Publishing Company, 1983, pp. 105–19.

"Symbolic Utility," in P. K. Pattnaick (ed.), *Essays in Honor of Amartya Sen*. Clarendon Press: Oxford, 1995, pp. 110–40 (extracted from the Tanner Lectures on Human Value).

10 PARFIT

JACOB ROSS

Derek Parfit is a British philosopher who has made major contributions to the study of ethics, practical reason, and the metaphysics of persons. Born in China in 1942, and educated at Oxford, he is now a senior research fellow at All Souls College, Oxford. He is also a regular visiting professor at Rutgers University, Harvard University, and New York University.[1]

Parfit's international reputation was already established in the early 1970s through a series of articles on personal identity. In his magnum opus, *Reasons and Persons* (1984), he presents his fullest account of this theme, as well as a wide-ranging exploration of rationality and morality. This work is recognized by many readers as the most important work in moral philosophy written since the early part of the twentieth century. It ranks in importance alongside the work that is its main inspiration, Henry Sidgwick's *Methods of Ethics* of 1874. *Reasons and Persons* set the agenda for many of the central debates in contemporary moral philosophy. It defined the terms for current discussions of personal identity and its moral significance, rational attitudes toward the past and the future, obligations to future generations, alternative conceptions of well-being, and the general structure of value. This book also served to initiate a number of important discussions by revealing new problems, some of which we will be discussing below.

Reason and Persons was followed by a number of articles, many of which have played a similar agenda-setting role. These have ranged from contributions to social and political philosophy, such as his work on the value of equality ("Equality or Priority?"), to his writings on philosophical cosmology, concerning the question of why the universe exists at all and has the orderly structure that it exhibits ("Why Anything? Why This?") He has now nearly completed a second book, tentatively entitled *Climbing the Mountain*, which concerns moral theory. Though this book is still forthcoming, it has been widely circulated in draft form.

1 The Fact of Reasons

Though Parfit's writings are broad in scope, to a large extent they are unified by the central theme of reasons. He is concerned with the reasons that bear on the question of how we should act, and on the question of what we should care about. This theme will therefore be the organizing principle of what follows; after discussing Parfit's general conception of reasons, we will turn to a discussion of prudential reasons (reasons of self-interest), then to reasons of beneficence (reasons to help others), and then to his recent work on the structure of moral reasons.

The reasons Parfit is concerned with are called *normative practical* reasons. They are *practical* because they bear on practical questions, and they are *normative* because they concern the question of what we *ought* to do, or *ought* to care about, rather than on the question of what we *in fact* do, or care about, or are motivated to do. An agent may fail to do what she ought to do, or she may fail to care about what she ought to care about, and so an agent may fail to be sufficiently motivated by her normative reasons. More generally, the *normative* force of reasons, or their force in favoring certain actions or concerns, must be distinguished from the *motivational* force of reasons, or their efficacy in motivating agents to act or to care. Parfit argues that there is a strong trend among philosophers to conflate, or to collapse the distinction between, normative force and motivational force, and that many of the central arguments in ethics and metaethics, from Hume and Kant to the present day, have involved such a conflation (see "Normativity"). If we lose sight of this distinction, then the question of how we should act is reduced to the question of how we are motivated to act, or of how we would be motivated to act under specified circumstances, and so ethics is reduced to a branch of psychology. And this, according to Parfit, is a serious misunderstanding of the object of ethical inquiry.

Even when the distinction between normative and motivational force is recognized, it is often held that the two are very closely connected. According to the dominant approach to understanding practical reasons, which is represented by what Parfit calls *desire-based theories*, an agent's normative reason for or against an action always consists in a fact concerning how this action would fulfill or frustrate the agent's present desires, and the motivational force of such a reason in explained in terms of the strength of the corresponding desire. On the simplest desire-based theory, the desires that determine what an agent has most reason to do at a given time are the ultimate desires she actually has at that time. According to this theory, nothing is by nature worthy or unworthy of desire, and so every consistent set of desires is on an equal footing, none being more rational than any other. An agent has reason to act in some way just in case doing so would promote the satisfaction of her desires *whatever they may be*. Parfit first criticizes such theories in *Reasons and Persons*, where he argues that certain patterns of desire are inherently irrational. One example of an irrational pattern of desire is "future Tuesday indifference," which consists in currently being indifferent to the prospect of painful experiences one may undergo on future Tuesdays, while desiring to avoid painful experiences on every other day of the week (*RP* 123–4). In *Climbing the Mountain*, Parfit discusses what he regards as the extremely implausible implications of the simple desire-based theory. This theory implies, for example, that if, at some particular time, one desires to drink sulfuric acid, and one has no desire to avoid the harmful consequences of doing so, then one is rationally required to do so, even if one is certain that one will regret having done so for the remainder of one's (possibly shortened) life.

In order to avoid such implications, many philosophers have adopted a more complex desire-based theory, according to which the desires one has reason to fulfill are not one's actual present desires, but the desires one would have if one knew and had carefully considered all the relevant facts. In particular, on this theory, the ends that one has non-instrumental reason to promote are not the ends that one currently desires for their own sake, but rather the ends that one would desire for their own sake if one had considered all the relevant facts. This theory, Parfit argues, is untenable. For desire-based theories must claim that facts about the objects of our desire can't give us reason to desire these objects as final ends. For a defining feature of such a theory is that it denies that facts about the objects of our desires can give us reason to desire these objects as final ends. Therefore it must claim that the ultimate desires we would have were we to consider all the facts would be no more supported by reasons than our actual desires. But if these hypothetical desires are no more supported by reasons that our actual desires, then there can be no grounds for asserting that it is these hypothetical desires, rather than our actual desires, that are the source of our reasons for action.

Instead of holding a desire-based theory of practical reasons, Parfit holds a *value-based* theory, according to which there are reasons for ultimate desires, namely facts about the objects of these desires that give us reason to desire them. And he holds that our reasons to promote an outcome are provided not by the fact that this outcome would satisfy our desires, but rather in the very same features of this outcome that give us reason to desire it. Thus, what gives us reason to want to avoid being tortured in the future, and to act in such a way as to prevent ourselves from being tortured in the future, is the fact that being tortured would be extremely painful. Since this fact is independent of our present desires, these reasons do not depend on our currently having any desires which would be frustrated by being tortured in the future.

The question remains as to what we have reason to desire for its own sake. One answer to this question is that one's ultimate aim should be to maximize one's own well-being, or to insure that one's life as a whole go as well as possible. This answer, which we shall discuss presently, is the target of many of Parfit's best-known arguments.

2 Prudential Reasons and Personal Identity

According to the *self-interest theory* of practical reason, all one has reason to care about for its own sake is one's own well-being, and what one has most reason to do is whatever would most promote one's well-being. Whenever there is anything else we should care about or promote, this is ultimately to be explained in terms of its contribution to our own well-being. While the desire-based theories of practical reason of the kind we discussed in the previous section are currently dominant among philosophers, Parfit holds that the self-interest theory has been the prevailing theory of rationality among people in general for more than 2,000 years. These two theories are often conflated, since it is sometimes assumed that each agent's fundamental desire is that her life as a whole go as well as possible, or that her own welfare be maximized. On this assumption, the action that most promotes the satisfaction of one's current desires always coincides with the action that would make one's life go best as a whole. But this assumption is false. For people often care more about the nearer future than about the more distant future, and so many people would prefer a life that is better in the short run, but worse on the whole, to a life that is worse in the short run, but better on the whole. The desire-based theory implies that such agents ought rationally to act in ways that make their lives go worse on the whole. Further, the desire-based theory implies that if today I desire some outcome, and I know that tomorrow my desires will change and I will desire some opposing outcome, then I will be rationally required today to promote an outcome while recognizing that tomorrow I will be rationally required to try to prevent this outcome.

But to the self-interest theorist, these implications are unacceptable. On her view, if we will ever have reason to care about some event or outcome, we already have this reason now. The force of a reason to promote an outcome, she insists, is transmitted over time, and its strength is not affected by the distance of this outcome from the present. And so our concern for how well we fare at future times must not be affected by the distance of these times from the present.

In Part II of *Reasons and Persons*, Parfit argues that, in making these claims, the self-interest theory occupies an unstable position between two alternative theories. On one side there are what we may call *fully relativistic* theories of reasons, like the simple desire-based theory, according to which what one has reason to care about, and to promote if one can, depends both on who we are and on where we are situated in time. In other words, practical reasons vary both from agent to agent and from time to time. On the other side there are *fully non-relativistic* theories, according to which what one has reason to care about and promote varies neither across agents nor across times. (An example of such a fully non-relativistic theory is rational consequentialism, according to which there is a single rational aim valid for everyone, namely that the history of the world go as well as possible as evaluated from an impartial point of view.) According to the self-interest theory, what one has reason to care about and promote varies from agent to agent (since each agent should be concerned with *his own* well-being) but it does not vary from time to time (since each agent should always have the aim of making his life as a whole go as well as possible). In order to defend this middle position between these opposing kinds of theory, the self-interest theories must show that there is a principled reason for treating agents and times differently, and hence for requiring a partial attitude toward agents but an impartial attitude toward times. She must show, in other words, that differences among persons have a rational significance that differences among times lack.

One argument, made by Sidgwick, Rawls, and Nozick, is that any supposed requirement to be impartial with respect to persons fails to do justice to the separateness of persons.[2] In Sidgwick's words: "It would be contrary to common sense to deny that the distinction between any one individual and any other is real and fundamental" and hence to deny that this distinction should be "taken as fundamental in determining the ultimate end of rational conduct."[3] By contrast, it might be claimed that the passage of time is merely a subjective illusion, and so the distinction between the nearer and further future should not be taken as fundamental in determining this ultimate end. Parfit argues, however, that no such defense of the self-interest theory can succeed.

For one thing, the most plausible version of the self-interest theory is not supported by any viable conception of the metaphysics of time. If one holds that the passage of time is an illusion and that this fact imposes constraints upon what patterns of concern can be rational, then the natural inference to draw is not merely that we should be impartial toward all *future* times, but that we should be impartial toward *all* times, including past times. But if we were impartial toward all times, then, other things being equal, we would have no preference for a situation in which a painful ordeal has occurred in the past over a situation in which this ordeal has yet to occur. But most of us have this preference: if we had amnesia, and could not remember the events of yesterday, and we knew that either we underwent a painful ordeal yesterday, or else this ordeal has yet to occur and is scheduled for tomorrow, most of us would be relieved if we discovered that the ordeal occurred yesterday. And most of us do not regard this bias as irrational. Thus, while a bias in favor of the nearer future over the further future may be irrational, it appears that a bias in favor of the future over the past is not. But if the self-interest theory is to be defended on the basis of the view that the passage of time is an illusion, then this theory must claim, counterintuitively, that these biases are equally irrational.

Parfit then argues that the self-interest theory, in addition to lacking support from any plausible conception of the metaphysics of time, is undermined by every defensible conception of the metaphysics of persons. His best-known argument against the self-interest theory is found in his discussion of personal identity in Part III of *Reasons and Persons*. Here Parfit argues that, on any defensible conception of personal identity, there are possible cases in which what we have ultimate reason to care about is not our own welfare.

In order to show that what we have reason to care about need not be our own future, Parfit employs a famous thought-experiment, which is among the many ingenious thought-experiments to be found in his writings. He first notes that, as we normally think about personal identity, the part of the body that matters for retaining personal identity is the brain, so that if one's brain were transplanted into another body, one would continue to exist within this new body. He further notes that, as we normally think about personal identity, a person could survive an injury in which much of her brain is destroyed, so long as enough of her brain survives in order for her to retain most of her beliefs, intentions, and other psychological characteristics. Thus, as we normally think about personal identity, one could survive an operation in which half of one's brain is destroyed, and the other half is transplanted into another body.

Now consider two cases. In the first case, called Single Transplantation, Van Cleve's brain is cloven in half, the left half of his brain is transplanted into another body, and the right half is destroyed. Let us assume that most of Van Cleve's memories and other mental states are encoded in both halves of his brain, so that the preservation of either half of his brain is sufficient for him to retain psychological continuity. In this case, we would normally think that Van Cleve survives the operation, and lives on in the body to which the left half of his brain was transplanted.

Now consider Double Transplantation. As in the case of single transplantation we just considered, the left half of Van Cleve's brain is preserved and transplanted into someone else's body. But in this case, the right half is also preserved, and is transplanted into someone else's body. Assume, further, that prior to the operation, both halves of Van Cleve's brain are nearly identical psychologically, since nearly all of Van Cleve's memories and other mental states are similarly encoded in each. Thus, after the operation, there will be one person (or one entity that appears to be a person), who has the left half of Van Cleve's brain, and who has most of Van Cleve's psychological characteristics, whom we may call "Lefty", and another person, or apparent person, who has the right half of Van Cleve's brain, and who likewise has most of Van Cleve's psychological characteristics, whom we may call "Righty." Suppose, finally, that after the operation, Lefty and Righty never interact. Does Van Cleve survive this operation? In other words, is there anyone who exists after this operation, and who is numerically identical with Van Cleve? It seems that there are five answers we could give to the question:

1   Van Cleve is the same person as Lefty, but not the same person as Righty.
2   Van Cleve is the same person as Righty, but not the same person as Lefty.
3   Van Cleve is the same person as Lefty, and Van Cleve is the same person as Righty.
4   Van Cleve survives the operation as a divided person, of which Lefty and Righty are both parts.
5   Van Cleve does not survive the operation.

It seems that we should reject (1) and (2), since in the case described there does not appear to be anything relevantly different between Van Cleve's relation to Lefty and his relation to Righty. Moreover, since Lefty is not the same person as Righty, they can't each be the same person as Van Cleve, and so we should reject (3). Further, since Lefty and Righty are each persons, or at least each would be a person in the absence of the other, and since we are assuming that the two do not interact after the operation, there is strong reason to reject the view that Lefty and Righty together constitute a single person. Therefore we should reject (4). Hence, there are only two remaining alternatives. One is to adopt the fifth answer and assert that Van Cleve does not survive the operation. And the other is to reject every determinate answer and conclude that there is no fact of the matter concerning relations of identity between Van Cleve and those who exist after the operation. In either case, we cannot affirm that Van Cleve survives the operation of double transplantation.

Although we cannot affirm that Van Cleve survives the operation, we should affirm that being divided into two persons is *as good as* survival, or at least it is not nearly as bad as ordinary death. Surely the preservation of both halves of one's brain can't be significantly worse than the preservation of only one; this hardly seems like a case in which a double success would amount to a failure. Similarly, although we cannot affirm that Van Cleve is identical with either of the people who result from the operation, we can affirm that he has reason to be concerned about the welfare of these persons for its own sake. For whatever reason Van Cleve has, in Single Transplantation, to be concerned about the welfare of the person who will have the left half of his brain cannot be negated by the fact that, in Double Transplantation, the right half of his brain will also be successfully transplanted.

But the self-interest theorist cannot make these claims, so long as she affirms that Van Cleve survives Single Transplantation, but does not affirm that Van Cleve survives Double Transplantation. For then, in Single Transplantation, she must affirm that Van Cleve has reason to care, for its own sake, about the person who will have the left half of his brain, but she cannot affirm this in the case of Double Transplantation. And this is an implausible position

One option open to the self-interest theorist is to deny that Van Cleve survives even in the case of Single Transplantation. So far we have been assuming that in Single Transplantation, Van Cleve survives because he retains enough of his brain to preserve most of his memories and other psychological characteristics. But one might adopt an alternative theory of personal identity according to which this is not enough for survival. One might therefore say that there is no asymmetry between the attitudes Van Cleve ought to have in the two transplantation cases toward the person who will have his brain after the operation: in both cases he should recognize that this person is not him, and so he has no reason to care about this person's welfare for its own sake. However, even if one regarded this as a tenable position, it would not solve the general problem Parfit raises. For Parfit argues that on any plausible theory of personal identity, there will be some thought-experiment involving division, analogous to the transplantation thought-experiment we have been considering, in which the self-interest theory has similarly counterintuitive implications (see "Experiences, Subjects, and Conceptual Schemes").

Thus, Parfit concludes, we should reject the self-interest theory. Though we may have special reason to care about the future person with whom we are identical, our reason cannot plausibly be said to derive from the fact that this person will be *us*, for if this were the case, then we would lack this reason in cases of division. Since, in both the case of Single Transplantation and in the case of Double Transplantation, Van Cleve has special reason to be concerned about the person who has the left side of his brain after the operation, it seems that the relation that explains his special reason for concern must be a relation that obtains in both cases. And this relation, as we have seen, does not appear to be the relation of identity. Rather, it is the relation of *psychological continuity*.

Parfit defines psychological continuity in terms of psychological connections, where these are the sorts of relations that exist between an earlier experience and a later memory of this experience, or between an earlier intention and a later fulfillment of this intention. In response to the charge that definitions of personal identity in terms of such relations as remembering and intending are circular, as these relations presuppose personal identity, Parfit, following Shoemaker's lead,[4] introduces the relations of *q-remembering* and *q-intending*, relations which are similar to those of remembering and intending but that are defined without presupposing personal identity. If we define a *person-stage* as a stage in the life of a person, then we may say that two person-stages are *strongly connected* just in case there are enough psychological connections between them. And two person-stages are *psychologically continuous* just in case they both belong to a sequence of person-stages such that each person-stage belonging to this sequence is strongly connected to the preceding one.

The relevant relations in which Van Cleve stands to the person who will have the left half of his brain in both the Single and the Double Transplantation cases are the relations of psychological continuity and connectedness. In both cases it is these relations, Parfit argues, that explain Van Cleve's special reason for concern. And it is also these relations, and not the relation of personal identity, that explain our own special reason to be concerned about our future welfare. And what is most important, Parfit argues, is the relation of psychological connectedness. Since we are connected to the future person-stages making up our lives to differing degrees, it can be rational, *pace* the self-interest theory, to be concerned about them to differing degrees.

Some have claimed that we cannot coherently deny the importance of personal identity. A prominent example is Christine Korsgaard, who gives an argument of the following form.[5] Any relation that we must necessarily take into account whenever we are deliberating is important from the practical point of view. But the relation of personal identity is such a relation. For when an agent deliberates, she is asking how *she* is to act, and the alternatives among which she is choosing always lie at some distance in the future. Hence, she must regard the actions that will be performed by an agent at some future time as *her* actions, which means that she must regard herself as identical with an agent who will exist in the future. But if any relation that we must take account of in practical reasoning is important from the practical point of view, and if the relation of personal identity is one such relation, then it follows that the relation of personal identity is important from the practical point of view. Thus, the practical importance of the relation of personal identity derives not, as Sidgwick suggested, from its being metaphysically real and fundamental, but rather from its being a necessary presupposition of the practical point of view.

But there is an obvious reply to this argument. Granted, in all actual cases of deliberation, we are deciding how *we* shall act in the future. But this is simply because there are no actual cases of fission. Suppose that Van Cleve knows that he will undergo Double Transplantation, and that the body into which the left half of his brain will be transplanted is in a hospital in which there is a dangerous gas leak. Suppose that after the operation occurs, Lefty will have no time to plan his escape, and will only be able to leave the building alive if he takes immediate and appropriate action. If, prior to the operation, Van Cleve is given a map of the hospital, it seems that he could and should consult this map and deliberate concerning how to escape. But in so doing, he would be deciding not how *he* shall escape from the building, but rather how Lefty shall escape from the building. And the conclusions of such deliberation would be q-intentions whose objects are the actions of Lefty. It seems, therefore, that in cases of division, one can deliberate concerning the actions of an agent with whom one is not identical, and with whom one does not take oneself to be identical. And so it appears that, contrary to Korsgaard, the concept of personal identity over time does not play an ineliminable role in practical reasoning.

Moreover, if Korsgaard is right that claims about the practical importance of a relation can be justified in virtue not of its metaphysical status but rather of its ineliminable role in practical reasoning, then this will strengthen rather than undermine Parfit's position. For as the division case illustrates, the fundamental distinction we must draw among future actions in the context of practical reasoning is not a distinction between actions that we may perform and actions that others may perform, but rather between actions that are up to us, or that we can cause to occur by q-intending that they occur, and actions that are not up to us in this sense. But this is a question of psychological connectedness, not of identity. Thus, what must be presupposed from the practical point of view is not personal identity, but psychological connectedness, which is precisely the relation to which Parfit thinks we should give most weight.

In Parfit's view, we can coherently regard the relation of personal identity as having no significance in relation to the question of how we ought to act. Indeed, this is how we ought to regard this relation. Parfit holds, with the Buddha, that when we free ourselves from the stranglehold of the concept of personal identity, then we can abandon the illusion that in order to act rationally we must act selfishly, and we can recognize that very often, what we have most reason to do is to act in such a way as to benefit others, even at the expense of our own well-being.

3 Reasons of Beneficence

According to Parfit, our reasons to benefit others, or *reasons of beneficence*, are among our most important moral reasons. Thus any adequate moral theory must recognize such reasons, and must also specify their content so that we can determine whether our reasons of beneficence favor one course of action or another. Parfit shows, however, in Part IV of *Reasons and Persons*, that this is no easy task, since all the prima facie candidate theories of beneficence have unacceptable implications.[6] This part of *Reasons and Persons*, though initially overshadowed by the part on personal identity, is increasingly becoming recognized for its fundamental importance.

One candidate conception of our reasons of beneficence includes the following claims:

(i) We have a greater reason of beneficence to choose outcome A than to choose outcome B just in case, on the whole, A would be better for people than B.

(ii) Unless there is someone whose level of welfare is higher in outcome A than in outcome B, A is not better for people than outcome B.

In cases where the same people will exist regardless of what we choose, or in what Parfit calls *same people choices*, (i) and (ii) have fairly plausible implications. But in cases where who will come to exist depends on how we act, these claims can have very implausible implications, for they fail to solve what Parfit calls the Non-Identity Problem.

Suppose we are choosing between two policies, *Conservation*, in which we conserve our resources so that they are available for future generations, and *Depletion*, in which we consume these resources in the near future. Suppose that Depletion would have slightly better consequences for some people who are alive now, and that it would not have worse consequences for anyone will be alive over the next two centuries. Suppose, however, that at all times later than 200 years from now, the prevailing level of welfare will be much higher if we choose Conservation than Depletion. Suppose, further, that our choice between these two alternatives will have very wide-ranging implications, significantly affecting the daily lives of everyone in the population. On these suppositions, Parfit argues that we can reasonably assume that in the population of those affected by our decision, *who* will exist at times later than 200 years in the future will depend on which of these policies we choose now, and that there is no one in this population who will exist more than 200 years from now regardless of which of these policies we choose.

In this case, it seems clear that, on the whole, people will be better off if we choose Conservation rather than Depletion, and that we thus have greater reason of beneficence to choose Conservation. But on the conception of beneficence we are now considering, we cannot draw this conclusion. For since there is no one in the affected population who will exist more than 200 years from now independently of which alternative we choose, there is no one whose level of welfare would be greater if we choose Conservation than if we choose Depletion. Hence the view under consideration implies that we do not have greater reason of beneficence to choose Conservation.

Thus, a common conception of beneficence runs into problems when faced with choices in which who will exist depends on how we act. Moreover, such cases present problems for a great many positions in moral philosophy. Parfit argues that they present serious problems for the moral theories of Gauthier, Harman, Mackie, Rawls, and Scanlon, among others (*RP* 523).

Any adequate moral theory must explain how an action can be wrong, and specifically wrong from the point of view of beneficence, even if there is no one for whom its outcome would be worse than any available alternative; or, in other words, any adequate moral theory must solve the Non-Identity Problem. One obvious solution to this problem is to conclude that the outcome that is best from the point of view of beneficence (and hence best simpliciter, all else being equal), is the outcome in which the total sum of human welfare or utility is greatest. Call this the Impersonal Total Principle. This principle implies that, other things being equal, conservation is preferable to depletion, since it would result in a greater sum of human welfare. Thus the Impersonal Total Principle gives the right answer in the case we have been considering.

Further problems arise, however, if we consider situations in which our choices will affect not only *who* will live, but also *how many* people will live. For the sum total of utility in a population can be increased either by increasing the average level of welfare in the population, or by adding people whose level of welfare is above the zero-level (the level below which lives cease to be worth living). Thus, one population can involve a greater sum total of welfare than a second population even if, on average, people are much better off in the second population, so long as the first population involves a sufficiently large number of people, and so long as everyone in this population has a life that is worth living. Hence the Impersonal Total Principle implies what Parfit calls the Repugnant Conclusion: "For any possible population of at least ten billion people, all with a very high quality of life, there must be some much larger imaginable population whose existence would be better, if other things are equal, even though its members have lives that are barely worth living" (*RP* 388).

To avoid this conclusion we can move to the Impersonal Average Principle, according to which the outcome that is best from the point of view of beneficence is the outcome in which people's lives go best on average. This principle avoids the Repugnant Conclusion, since the average level of welfare is clearly higher in a population in which everyone has a very high quality of life than in a population, however large, in which everyone lives a life that is barely worth living. But the Average Principle has its own problematic implications. The worst of these arise in cases in which one must choose the lesser of two evils. Suppose we are choosing between Hell A, which consists in a population of a billion innocent people, all of whom experience extreme agony throughout their lives, and Hell B, which consists in these same billion people undergoing this same degree of agony, plus an additional billion innocent people who likewise experience extreme agony throughout their lives, but to a slightly lesser degree. The Average Principle implies that since the average level of welfare is slightly higher in Hell B than Hell A, our reasons of beneficence favor the choice Hell B.

We can avoid this conclusion, while at the same time avoiding the Repugnant Conclusion, if we suppose that there is an asymmetry between the positive value of lives that are worth living, and the disvalue of lives that are wretched, or not worth living. We might hold, contrary to the Impersonal Average Principle, that numbers matter, so that by adding people with positive levels of welfare (people whose lives are worth living), we improve an outcome, regardless of whether we increase the average level of welfare, and that by adding people with negative levels of welfare, we make an outcome worse. And yet – and this is where the asymmetry enters – we may hold that there is a limit to how much we can improve a situation by adding people at any given positive level of welfare, but no limit to how much we can make an outcome worse by adding people at any given negative level of welfare. By assuming that there is a limit in the first case, we avoid the Repugnant Conclusion, and by assuming that there is no limit in the second case, we avoid the conclusion that Hell B is preferable to Hell A. However, we now face another unacceptable implication. For now our view implies that if we begin with a population of ten billion people, all but one of whom has an absolutely wonderful life, but one of whom has a life that is not worth living, and we then progressively multiply this population, retaining the proportion between those with wonderful lives and those with lives not worth living, then the disvalue of the tiny fraction of bad lives will come to swamp the positive value of the wonderful lives, so that we eventually reach a world that is worse than a world in which no one exists at all. Parfit calls this the Absurd Conclusion.[7]

Thus, in attempting to formulate an adequate principle of beneficence, we seem to be caught between the Scylla of the Repugnant Conclusion and the Charybdis of the Absurd conclusion. Naturally, Parfit considers ways in which we might attempt to navigate a course between them. We might distinguish between three kinds of lives: bad lives (lives that are not worth living), good lives (lives that are well above the level at which they cease to be worth living), and mediocre lives (lives that are only marginally above the level at which they cease to be worth living). And we might hold that while the positive values of good lives and the disvalues of bad lives should be added up in a similar manner, the positive values of mediocre lives should be added up differently. One solution is to say that while there is no limit to the value or disvalue of additional good or bad lives, there is an upper limit to the value of additional mediocre lives. By placing a limit on the value of additional mediocre lives, we avoid the Repugnant Conclusion, and by placing no limit on the value of additional good lives, we avoid the Absurd Conclusion. Call this the *non-lexical solution*.[8] An alternative solution is to say that while there is no upper limit to the value of additional lives of any kind, the value or disvalues contributed by good and bad lives infinitely outweigh, and hence always take precedence over, the value contributed by mediocre lives, so that the only significance of mediocre lives is to break ties between outcomes that are equally good with respect to good and bad lives. Since, on this view, the value of good lives always has precedence over the value of mediocre lives, we avoid the Repugnant Conclusion, and since the disvalue of bad lives does not always take precedence over the value of good lives, we avoid the Absurd Conclusion. Call this the *lexical solution*.

Parfit argues, however, that these solutions are unsatisfactory. He demonstrates that while they enable us to avoid the dilemma between the Repugnant Conclusion and the Absurd Conclusion, they leave us with a dilemma between a variant of the Repugnant Conclusion and a variant of the Absurd Conclusion. And since the variants of these conclusions are nearly as counterintuitive as the original conclusions, these solutions, Parfit argues, remain unacceptable.

And there are, I believe, further reasons for rejecting these two solutions, in addition to those given by Parfit. First, there is strong reason to deny that the value of good lives infinitely outweighs the value of mediocre lives. For given any good life, G, there is some possible mediocre life, M, such that G and M can be connected by a chain of possible lives wherein no two successive lives differ from one another significantly in any important respect. And if two lives do not differ from one another significantly in any important respect, then neither of these lives will be infinitely outweighed in value by the other. And if two lives, G and M, are connected by a finite chain of possible lives, such that no life belonging to this chain infinitely outweighs the next life in value, then it follows that the value of life G cannot infinitely outweigh the value of life M.[9] So, the value of good lives cannot infinitely outweigh the value of mediocre lives. And so we should reject the lexical solution.

But there is also strong reason to reject the non-lexical solution. For it has the implausible implication that we should give more weight to improving the lives of the better off than to improving the lives of the worse off. Let P_1 and P_2 be two populations of equal size such that everyone in P_1 has a level of welfare that is at the dividing line between good lives and mediocre lives, and everyone in P_2 has a level of welfare that is slightly below this dividing line. Formally speaking, if we let g represent the minimum level of welfare for a good life, then we can say that everyone in P_1 has a level of welfare of g, and that everyone on P2 has a level of welfare of $g - \Delta$. Now suppose we have two options: we can either raise the level of welfare of everyone in the better-off population, P1, by a margin of Δ, so that they all attain a level of welfare of $g + \Delta$, or we can raise the level of welfare of everyone in the worse-off population, P2, by this same margin, so that they all attain a level of welfare of g. Intuitively, if either alternative is better than the other, then it's the alternative of improving the lives of those in P2, since they are worse off to begin with. But if we adopt the non-lexical solution, we must accept the counterintuitive implication that, so long as the two populations are large enough, it would be better to improve the lives of the better off people (P1) than to improve the lives of an equal number of worse off people by an equal margin.

This conclusion follows because, on the non-lexical view, it is true of both population P1 and P2 that, as we increase its size, we increase the amount of good we could do by improving the lives of everyone in it by a margin of Δ. However, on this view, since, initially, people in P2 have mediocre lives, as we increase the size of this population, the amount of good we could do by improving the lives of everyone in it by Δ approaches an upper limit. But since people in P1 initially have good lives, this view implies that as we increase the size of this population, there is no upper limit to how much good we could do by improving the lives of everyone in this population by Δ. Therefore, if we make the two populations large enough, there will come a point where it will be better to improve the lives of those in the better-off population, P_1 by a margin of Δ than to improve the lives of those in the worse-off population, P_1 by this same margin.[10]

Parfit's explorations of our reasons of beneficence demonstrate a great difficulty of moral theory. The problem is not that there are too many plausible alternative moral theories, and hence that there is too much room for reasonable disagreement. The problem is rather that there is no moral theory that appears to be plausible. For any plausible moral theory would need to account for our reasons of beneficence, and every account of such reasons that has yet been offered has intolerable implications.

4   Impartial Reasons and Morality

Reasons of beneficence are what we may call *teleological* reasons, in the sense that they are reasons to promote ends. And they are also *impartial* reasons, in the sense that if anyone has a reason of beneficence to desire and promote some end, then everyone has this reason to do so. But while reasons of beneficence are teleological and impartial, they are not the only reasons of this kind, since there are other social, cultural, and ecological ends that we have impartial reason to promote for their own sake. Moral theories differ, however, concerning the moral significance they attribute to such impartial teleological reasons. According to consequentialist moral theories, such reasons are absolutely fundamental, as they are the basis for all moral requirements. Such reasons have not traditionally played a central role in the kinds of moral theories that are the main rivals to consequentialism, such as contractualism and Kantianism. Contractualists and Kantians attempt to ground moral obligations not in impartially valuable ends, but rather in terms of principles that could be rationally chosen or rationally willed, and the rationality of the choice in question is in turn understood without reference to impartial teleological reasons. Parfit argues that no adequate moral theory can be grounded in this manner. If moral obligations are to be derived from principles that we could rationally choose, then the rationality of this choice must be understood in terms of *all* the relevant reasons, including reasons of the impartial, teleological variety. And he goes on to argue that when the Kantian and contractualist theories are formulated in this way, then Kantians, contractualists and consequentialists will all converge on theories that are equivalent from the practical point of view. Thus, while the proponents of Kantianism and contractualism may have intended their theories to support the rejection of consequentialist principles, the best versions of their theories in fact constitute the strongest defense of such principles. And so, in Parfit's view, these different and seemingly rival theorists have all been climbing the same mountain from different sides.[11]

Parfit's argument begins with a critical discussion of Kant's moral philosophy. Kant claims that the fundamental moral principle, or the categorical imperative, can be given a variety of formulations, but that all of these are equivalent. Parfit shows, however, that on any reasonable assumptions, Kant's various formulations of the categorical imperative are not in fact equivalent, and that some of these formulations could not possibly serve as the fundamental principle of morality. According to the best-known formulation, the Formula of Universal Law, one acts rightly just in case one acts on a maxim that one could will to be a universal law, where "could" here means "without incoherence." Parfit shows that this fails to rule out many impermissible actions. Consider the following maxim "If one is white and one is able to enslave a black person, do so." Acting on this maxim would clearly be wrong. But a white person could, without incoherence, will that this maxim be a universal law, or in other words that white people enslave black people whenever possible. For even if there is a kind of rational incoherence involved in willing one's own enslavement, there does not seem to be any rational incoherence involved in willing the enslavement of someone else. The problem with the maxim under consideration is not that it couldn't be willed as a universal law by *anyone*, but rather that it could not be willed as a universal law by *everyone*, and in particular, that it couldn't be so willed by blacks.

A better candidate for the fundamental principle of morality is thus the following: one acts rightly just in case one acts on a maxim that everyone could coherently will to be a universal law. But even this is too permissive, since far too many immoral maxims could be willed by everyone to be universal laws without incoherence – there is no contradiction, for example, in universalizing a maxim of causing as much pain as possible. Hence, according to Parfit, the best formulation of a principle of universal law concerns not what everyone could will *coherently*, but rather what everyone could will rationally, in the sense of *having sufficient reason* to will. The best formulation, Parfit argues, can be stated as follows: one acts rightly just in case one acts on principles whose universal acceptance everyone would have sufficient reason to will, or to choose. Parfit calls this the Kantian Contractualist Formula, since it bases the rightness or wrongness of an action on principles that all agents could rationally agree to. Parfit argues that the Kantian Contractualist Formula represents not only the best version of Kantianism, but also the best version of contractualism.[12]

The Kantian Contractualist Formula presupposes that there are principles whose universal acceptance each of us would have sufficient reason to will, or to choose, were we in a position to choose the principles that are to be accepted by everyone. But whether there are any such principles depends on what our reasons are, and on the strength of these reasons. Suppose, for example, that our only reasons are prudential reasons. In this case, it is unlikely that there would be any principles whose universal acceptance everyone would have sufficient reason to choose, since everyone would have decisive reason to choose the universal acceptance of principles that would be optimal in relation to *her own* interests, and it is unlikely that any principles would be optimal in relation to everyone's interests. Suppose, however, that apart from any prudential or other partial reasons we may have, we also have impartial teleological reason to choose outcomes that are best from a point of view that is valid for everyone. And suppose, further, that it is always rationally permissible (though perhaps not rationally obligatory) to give significant weight to these impartial reasons. In this case, Parfit argues, there will be principles whose universal acceptance everyone would have sufficient reason to will. And these will be precisely those principles whose universal acceptance would have the best consequences from an impartial point of view; that is, these will be the rule-consequentialist principles. For these rule-consequentialist principles are the ones that each agent would have strongest impartial reason to choose, and these impartial reasons would in each case constitute sufficient, though perhaps not decisive, reason for the agent in question to choose these principles. But if the acceptance of these principles would not make things go best from an impartial point of view, then there will always be someone who has decisive reason not to choose their universal acceptance. Thus, the only principles that everyone has sufficient reason to choose that everyone accept are the rule-consequentialist principles. And so it follows from Kantian Contractualism that one acts rightly just in case one acts on rule-consequentialist principles.

There are, however, strong objections to rule-consequentialist principles. Therefore, if the best versions of Kantianism and of contractualism imply that we act rightly just in case we act on such principles, these objections will count equally against Kantianism and contractualism. Indeed, one of the strongest objections to rule-consequentialist principles can be found in chapter 12 of *Climbing the Mountain*. The problem is that there are principles whose universal acceptance would make things go best or equal-best, but that it would be clearly immoral to act on. Consider the following: "Never use violence, unless some other people have used aggressive violence, in which case kill as many people as possible." This principle might well be one whose universal acceptance would make things go as well as possible, and hence a principle whose universal acceptance everyone would have sufficient reason to choose. For if everyone followed this principle, then no one would ever use violence. But to follow it in the actual world, where there will always be others who have used aggressive violence, would involve killing as many people as possible.

To avoid this problem, Parfit claims, we must revise rule-consequentialism, so that it states that we act rightly just in case we act on principles whose acceptance *by any number of people* would make things go best. We must similarly revise Kantian contractualism, so that it states that we act rightly just in case we act on principles whose acceptance *by any number of people* everyone would have sufficient reason to choose. That is, in order to act rightly, we must act on principles whose acceptance we could rationally will not only in a situation in which we are choosing the principles to be acted on by everyone, but also in a situation in which we are choosing principles to be acted on by any smaller number of people. And according to Parfit, when consequentialism and Kantian contractualism are reformulated in this way, they once again converge.

It is doubtful, however, that there are sufficiently many principles satisfying the descriptions in these revised formulation. That is, it is doubtful that in every choice situation there is some principle one could act on whose acceptance by any number of people would make things go best, or whose acceptance by any number of people everyone could rationally will. Consider, for example, the following two rules:

P1:   Make a reasonable effort to benefit the poor, but give significant priority to the interests of the near and dear.

P2:   Act in such a way as to maximally benefit humanity as a whole, without favoring anyone's interests over anyone else's.

If our choice concerned what principle would be followed by only a single individual, then we may have stronger impartial reason to choose that she accept P2 rather than P1, since in the actual world, there are countless desperately poor people who would benefit far more from her accepting P2 than from her accepting P1, and this benefit would, from an impartial point of view, more than outweigh any loss to the agent in question, or to her near and dear, that would result from her accepting P2. But if we were in a position to choose the principle to be accepted by everyone, then we might have stronger impartial reason to choose P1 than P2. For regardless of whether everyone accepts P1 or P2, poverty will be eliminated or nearly eliminated. But if everyone were to accept P2, then no one could have close personal relations with the near and dear, and this would arguably be a significant, uncompensated loss. Thus, it seems that the rule that we would have strongest impersonal reason to choose that one person accept differs from the rule we would have strongest impartial reason to choose that everyone accept.[13]

Parfit suggests that we can solve this problem, and arrive at principles whose acceptance by any number of people would be optimal, if we allow for conditional principles of the form "Do A, unless the number or proportion of A-doers is or will be below some threshold, in which case do B."[14] Thus, in the present case, the relevant conditional principle might be the following:

P3:   Make a reasonable effort to benefit the poor, while giving significant priority to the interests of the near and dear, unless there are insufficiently many people who make such a reasonable effort to benefit the poor, in which case act in such a way as to maximally benefit humanity as a whole.

But would the acceptance by everyone of P3 be as good as the acceptance by everyone of P2? In both cases, everyone would give significant priority to the near and dear. But in the former case, this priority would be conditional. That is, if everyone accepted P3, they would be willing to sacrifice the interests of the near and dear if insufficiently many people made a reasonable effort to benefit the poor. And it may be that personal relationships that involved this kind of conditional commitment would be less valuable than ones involving unconditional commitment.

And so we appear to be faced with a dilemma: if we say that the moral principles are those whose universal acceptance would make things go best, then we get the result that too many alternative principles count as moral, many of which are clearly dreadful. If, on the other hand, we say that the moral principles are the ones whose acceptance by any number of people would make things go best, then we may get the result that principles count as moral, or at least that too few principles count as moral.

We can solve this problem by defining the relevant principles in terms of *compliance* rather than acceptance. For a person might happen to comply with a rule, in the sense that all his actions happen to be in accordance with this rule, without his accepting or being guided by this rule. Hence, we might define the moral principles as the principles compliance with which by any subset of people would make things go best. For conditional principles such as P3 might well be principles compliance with which by any number of people would make things go best, or equal-best, even if their universal acceptance would not make things go best. After all, in a world in which sufficiently many people make a reasonable effort to benefit the poor, P1 and P3 make the same prescriptions, and so anyone who complies with P1 will also comply with P3. Thus, universal compliance with P3 would be just as good as universal compliance with P1. If a principle has the feature that compliance with it by any number or people would make things go best, then we can call this principle *adaptable*.[15]

Thus, we can avoid the dilemma indicated above if we reformulate consequentialism so that it states that an act is right just in case it accords with *adaptable* principles. And we should similarly revise the Kantian Contractualist Formula so that it states than an act is right just in case it accords with principles compliance with which by any subset of people everyone could rationally will. If Parfit's arguments are sound, the resulting formulations will be equivalent: both formulations will permit just those actions that conform with adaptable principles. But if we make these revisions, then we come very close to adopting act-consequentialism, since it can be shown that any action that is permissible according to adaptable principles must be an action that makes things go best, and so it must also be permissible according to act-consequentialist principles. We may, therefore, be faced with the conclusion that in their best formulations, consequentialism, Kantianism, and contractualism converge on a view that in many ways resembles act-consequentialism. If this is so, then Parfit's thesis that the three main schools of moral thought converge will still be vindicated. But the summit at which they converge as they climb the moral mountain will turn out to be very far from two of the three base camps from which they began their ascent.

5   Conclusion

Parfit's works have been tremendously influential. Their significance lies not only in the ideas they present, but equally in the manner in which these ideas are presented. His works contain a clarity of prose, a rigor of argumentation, a thoroughness in the exploration of theoretical alternatives, an ingenuity and imaginativeness in the construction of examples, and a breadth of argument-ative strategies that had never before been seen in moral philosophy. Countless readers of Parfit, including many of today's leading ethicists, have found in his works a revelation of how moral philosophy can fruitfully be done, and of how undeniable progress in moral philosophy can be made.

Parfit begins *Reasons and Persons* with the following epigraph from Nietzsche: "[A]ll the daring of the lover of knowledge is permitted again; the sea, our sea, lies open again; perhaps there has never been such an 'open sea'."[16] We can only expect that much of the future progress in moral philo-sophy, like much of its recent progress, will be made in the exploration the open sea that Parfit's writings have revealed.

Notes

1   I am indebted to Derek Parfit and to Larry Temkin for very helpful comments on an earlier draft of this paper.

2   See Henry Sidgwick, *Methods of Ethics*. London: Macmillan, 1874, p. 498; John Rawls, *A Theory of Justice*. Cambridge. MA: Harvard University Press, 1971, sects. 5–6; and Robert Nozick, *Anarchy, State, and Utopia*. New York: Basic Books, 1974, pp. 32–3.

3 Sidgwick, *Methods of Ethics*.
4 Sidney Shoemaker, "Persons and Their Pasts," *American Philosophical Quarterly* 7 (1970).
5 In "Personal Identity and the Unity of Agency: A Kantian Response to Parfit," *Philosophy & Public Affairs* 18/2 (Spring 1989): 101–32.
6 Some of the arguments from this part of *Reasons and Persons* are developed further and strengthened in "Overpopulation and the Quality of Life."
7 For a more precise characterization of this conclusion, see *RP* 410–11.
8 This corresponds to what Parfit calls the "appeal to the valueless level;" see *RP* 412–14.
9 Ruth Chang presents a related argument in her introduction to *Incommensurability, Incomparability, and Practical Reason*. Cambridge, MA: Harvard University Press, 1998.
10 In "Equality or Priority," Parfit presents and defends a view, called *prioritarianism*, according to which we ought to give priority to the welfare of the worse off. Since the non-lexical solution has the opposite implication, we may call it *antiprioritarian*.
11 Parfit's arguments for this conclusion receive their fullest presentation is in *Climbing the Mountain*, but they were first sketched in "What We Can Rationally Will."
12 See chapter 13 of *Climbing the Mountain*.
13 Michael Ridge argues very forcefully for this conclusion in "Climb Every Mountain?" forthcoming in *Ratio*.
14 See *Climbing the Mountain*, ch. 12.
15 See Donald Regan, *Utilitarianism and Cooperation*. Oxford: Oxford University Press, 1980.
16 This quotation is from *The Gay Science*, section 343.

References

"Equality or Priority?" delivered as the Lindley Lecture at the University of Kansas, November 21, 1991; repr. in M. Clayton and A. Williams (eds.), *The Ideal of Equality*. Basingstoke: Palgrave MacMillan, 2000.

"Experiences, Subjects, and Conceptual Schemes," *Philosophical Topics* 26/1&2 (Spring & Fall 1999).

"Normativity," in R. Shafer-Landau (ed.), *Oxford Studies in Metaethics*, vol. 1. Oxford: Oxford University Press, 2006.

"Overpopulation and the Quality of Life," in P. Singer (ed.), *Applied Ethics*. Oxford: Oxford University Press, 1986.

Reasons and Persons [*RP*]. Oxford: Oxford University Press, 1984.

"What We Could Rationally Will," *The Tanner Lectures on Human Values*. Salt Lake City: University of Utah Press, 2004, pp. 285–369.

"Why Anything? Why This?" *The London Review of Books*, January 22 and February 5, 1998.

Other works by Parfit

"Personal identity," *The Philosophical Review* 80/1 (1971): 3–27.

"Rationality and Reasons," in Dan Egonsson et al. (ed.), *Exploring Practical Philosophy*. Aldershot: Ashgate, 2001.

"Reasons and Motivation," *Proceedings of the Aristotelian Society*, Supplementary Volume, 1997.

"The Unimportance of Identity," in H. Harris (ed.), *Identity*. Oxford: Oxford University Press, 1995.

McDOWELL

MARIE McGINN

1 Introduction

John McDowell's (1942–) contribution to philosophy includes work on Greek philosophy, philosophy of language, philosophy of mind, epistemology, metaphysics, and ethics. The publication of *Mind and World*, in 1994, made him one of the most widely read and critically discussed contemporary philosophers. The book brought together ideas that McDowell had been developing over the previous two decades, and although he has developed these further since the book's publication, it may still be regarded as providing an account of the principal themes of his philosophical reflections. Looked at in one way, the scope of these reflections is exceptionally ambitious: McDowell sets out to diagnose and overcome the philosophical tradition that has emerged in the context of the rise of modern science. This philosophical tradition, which I will call the post-Cartesian tradition, is characterized, on the one hand, by its commitment to a certain form of naturalism, one which identifies the natural world with what can be treated within the conceptual resources of the natural sciences, and, on the other, by its preoccupation with a characteristic set of philosophical problems. These problems include the mind–body problem, skepticism about the external world, skepticism about other minds, and the problem of freedom and determinism. All these problems can be seen as aspects of the fundamental problem that defines the post-Cartesian tradition: to understand how conscious, sapient, rational, active subjects fit into nature, as it is conceived within this tradition.

The approach that post-Cartesian thought has taken to the problems that in part define it is essentially constructive. The fundamental problem – understanding how conscious, rational agents fit into nature – is seen to call for an explanation: we need to explain how sentience, sapience, rationality, and agency are possible in a world that is conceived as physical in nature. McDowell's work is ambitious to the extent that it sets out to criticize the presuppositions on which this naturalistic, constructive tradition in philosophy rests. His aim is to reinvigorate an alternative philosophical approach, broadly Aristotelian in nature, in which the "How possible?" questions that characterize post-Cartesian philosophy no longer present themselves as calling for an answer. McDowell is, in a sense, out to change our philosophical paradigm. In another sense, however, his aims might be described as philosophically modest. For it is fundamental to his approach to the problems of the philosophical tradition he rejects that he does not provide any solution to the problems that have characterized it. He does not, in other words, answer the "How possible?" questions which define that tradition. His aim is to exorcise, rather than answer, them. Exorcism is not a way of answering the questions and nor, he believes, is it a way of proving that they make no sense, or that they cannot be answered. Exorcism is achieved by, on the one hand, working to reveal the presuppositions that form the framework for the tradition and exploring the source of their power over us, and, on the other, working to loosen the grip that these presuppositions have on our thought and provide an alternative way of thinking, one on which the "How possible?" questions no longer seem urgent.

2 Aristotelianism vs. post-Cartesianism

At the heart of McDowell's project is an attempt to articulate an alternative, Aristotelian version of naturalism, which opens up ways of understanding rational agents and their relation to the world that simply don't present themselves as possibilities within the post-Cartesian tradition. McDowell sets out to present an alternative framework within which to think about the relation between mind and world, and within which we can achieve a form of philosophical understanding that offers relief from the problems and para-doxes that characterize post-Cartesian philosophy. The traditional philosoph-ical problem that principally bears on the topics discussed in *Mind and World* is skepticism about the external world. McDowell's aim is to provide an understanding of the relation between mind and world, made available by the framework of an Aristotelian version of naturalism, on which it no longer seems to us that we have to respond to the skeptic's doubt in order to under-stand how knowledge of the world is possible. The apparent urgency of the skeptical problem will be shown to have its source in the very preconceptions to which McDowell is providing an alternative. With that alternative in place, our ability to know about the world, McDowell believes, will no longer seem under skeptical threat.

Although it is one of the central aims of *Mind and World* to deliver a philo-sophical understanding within which skeptical doubts no longer appear pressing, McDowell does not begin by focusing on epistemological questions directly. He believes that the epistemological anxieties that find their expression in skeptical doubt – i.e. in the idea that we cannot explain how knowledge of the world is possible – are grounded in a deeper problem: the perceived threat that our way of thinking leaves minds out of touch with the world. The deeper problem, McDowell believes, is the problem of understanding how our thoughts can be about a mind-independent world. How are we to make sense of our thoughts having a content such that their truth or falsity depends upon how things are in a mind-independent world? How the mind makes contact with the objective world is not in the first instance, McDowell argues, a question about how we can *know* about the world, but of how we can *think* about it: how does thought "catch reality in its net"?

McDowell argues that reflection on this question leads us to accept a "minimal form of empiricism." The idea that our thoughts bear on reality is essentially the idea that whether our thoughts are true or false depends on something that is independent of thought. It is the idea that our thoughts are *answerable* to the world, to something outside thought. There must, there-fore, be something outside thought that governs whether accepting a thought as true is correct or incorrect; our thought must actually be guided by some-thing that is independent of it. It follows that there must be some tribunal that is independent of our system of beliefs against which we can judge our beliefs for correctness or incorrectness. This notion of an external constraint on judgment is, McDowell argues, essential to the very idea that our thoughts are about an objective, mind-independent world. Given that the only plaus-ible candidate for the role of external constraint on our system of beliefs is experience, this leads to a minimal form of empiricism: our beliefs must be *rationally responsive* to what is given in experience. Experience must be the final test of whether a belief ought to be accepted as true. This, McDowell argues, is the only intelligible picture of what it could be for beliefs to be answerable to something outside the system of beliefs. He believes that the philosophical tradition that he is out to reject is unable to achieve this minimal form of empiricism; that is to say, it is unable to provide any satisfactory understanding of how experience can act as a rational constraint on belief. This tradition is faced with an antinomy: on the one hand, it seems that experience *must* function as a tribunal if thought is to bear on reality (minimal empiricism); on the other, with the presuppositions of the tradition in place, we cannot see *how* experience can function as a tribunal.

3 Normativity and Nature

McDowell presents the case for the antinomy as follows. First of all, he points out that the concept of belief is essentially a *normative* one – that is to say, it has its place within a system of concepts that is governed by the constitutive principle of rationality. To describe an episode in a subject's history as one of expressing, say, the belief that world temperatures are rising is thereby to commit oneself to holding that the subject is aiming to express what is true, that McDowell bases his assertion on evidence that counts in favor of the belief he has expressed, that he holds himself responsible for addressing any counter-evidence that might be produced, and so on. McDowell uses an expression of Wilfrid Sellars to capture this idea: describing an episode as an instance of someone's expressing a belief is to place that episode "within the logical space of reasons." The intelligibility that we thereby confer on the episode is one that arises from seeing it as an episode in the life of a rational agent. The concept of experience, as it is conceived within the set of presuppositions McDowell is concerned with, does not belong in the same conceptual category as the concept of belief. Experience is conceived as sensory impressions that are the result of the causal impact of the world on our sensory surfaces. To describe a subject as enjoying a particular experience is to place that episode in the subject's history, not within the logical space of reasons, but within the logical space of nature. The intelligibility that is appropriate to a sensory episode is one that places it within the space of natural law, that is to say, it is intelligible insofar as it can be described and understood naturalistically, as the outcome of natural processes whose operation is completely independent of rational capacities.

McDowell's fundamental idea is that what is thus conceived as a mere happening in the space of nature, or in the realm of law, cannot stand in normative relations to our system of beliefs. Rational – that is to say, evidential and logical – relations hold between states whose contents are expressed in the form of a proposition. Rational relations between states are relations that hold in virtue of the relations between the propositions that describe the content of the relevant states. States that are understood as lacking any propositional content, i.e. that are conceived as brute occurrences that are the outcome of a causal impact of the world on a sensory surface, cannot stand in a rational relation to anything. Such states cannot, therefore, serve as a rational constraint on beliefs. The traditional conception of experience as a non-conceptual episode whose occurrence is intelligible from within the logical space of nature puts experience out of play to the rational structures within which the process of justifying beliefs essentially occurs. It is, McDowell argues, only insofar as we have an episode whose content places it in normative relations to other events and episodes that we are operating within the space of reasons, and thus within the space in which the concepts of justification, answerability, warrant, and so on have their place. If we conceive of experience as a brute Given, devoid of conceptual or propositional content, then we cannot understand how it plays a rationally constraining role on our system of beliefs. That is to say, we cannot achieve the minimal form of empiricism that has been revealed as a requirement on the intelligibility of the concept of empirical judgment.

To attempt to make experience, conceived as the causal impact of the world on our sensory surfaces, play the role of tribunal is to fall into the Myth of the Given. It is to try to hold on to the unintelligible idea that there is something that lies entirely outside the conceptual sphere (brute impressions) that can stand in the relation of rational warrant to something that lies within it (a belief or a judgment). The idea, McDowell argues, is incoherent. There is simply no making sense of the idea that a state that lacks a conceptual content – i.e. whose content is not describable by means of a that-clause – could stand in the rational relation of warranting or justifying a belief. In his paper "A Coherence Theory of Truth and Knowledge," Donald Davidson argues against the Myth of the Given.[1] He agrees with McDowell that the idea of evidential relations between states that do not both have propositional contents is unintelligible. However, Davidson's response to this is not to abandon the conception of experience as brute impressions, but to deny that experience plays any epistemic role. An experience, Davidson claims, may cause someone to acquire a belief, but it cannot justify them in doing so. When it comes to the process of justification, the only thing that can justify a belief is another belief. According to McDowell, the position Davidson ends up with is a form of coherentism, in which our thought has altogether lost touch with the world. McDowell has argued that it is only insofar as we can make sense of the idea that our beliefs are answerable to, or governed by, what is given in experience that we can make sense of our beliefs having an empirical content at all. Abandoning minimal empiricism is, in McDowell's view, not an option. Thus, we are faced with two unsatisfactory alternatives: the Myth of the Given or coherentism.

4 Experience as Conceptually Articulated

McDowell has argued that in order for acts of judgment to have an empirical content at all, they must ultimately be rationally responsive to what is given in experience. If our system of beliefs is conceived as a self-contained system of rational linkages, with at most causal connections to what lies outside, it could not constitute a system of beliefs. It is only insofar as a subject forms beliefs as a matter of a rational response to what is given in experience that he can be understood as engaging in acts of judging what is the case. The capacity for active thought thus essentially involves a capacity to make observational judgments based on experience. For an episode in a human being's life to constitute an observational judgment, it has to be the case that the subject who makes the judgment understands it as a rational response to what he observes to be the case. It is, McDowell argues, therefore essential that we can see human experience as directly disclosing what is the case: facts, bits of the world. Only then can we see an observational judgment that things are thus and so as a judgment that is made in the light of the subject's observing that things are thus and so.

McDowell's aim is to articulate a conception of experience on which it has *both* the passivity and sensory immediacy that is held to characterize sense impressions *and* the conceptual structure that is held to characterize judgments and beliefs. The content of my visual experience is, for example, that the cup is empty. In visual experience, McDowell holds, this objective circumstance – that the cup is empty – is made manifest. On this conception, experience is not conceived as a mere sensory episode, a non-conceptual given, occurring in the space of nature, but as a form of "openness to the world." Conceived in this way, the idea of experience as a normative constraint on belief – as something to which belief is rationally answerable – is unproblematic: a subject is in a position to constitute his experience of the fact that the cup is empty as a reason to judge that the cup is empty. If experience is understood as making manifest to perceptual consciousness that a fact obtains, then we can make sense of an observational judgment, and thus of a system of empirical beliefs. Minimal empiricism is secured and we achieve a satisfactory understanding of how thought bears on reality. McDowell's way out of the antinomy described in the previous section is to recommend a conception of experience on which, in the case of creatures with the relevant conceptual capacities, it is itself conceptually articulated, so that in experience a subject understands himself to be aware of states of affairs that are described by means of true propositions. The content of experience is something that is expressed by means of a proposition that represents an objective state of affairs, i.e. a state of affairs that the subject of experience understands to obtain independently of his experience of it.

The conception of experience that McDowell recommends as the only way out of the antinomy is tied up with a particular conception of the world: the world is the totality of facts, where the notion of a fact is internally or essentially connected with the idea of a true proposition. His attack on the idea of experience as a non-conceptualized Given is essentially an attack on the very idea of something outside the conceptual sphere that constitutes objective reality. Part of the source of the power that this problematic conception of experience has over us lies in the appeal of the idea that how things are objectively, in themselves, is independent of how they strike the occupant of this or that particular point of view. Insofar as the system of concepts in terms of which we conceptualize the world is clearly a product of our distinctively human history and perspective, McDowell's claim that the concept of the objective world is intelligible only insofar as it is conceived or described from within our conceptual system may appear unacceptably idealist. The world in itself, we feel, is surely something that is there independently of, and prior to, human thought and experience. Experience must, therefore, be seen as the result of the mere causal impact of this brutally independent world on our senses; our conceptual scheme can then get to work on ordering or structuring this non-conceptualized given. It might seem that it is only in this way that we do justice to the idea that objective reality is independent of us and our ways of conceiving matters.

McDowell's resistance to this sort of picture is at one with his resistance to the Myth of the Given. If we place the world and experience outside the space of concepts, then we cannot make intelligible how experience warrants or rationally constrains experiential beliefs. Experience conceived as non-conceptual content, as the brute impact of a world that lies outside or is independent of our conceptual perspective, must disappear completely if we are to achieve the minimal form of empiricism that McDowell argues is obligatory. There must, McDowell argues, be no stage at which our concepts get to work on something that is conceived as absolutely independent or just there. The content of experience is to be conceived as an open-ended multiplicity of judgable contents. And insofar as a judgable content is precisely something that can be the case – a fact – experience is conceived as bringing the world – the totality of facts – into view for a subject. For McDowell, the idea of the objective world is intelligible only as what is revealed to be the case from the point of view of someone who has a perspective on it. There is no other conception of the world that is either intelligible itself, or which makes it intelligible how we can have such a conception – i.e. think about the world – at all.

5 What Are Concepts?

Why, on McDowell's view, does the acquisition of a conceptual scheme amount to the acquisition of a perspective on the world? Why, in virtue of its being within the conceptual sphere, does experience constitute a form of openness to the world? The passivity of experience, the fact that we have no control over what is given in experience, plays a role here. It is our passivity in relation to experience that in part gives content to the idea that our beliefs are constrained by something outside the sphere in which the rational agent exercises active control. However, McDowell stresses that passivity alone is not the whole story: "The general context [of the distinctive passivity of experience] matters for the availability of the image [of experience as openness to the world]" (*MW* 29). This "general context" is provided by the nature of our conceptual scheme, in particular, by the idea that it essentially amounts to a world-view. But why, we might now ask, does anything that could be recognized as a system of concepts constitute a view of the world? To answer this question, we need to get a clearer idea of how McDowell understands the nature of concepts, and of what he takes to be involved in the existence of a conceptual scheme.

First of all, McDowell is committed to the idea that a concept is essentially something that is applicable to more than one instance. A concept is essentially something that brings together items as *the same*. This is known as the Generality Constraint: concepts are essentially applicable in a succession of judgments which serve to bring different instances under the same concept. The idea of a concept is thus internally connected with the idea of doing something correctly or incorrectly on a succession of occasions; it involves the idea of using a sign in accordance with a rule, correctly or incorrectly. The influence of the later Wittgenstein on McDowell's thought comes in the shape of a commitment to the idea that the existence of a rule with which the use of an expression can be in accord, or fail to be in accord, depends essentially upon the existence of a practice of using it. We can make the concept of the correct or incorrect application of an expression intelligible, McDowell holds, only against the background of an established practice of employing it, a customary use of it. It is very important to McDowell's interpretation of Wittgenstein's thought here that the notions in terms of which we try to shed light on the notion of a rule for the use of an expression are themselves normative. Thus, the practice against the background of which a particular use of an expression can count as correct or incorrect is one that is essentially characterized in normative terms. We cannot characterize either the practice, or the behavior of someone who participates in it, in a way that does not employ normative notions such as rule, custom, institution, and so on. The practices we're concerned with are essentially practices in which the participants understand themselves as following rules, as complying with a customary way of employing a word, as using linguistic techniques that are in their nature normative.

Implicit in this entire conception is the idea that going by a rule, or being master of a concept, is essentially public: it is the existence of an established way of *acting*, i.e. of employing expressions in acts of judgment, which grounds the notion of a rule. Thus, the concept expressed by the word "red," say, is fixed by a custom – a public practice – of employing the word, into which I must be initiated, if I am to come to understand it. The question of whether the concept applies in a particular case must be an objective question that can be determined by anyone who is a master of the relevant linguistic technique. Thus, the color concepts are essentially tied up with the idea of a visible object whose color is a matter for objective determination. In the case of color concepts, the criteria for determining the color of a visible object are linked with the idea of standard conditions of observation, in particular with the idea of a standard observer who views the object in standard illumination conditions. It is essential to what makes it intelligible that the words of our language express concepts, or have a meaning, at all, that our concept of color is integrated into a conception of the world as comprising physical objects whose visible surfaces are, in suitable circumstances, objectively (i.e. correctly or incorrectly) characterizable as being of a particular color. In a secondary employment of them, we can apply color concepts to, for example, after-images or to the sensations caused by pressure to the eye, but, according to McDowell, their primary use is essentially as an element in a conceptual scheme that amounts to a view of the world, insofar as the state of affairs it is used to describe is one that a speaker understands to obtain objectively, independently of his act of judgment. The idea of an object's appearing to have a color, e.g. of its looking red, is entirely parasitic on the shared practice of employing color concepts in objective judgments of color.

6 A Relaxation of the Concept of Nature

On the conception McDowell recommends, what a subject takes in in experience is that something is the case; the content of experience is something that is expressed by means of a proposition that essentially represents an objective state of affairs. A subject who enjoys experience in this sense understands himself to be aware, in experience, of a state of affairs that exists independently of his experience of it. However, McDowell recognizes that there are serious obstacles to our recognizing this conception of experience as one that is available to us in philosophy. In the previous sections, we looked at the way in which a commitment to a robust form of realism might make McDowell's conception of experience as openness to the world appear unacceptably idealist, and the response that he makes to this. McDowell suggests that the appeal of what he sees as a deeply problematic form of realism is an expression of a form of dualism that constitutes one of the framework presuppositions of post-Cartesian thought: the dualism of reason and nature. One of the central aims of McDowell's work is to criticize the conception of nature that is one half of this dualism and to recommend, in its place, a conception of the natural world within which the concept of reason and the concept of nature are no longer inimical to one another. McDowell claims that once this "more relaxed" conception of nature is in place, we will have made room for the idea of a natural perceptual capacity that is shaped by the characteristically rational structure of an acquired system of concepts.

As we saw at the beginning, McDowell holds that the sort of understanding that is appropriate to the performances of a rational agent is logically distinct from the sort of understanding that is appropriate in the natural sciences. The contrast was expressed in terms of a form of understanding that makes an occurrence intelligible by placing it in the logical space of reasons and a form of understanding that makes an occurrence intelligible by placing it in the logical space of nature. McDowell holds that these are two different and logically distinct ways of making an event intelligible: by seeing it as the performance of a rational agent who is rationally in control of his life, as against seeing it as a natural phenomenon whose occurrence is explicable in terms of a natural law. McDowell suggests that this clear contrast between two ways of making an event intelligible has its origins in the development of modern science. The clear contrast between the two forms of intelligibility, or logical spaces, was not available before modern times. The sharp distinction between nature and reason had not previously been made, and the tension between the idea of normative capacities and the idea of natural powers was, consequently, not felt.

To accept that there are two logically distinct ways of making things intelligible is to accept that the concepts that are employed when we place something in the space of reasons – judgment, belief, intention, etc. – cannot be captured in terms of the concepts that are employed when we place something in the space of nature. This is what McDowell means by the idea that reason is *sui generis*: concepts that are governed by the constitutive ideal of rationality constitute an autonomous conceptual region that cannot be explicated or understood in terms of concepts that lie outside it. This is not, however, equivalent to accepting a dualism of reason and nature. The dualism of reason and nature depends upon our also accepting the further assumption that nature is equivalent to the subject-matter of the natural sciences, i.e. of what is intelligible within the realm of law. Once we accept this assumption, then, insofar as experience is a natural capacity, it cannot be conceived in a way that makes it intelligible how it can act as a rational constraint on belief. It is, therefore, the dualism of reason and nature, and the conception of nature that it presupposes, that is the real source of our inability to see the conception of experience, which McDowell recommends, as a possibility.

McDowell recognizes that there are two ways to respond to this difficulty. One is to deny that the logical space of reasons constitutes an autonomous conceptual domain. This would be to embrace some form of naturalism, with the post-Cartesian conception of nature still in place. This is not, however, a route that has any appeal for McDowell, who accepts that the form of intelligibility that places occurrences in the logical space of reasons is, in the required sense, *sui generis*. His aim is to arrive at an alternative conception of nature, one that permits us to feel at ease with the idea that conceptual or rational capacities are *sui generis*, not explicable in terms of the conceptual resources of the natural sciences, and the idea that they are nevertheless understandable as the natural capacities of a certain sort of animal. Once this move has been made, McDowell believes, there is no longer any difficulty in accepting a conception of human perception as a capacity in which conceptual abilities are already at work, and thus as a form of openness to the world.

It is at this point that McDowell appeals to Aristotle's ethics as a philosophical prototype for the form of naturalism that he wants to recommend. McDowell's conception of the relation between mind and world may be seen as a generalized form of Aristotle's conception of the relation between the ethical agent and ethical reality. Thus, the kind of ethical realism that McDowell finds in Aristotle's ethics mirrors the form of realism that constitutes McDowell's relaxed form of naturalism, which allows us to conceive of experience as a form of openness to the world.

7 Aristotelian Realism

For McDowell, this form of Aristotelian realism goes along, as we've already seen, with a suspicion of the idea that we have a grip on the notion of what constitutes a fact that is independent of the conceptual resources that we understand to be available for the expression of true propositions. McDowell holds that we have no vantage point from which we can ask the question what constitutes a fact that is external to the perspective from which we determine what is true and what is false. This is a position that, on McDowell's understanding, Aristotle also occupies. Aristotle un-self-consciously inhabits our human point of view and the ethical outlook that it gives us. From within that perspective, he provides a naturalistic account of how it comes about that a human being comes to have that outlook, or to have his eyes opened to ethical facts. Aristotle thinks of this as a form of cognitive accomplishment, which is acquired through a process of habituation and training that develops ways of seeing and responding to the world. These ways of seeing and responding constitute what Aristotle calls *second nature*. McDowell's idea is that we can see this as a model for the acquisition of conceptual capacities more generally: it is through a certain sort of training in practices, in which the acquisition of ways of seeing and responding to states of affairs that are understood to obtain independently of acts of judgment is fundamental, that a mature human being comes to have a perceptual perspective on the world.

McDowell wants us to accept Aristotle's more relaxed attitude toward what constitutes the world and to use Aristotle's account of ethical education as a model for understanding the transition that a human being makes, from a position in which he has no access to the relevant facts to a position in which his eyes have been opened to them. In order to achieve this, McDowell has had to undertake work that Aristotle didn't have to: he has had to articulate a conception of experience as openness to the world that was no longer visible as a possible position within the philosophical tradition that is defined by a scientistic conception of nature. In carrying out this task he draws not on Aristotle, but on Kant. He has used Kant's idea that intuitions without concepts are blind and concepts without intuitions are empty to remotivate a form of Aristotelian realism, on which facts are made manifest in experience and reality is objective in this sense: it is conceived as something that is the way it is independently of any particular agent's either experiencing or judging it to be that way. This is the kind of objectivity that is connected with the idea of our being right or wrong about how things are, and with our being under a standing obligation to insure that our beliefs and actions are appropriately responsive to how things are. There is no sense, however, that what is objective, on the Aristotelian understanding of this notion, is something that can be grasped or characterized, or that is understandable, independently of the human point of view from which it is revealed as an objective state of affairs, as a bit of the independent world. What counts as a fact, and thus as part of the fabric of the world, is, for McDowell, whatever counts as a topic for correct or incorrect judgment. It is not required that the subject-matter of the correct judgment should be graspable from outside the conceptual perspective from which the judgment is made. He claims that this is not to make reality dependent on our thinking of it; it is simply to acknowledge that objective facts are thinkable and can be taken in in experience by a creature with the requisite conceptual capacities.

8   Conclusion

The project of *Mind and World* is to present a framework for philosophical reflection on which the central questions of traditional philosophy, including the obsession with the problem of skepticism about the external world, become obsolete. McDowell claims to have provided an understanding of the relation between mind and world on which the traditional skeptical argument may be properly ignored. This claim is clearly much more modest than a claim to have answered skepticism outright; that would require him to prove, from a starting point that the skeptic himself accepts, that there is an external world and that we have knowledge of it. McDowell does not only not claim to answer the skeptic in this sense; he also holds that no answer of this sort is possible. However, he does not believe that, in conceding this, the response that he does make is rendered question-begging or philosophically unsatisfactory. For his claim is that the skeptic's ability to worry and confound us depends upon our operating within the philosophical framework he rejects. The principal motivation for the alternative framework that McDowell provides is that it makes intelligible our ordinary understanding of ourselves as having thoughts that bear on reality. The claim is that, in making sense of empirical thought, and by accepting the conception of nature and of experience that McDowell recommends, we have, at the same time, put ourselves in a position to ignore the skeptical worries of the post-Cartesian tradition.

McDowell argues that the traditional problem of skepticism about the external world emerges in the context of the tradition's tendency to interiorize the mental: to see the mind as an inner realm whose layout is fully transparent to the subject whose mind it is. McDowell argues that the disastrous step that leads to the fatal interiorization of the space of reasons is one that is taken in response to the Argument from Illusion. If I see that something is so – that there is a hand in front of me, say – then this would normally be understood to give me a reason to judge that this is a hand. But, the reflection runs, it is surely the case that when I judge that this is a hand, I'm taking it that this is a hand on the basis of its looking to me as if there is a hand in front of me. And, clearly, things can look to be the case when they are not. It can look to me that there is a hand in front of me in a dream or in a hallucination. If matters in the subjective realm are fully transparent to the subject, then it seems that what McDowell calls "the first standing in the space of reasons" must be merely that it looks to me as if there is a hand in front of me, i.e. something that falls short of my taking in the fact that there is a hand in front of me. Making the judgment that there is a hand in front of me must now be conceived as an inference that I make on the basis of its looking to me that this is so. However, it is clear that this inference is warranted only on the assumption that my current experience is a reliable guide to how things stand in reality. And now the skeptical hypotheses begin to bite, for it seems that it is only if I am in a position to rule them out that I am warranted in making any judgment about what is the case on the basis of my experience. McDowell argues that once the interiorizing move in response to the Argument from Illusion is made, there is simply no way to make our capacity to know about the world intelligible.

One of the central aspects of McDowell's alternative framework is that mindedness is conceived in terms of capacities that are essentially understood as world-involving. Thus, experience is conceived as the capacity to take in facts, to see, for example, that this there is a hand in front of me. The question is, how is McDowell to retain this conception of experience in the face of the Argument from Illusion? In the deceptive case – e.g. a case where I am simply dreaming of a hand – it merely appears to me that I am seeing a hand in front of me; in this case my experience is a matter of a mere appearance. McDowell argues that accepting this account of the deceptive case gives us no reason to accept that a description of the non-deceptive case is limited in the same way. It is true that in the non-deceptive case that it appears to me that I am seeing a hand in front of me, but in this case the appearance is a matter of the fact that there is a hand in front of me making itself manifest, and, McDowell argues, it can correctly be described as a case of my seeing that there is a hand in front of me. Thus, cases of its appearing to me that there is a hand in front of me can be constituted by two quite different kinds of mental state: in one case it is a kind of state in which it merely seems to me that I'm seeing a hand (a matter of mere appearance) and in the other it is a kind of state in which I take in in experience the fact that there is a hand in front of me. In the latter case, the experience does not fall short of the fact. There is, as McDowell puts it, no highest common factor that constitutes the content of both the deceptive and the non-deceptive case.

McDowell sees what is known as "disjunctivism" as showing us how to detach the correct intuition, that how things are subjectively cannot depend on how matters stand in a realm blankly external to the subjective, from the mistaken requirement that the subject be able to give a non-question-begging demonstration that this is how things are subjectively. How things are subjectively depends on whether one is perceiving that things are thus and so, or merely dreaming that things are thus and so. That is not a matter of how things are in a blankly external realm, but it does not follow from this that the subject must be in a position to give a non-question-begging demonstration that he is seeing a hand and not dreaming that he is seeing a hand. McDowell argues that, once we accept this, then we are in a position to recognize that when I am in a state of seeing that there is a hand in front of me, this is in itself a satisfactory standing in the space of reasons, one that justifies the judgment that there is a hand in front of me, without any need for support from general beliefs about how one is placed in the world. My seeing that there is a hand in front of me is an encounter with the world that, other things being equal, warrants my judgment that this is a hand. Of course we are fallible; that, as McDowell says, is something that we have to learn to live with. If there is a special reason to think that I might be deluded or deceived, I am under an obligation, as a responsible epistemic agent, to carry out appropriate checks. However, when there is no special reason for doubt, in those cases in which experience is a matter of taking in the facts as they stand, experience provides reasons for judgment; it constitutes a direct mode of cognitive contact with the world that provides a satisfactory grounding for belief. This picture, McDowell claims, enables us to make the idea of ourselves as subjects of knowledge intelligible, and to escape from the idea that it is only by answering the skeptic's doubts that we can understand how knowledge of the world is possible.

McDowell argues further that it is only if we accept this conception of reason as world-involving, so that the shape of the space of reasons is just the shape of the world as we encounter it in experience, that we can properly think of it as having a shape, or as consisting of contentful states, rationally linked to one another, at all. If we don't conceive of reason as a world-involving capacity, then the whole idea of content – and thus of appearances – is under threat. Reality is, he has argued, essentially prior in the order of understanding to appearances: we cannot take the interiorizing step that provides the essential framework for skepticism without making the very notion of reason and content unintelligible. Thus, we have a motivated philosophical framework within which our sense that we ought always to remove skeptical doubts before being able to make a warranted judgment about the material world subsides. It is not that McDowell has shown that we can answer the skeptic's challenge, but that we have a well-motivated philosophical framework within which the sense that it is required that we should answer it if our ability to know about the world is to be intelligible has disappeared.

Note

1   Repr. in Donald Davidson, *Subjective, Intersubjective, Objective*. Oxford: Oxford University Press, 2001, pp. 137–53.

Reference

Mind and World [*MW*]. Cambridge, MA: Harvard University Press, 1994.

A selection of other works by McDowell

Book symposium on *Mind and World*, in *Philosophy and Phenomenological Research* (1998).
Meaning, Knowledge and Reality. Cambridge, MA: Harvard University Press, 1998.
Mind, Value and Reality. Cambridge, MA: Harvard University Press, 1998.

12 SINGER

LORI GRUEN

"Philosophers have only interpreted the world, the point is to change it" (Marx)

Peter Singer may very well be the most influential living philosopher, perhaps of any philosopher in recent history. He certainly is the most controversial. Debate tends to follow him around the globe, and that is just what he and his work seek to provoke – rational reassessment of many of the beliefs we hold dear. Encouraging the reconsideration of popular moral attitudes is a task philosophers have always taken on, often generating some sort of stir. While the turbulence he causes is not quite as extreme as that which ultimately led to Socrates' imprisonment and death, Singer has been subject to more than just heated disagreements. On occasion, protests have halted debate and silenced discussion; conferences he was to speak at have been cancelled in Austria and Germany; and he has even been physically assaulted ("On Being Silenced in Germany," 1991). When it was announced that he was to be appointed Ira W. DeCamp Professor of Bioethics at Princeton University, the commotion was almost uncontainable. Major US newspapers ran stories describing him as the "most dangerous man on the planet," he was dubbed "professor death," and many compared him to a

Nazi.[1] Steve Forbes, one-time presidential candidate and a member of the Princeton board of trustees, urged the school's president to rescind the appointment. Despite the outcry, Singer did move from Monash University, Melbourne to take up his new position in New Jersey, where his mail was scanned for explosives and other dangerous substances and he was accompanied by bodyguards on the Ivy League campus, which was littered with protestors. Though things have quietened down since his arrival in the United States in 1999, it is not because people have come to accept his views.

Singer was born in 1946 in Melbourne, Australia, and still makes Melbourne home for half of each year. He was educated at Melbourne University, where he studied law, history, and philosophy. After he earned his Master's degree in 1969, he went to Oxford where his thesis work with R. M. Hare became his first book, *Democracy and Disobedience* (1973). It was also while at Oxford that Singer began to think critically about the scope of our moral obligations and to challenge traditional notions of what matters ethically and why.

Much of the furor over Singer's philosophy stems from his criticism of sanctity-of-life views. Singer argues that not only are these views ethically problematic, but that those who claim to hold all human life as sacred do not do so consistently. He views some of those who espouse the sanctity of human life as "hypocrites" – they appeal to the view when it suits their ends and ignore it when it doesn't (see *The President of Good and Order*). He has also raised more than a few eyebrows because of his views about equality. For he argues that equal interests should be considered equally, whether the being that has the interests is a black man or a white woman, lives near or far away, is a teenage boy or an aging aardvark. If an individual is suffering, no matter their location or their species, their suffering must be taken into account. His arguments that the affluent are morally obligated to give to those living in poverty have led some to question whether one can lead a meaningful life and still be ethical. Singer believes living up to our ethical obligations to attend to the suffering of others is precisely what provides meaning in our lives. Those who work to make the world a better place will know they have done something beyond themselves, and it is by doing something beyond oneself that real satisfaction with one's life can be found (see *How Are We to Live?*).

Singer's book *Animal Liberation* (1975) jump-started the modern animal rights movement, but his claim that animals deserve to be ethically considered, though convincing to thousands, has led some to dismiss him as having gone too far. Ironically, Singer's views have even caused controversies within the very movement he helped to start. For example, in conversation with an Oxford researcher who creates Parkinson-like symptoms in monkeys to study movement disorders, Singer suggested that some of that work might be justified.[2] Many in the animal rights movement were shocked; others were disgusted. One radical website exclaimed: "The man talks rubbish and the sooner the notion that he has any place in the modern animal rights movement is dispelled the better."[3] Others were surprised by the outrage, rightly acknowledging that Singer was never actually a proponent of animal rights because he is, after all, a utilitarian.

Before looking in more depth at Singer's views on life, death, and suffering, which are the source of such controversy, it is important to understand the utilitarian ethical theory that informs his conclusions about the scope of our moral obligations and the life and death decisions we are often forced to make.

1   Utilitarianism

Utilitarianism, as it was initially formulated by philosopher and social reformer Jeremy Bentham (1748–1832), holds that when considering what to do, one ought to take the action that will bring about the greatest happiness over suffering for all affected, given the options available. This classical utilitarian principle, though simply stated, has a number of implications that are worth spelling out. First, utilitarianism is consequentialist: the rightness or wrongness of an action is determined solely by the consequences that action produces. The right action (or rule, or policy) is that which leads to the best consequences. That the consequences should be the best, or greatest, means that the theory is maximizing. A utilitarian is committed to trying to bring about the best consequences she can given the options that are open to her. It is not enough to bring about some good outcomes if, by doing more, even better outcomes follow. The theory is also an aggregative theory – that is, the right action will be determined by adding up all the good consequences that result from the action (and then subtracting any of the bad consequences from that sum). The theory is also impartial – as another utilitarian William Godwin (1756–1836) noted, there is nothing special about the pronouns "me" and "mine." Classical utilitarians believe that everybody who is affected by an action should have that effect included in the utilitarian calculation of the rightness of the action. As Bentham put it: "Each to count for one, none for more than one."

To illustrate how a utilitarian would reason about the right action, consider the following sort of case. You are a firefighter who is standing in front of a burning building. You see that there are two people still inside on different parts of the third floor and, given the nature of the blaze, it seems clear that only one of them can be saved. On the right side of the building is the fire chief's daughter, who was unable to escape from her apartment as the fire intensified; on the left side is a visiting diplomat who is in town to report on the success of delicate negotiations with the leadership of a country that has previously been isolated from the rest of the world and whose rulers are known for serious human rights violations and escalating, and potentially violent, xenophobia. If you save your boss's daughter, you will clearly be a hero at the station house and may even get promoted. On the few occasions when you met her, you found her compassionate and quite endearing and leaving her to die in the fire will have a significantly negative effect on your mental health, at least in the short term. If you save the diplomat, you will be providing him with the opportunity to continue to make progress with this troubled nation and so you may help prevent further torture and death and perhaps too the outbreak of a dangerous war. Who should you save?

According to the classical utilitarian perspective, you should save the diplomat. By saving him, you will be creating better consequences and thus more good than you would by saving the chief's daughter. And even though it will be personally difficult for you, that shouldn't matter from an ethical point of view. Saving the diplomat, and thus preventing further human rights violations and war, is likely to lead to greater happiness and less pain for more people – these are better consequences than the alternatives.

Of course, actual ethical problems faced by real people in the world rather than hypothetical characters in a book chapter are rarely as simple as this example. There is usually much more to think about and more issues that need to be considered. Utilitarians are not oblivious to the difficulties associated with translating theory into practice. While Bentham may have had an overly simplified view of how ethical agents would perform the utilitarian calculus (he thought a utility meter would be invented, a device like a thermometer, except that it would measure happiness) his principle seems to have the virtue of helping increase social welfare. Unlike some other ethical theories, utilitarianism is direct and practicable – do what promotes overall utility – and it is often relied on explicitly or implicitly by policy-makers, who, by necessity, must overlook some nuances, since policy is a blunt instrument.

Over the years, the theory has been revised in various ways, in part to address the perception that it oversimplifies complex ethical problems. The value theory that underlies utilitarianism has also been altered, as philosophers and some economists have argued about precisely what constitutes the "utility" that is to be promoted. Even among the early utilitarians there was debate about the value that was to be maximized through right action. Bentham was a simple hedonist. For him, happiness, no matter its source or content, was to be promoted. He was concerned with the quantity and strength of pleasures, not their quality. If one person was happier watching baseball than another person was listening to Beethoven, then if we were to be in a position where we could only allow one of these individuals to experience their pleasures, we would be right to promote the baseball watcher's happiness. Other early utilitarians, like John Stuart Mill (1806–73) and Henry Sidgwick (1838–1900), had more developed views of utility. Mill distinguished between higher and lower pleasures. He argued that when most educated people, people who had truly experienced different kinds of pleasures, had to choose between, say, the pleasure of creating something beautiful that garnered social admiration and respect, and the pleasure of sitting alone eating chocolate and watching reality television, most would pick the former over the latter. So for Mill, higher pleasures are what a utilitarian should maximize. Sidgwick, who was also a kind of hedonist, made another distinction: it isn't just higher pleasures or happiness that utilitarians should be maximizing, but what he called "desirable consciousness," a complex mental state that corresponds to the experience of having a desire that one wants to have satisfied, in fact satisfied.

Singer has been influenced by each of the classical utilitarians. Like Bentham, he believes that we must take into account the consequences of our action on all those who experience pleasure or pain as a result of that action, and that accounting requires that like interests be treated equally, no matter who has them. Sentient beings have interests, particularly interests in experiencing pleasure and avoiding pain. Since most humans and non-human animals are sentient beings capable of feeling pleasure and pain, the happiness and suffering of most humans and non-human animals should be taken into account. Rocks, plants, and eco-systems, because they are not sentient, do not have interests that can or should be taken into account. Singer often quotes Bentham's powerful text in support of his own views about the proper scope of ethical concern:

The day may come when the rest of the animal creation may acquire those rights which never could have been withholden from them but by the hand of tyranny. The French have already discovered that the blackness of the skin is no reason why a human being should be abandoned without redress to the caprice of a tormentor. It may one day come to be recognized that the number of the legs, the villosity of the skin, or the terminations of the os sacrum, are reasons equally insufficient for abandoning a sensitive being to the same fate. What else is it that should trace the insuperable line? Is it the faculty of reason, or perhaps the faculty of discourse? But a full-grown horse or dog is beyond comparison a more rational, as well as a more conversable animal, than an infant of a day, or a week, or even a month, old. But suppose they were otherwise, what would it avail? The question is not, Can they *reason*? Nor Can they *talk*? But Can they *suffer*? (Bentham cited in Singer *PE* 49–50)

While the interests of all sentient beings must be considered from an ethical point of view, Singer, like Mill and Sidgwick, wants to allow that different types of interests, and different attitudes towards those interests, matter in determining what counts as ethically justifiable action. In particular, Singer is concerned not simply with interests in avoiding pain and experiencing pleasure, but also with interests and desires that are projected into the future. When you or I have our future desires frustrated, the disappointment and mental suffering that may result is different from what it would be for a being who doesn't have a concept of the future. Without a concept of time, or of existence into the future, one cannot suffer a particular kind of harm – that of having one's future interests thwarted.

This is particularly important when considering the issue of killing, a topic that has been the source of much of the controversy that Singer generates. Many have argued that one of the most serious shortcomings of classical utilitarianism is that it cannot provide an account of the wrongness of killing. If a person is secretly and painlessly killed, then there is no negative utility generated because there is no pain to take into account, and thus there is apparently nothing ethically objectionable about the killing. It may cause friends and family members sadness or, if it wasn't kept secret and people found out that they too could be painlessly killed, then that may generate fear and anxiety. But these are "side-effects" of the killing and they may be outweighed in the utilitarian calculus if the killing in fact promoted greater good. So, there is nothing directly wrong with painless killing and this strikes most people as problematic. As Singer notes: "One has to be a tough-minded classical utilitarian to be untroubled by this oddness" (*PE* 79).

Singer, though certainly tough-minded, advocates a modification on classical utilitarianism to avoid this odd conclusion. His version of utilitarianism, "preference utilitarianism," judges actions not solely by their tendency to maximize happiness and minimize pain, but also by their role in promoting interests or satisfying preferences (and avoiding violations of interests or frustration of preferences). For a preference utilitarian, it is wrong to kill a being who has an explicit preference for continued existence and it may even be wrong to kill a being who has desires and preferences that extend into the future, even if they haven't explicitly formulated a preference to continue to live. Beings that have the ability to formulate preferences for continued existence or who are capable of seeing themselves as existing over time are considered "persons." Like many philosophers, Singer uses the term "persons" to mean beings who have reached a certain level of cognitive sophistication. Persons are self-aware and self-motivated and they recognize themselves as individuals who continue over time. Some humans are not persons in this philosophical sense (e.g. fetuses, newborn infants, and people with severe cognitive impairments), and some non-humans may be persons (e.g. great apes and dolphins). By shifting from a hedonistic theory of value to a preference satisfaction theory of value, Singer is able to accommodate what is wrong with painlessly and secretly killing a person. Non-persons have interests and preferences to avoid pain so, other things being equal, it is wrong to cause pain and suffering to them. Yet persons have desires not just to avoid pain but also to avoid death, so it is not only wrong, other things being equal, to cause them to suffer, but it is also ethically problematic to kill them.

2 Practical Ethics

With the theoretical groundwork for Singer's preference utilitarianism laid, we can now turn our attention to its specific implications for the three areas of practical ethics on which Singer has had such a tremendous impact.

Animals[4]

Given that Singer's preference utilitarianism is concerned with promoting the most preference satisfaction over frustration all things considered, it follows that his theory applies to all of those who can have preferences and that includes non-human animals. Some non-humans, such as great apes, dolphins, and elephants, are thought to have relatively complex sets of preferences, and may be considered persons. There is growing evidence that these animals have long memories, that they strategize and plan, that they engage in complex social behaviors, and that they have cultural practices which they can pass along to others, all of which support the view that they have a sense of themselves as existing over time. We may never know whether they are able explicitly to formulate a desire for continued existence, but they do have preferences that extend into the future, preferences that are frustrated when they are killed. And, in the wild, great apes, elephants, and dolphins are being killed at alarming rates. Scientists predict that orangutans, great apes that live only in Borneo and Sumatra, will be extinct in the wild by 2015 if the unsustainable destruction of Indonesian forests continues at its current pace. Gorillas in Africa are extremely endangered, as are bonobos; chimpanzee populations are also in precipitous decline. The African great apes and elephants are the victims of habitat destruction and the illegal trade in their body parts. Dolphins too are in peril as they are drowned in tuna fishing nets and are killed by other forms of human encroachment into the sea. The slaughter of these non-human persons, on Singer's view, is just as ethically objectionable as the slaughter of human persons would be when done to satisfy exotic tastes or to increase corporate profits.

While killing non-human animals in the wild, particularly those that may be considered persons, is ethically problematic from a utilitarian perspective, at least for many wild animals their lives are their own, free of human inflicted pain and frustration until that unfortunate encounter with humans. For billions of animals that are in some form of human captivity, the situation is much more troubling, whether or not they are beings with the same sort of capacities as persons. As sentient beings, their suffering matters, and, at present, the vast level of suffering of non-human animals in captivity is almost unthinkable.

An estimated 10 billion animals are killed or die on factory farms in the US each year; global estimates put the annual number of animals raised and killed in intensive agriculture at 26 billion.[5] That is a staggering number, and while some of the deaths may be painless, most animals sent to slaughter suffer as they are being transported and as they wait in line to be killed. Most are hung upside-down on a conveyer belt and only occasionally are their throats slit cleanly enough that their death is instantaneous. Even if animals used for food were to be killed painlessly, intensive rearing methods used in most of the industrialized world (and increasingly being copied in industrializing societies) cause extreme suffering. Most animals are confined indoors for their entire lives in areas that prevent them from moving around; they are denied species-typical social interactions, including being able to raise their young, who are removed at birth; and they are subjected to a variety of painful procedures – tails and ears are cut off and males are castrated without anesthesia, animals are branded with hot irons, birds have their beaks cut off with hot knives. The lives of animals used for food are full of suffering and the slaughterhouse often doesn't bring immediate relief as many linger in pain bleeding to death until they finally lose consciousness.

That huge numbers of sentient creatures suffer so greatly in order to provide cheap meals for humans is very hard to justify on utilitarian grounds. When the negative health, environmental, and other consequences of factory farming are taken into account, the calculus seems simple. Since there are tasty, nutritious, inexpensive, and far less destructive options available, purchasing and eating factory farmed meat, dairy, and eggs is ethically wrong.

The magnitude of the suffering that animals endure makes Singer's arguments about our food choices particularly pointed. Most people can forgo eating animals much of the time and directly contribute to overall happiness. Yet there are other ways in which animals suffer in captivity and, although Singer is most concerned about the terrible distress caused by factory farming, this further suffering also needs to be considered from an ethical point of view. For example, 20–40 million animals and birds are used for medical research purposes in the US each year, a number that is equivalent to "less than two days' toll in America's slaughterhouses," and there are very important ethical concerns raised about the benefit to humans as a result of this research (*WWE* v).

Singer has argued for a particular way of assessing whether or not an experiment with a non-human animal is ever justifiable. It is what I will call the "non-speciesist utilitarian test" or NSUT. According to NSUT, an experiment would be justified if and only if:

1 Of all the options open, the experiment generates more pleasure or benefit than pain or cost on balance, for all affected. (This is a straightforward utilitarian assessment.)
2 The justification for the experiment does not depend on irrelevant species prejudice or speciesism. Equal interests are to be considered equally no matter who has them.

Formulated thus, NSUT appears to allow one to make a relatively clear determination about whether an experiment might be justified.

Consider the experiment alluded to earlier that caused some animal rights proponents to become outraged with Singer. An Oxford experimenter claimed that 40,000 people suffering from Parkinson-like symptoms were helped by surgically damaging the brains of 100 otherwise healthy monkeys. The monkeys were tested for a period of time after their brains had been injured, after which they were painlessly killed and their brains studied. The monkeys lived in small, indoor cages, were not allowed to interact with each other or engage in any type of species-typical behaviors, but they were provided with food and water and the painful surgical procedures were performed while the monkeys were anaesthetized.

Does NSUT condone this research? In order to answer this question, one would first have to calculate pleasures and pains across species. Assuming that the facts are as presented, there would be a great benefit to 40,000 humans at great cost to 100 monkeys.[6] Even with such good consequences, however, there is more to determining whether the research is justifiable. One would have to know that this was the only way to achieve this greater balance of pleasure over pain and, perhaps most importantly, would also have to establish that the use of monkeys was not based on speciesist reasoning. Speciesist reasoning puts the interests and needs of one's own species ahead of the like interests of other species, based only on species membership. A speciesist favors human interests merely because they are human. This sort of reasoning is as prejudicial as racist or sexist reasoning, putting the interests of members of one's race or gender ahead of the like interests of others. Being born a certain race, or gender, or species is not an ethically relevant factor in determining how to act; what matters is the ability to suffer. In determining whether speciesist reasoning is operating, Singer suggests: "You should ask yourself: Do I think this experiment is so important that I would be able to perform it on a human being at a similar mental level if that alternative were open to me?"[7] If the experiment would not be justified if it were to be done on a human with the same mental capacities as a monkey, then a form of indefensible species prejudice is operating and the experiment would not be justified, even if it did lead to good consequences. In order to justify any experimentation, whether on humans or non-humans, both parts of NSUT must be satisfied. According to Singer, the institutional practice of animal research, much like all institutional uses of sentient beings, is largely influenced by species bias, so most experiments do not pass (2). "Experimenters show bias in favor of their own species whenever they carry out experiments on nonhuman animals for purposes that they would not think justified them in using human beings at an equal or lower level of sentience, awareness, sensitivity, and so on. If this bias were eliminated the number of experiments performed on animals would be greatly reduced" (*PE* 59). In addition, work toward developing alternative ways to achieve knowledge to promote health and well-being would increase, which in turn would increase overall good consequences with even less suffering. So while there may be some forms of experimentation on non-human non-persons that could be justified by NSUT, most experiments being performed today are not ethically permissible.

Singer's views about our treatment of non-human animals do not lead to absolutist conclusions. He is not opposed to all experimentation; some experiments on humans and non-humans may be defensible if they pass NSUT. Neither does his position demand that one always refrain from eating animals, but rather that one refrain from consuming products that promote the suffering of animals when there are options available. Though Singer is a strong advocate for vegetarianism – especially among those living in Western industrialized nations – this advocacy is not based on absolutist reasoning. His ethical position is critical of the way that non-human animals are mistreated in most societies. A non-human animal's interest in avoiding suffering must be considered in any moral deliberation, just as a human's interest in avoiding suffering must be considered. And a person's interest in continued existence must also be considered if killing is involved, whether the person is human or a chimpanzee (*Writings on an Ethical Life*). When all the relevant interests are considered, some uses of non-humans, and perhaps some uses of humans, may be ethically permissible, depending on the alternatives available and the good consequences produced by the action. However, the number of cases where the use of animals may be justified is quite small compared to the current level of suffering that we cause.

Euthanasia[8]

The distinction between persons and non-persons has important implications for a position that holds all human life sacred. Persons are those humans and non-humans who have the capacity to project their desires into the future and who have an interest in continued existence; they are beings who recognize, in some sense, the value of their lives. Non-persons are those humans and non-humans who are sentient but whose mental capacities are limited to the here and now, if that. Some sentient beings may only experience pleasure or pain and have no greater sense of what it is that they are experiencing other than that painful stimuli are unpleasant. Some are simple sensory beings who may not even be capable of moving away from painful stimuli.[9] They are not the sorts of creatures who recognize themselves and thus cannot view their lives as valuable. Nonetheless, to cause these individuals pain or to allow them to suffer is morally objectionable, particularly when there is no greater good that results from their pain and suffering. In the case of some severely disabled human infants, for example, those who will never develop into persons and whose short lives will be miserable, Singer has argued that it is best, from an ethical point of view, to painlessly kill them, assuming that the parents are prepared to make that decision under the guidance and advice of their doctor. This is clearly the right thing to do if the infant will otherwise be left to dehydrate and starve as "nature takes its course." Death from benign neglect causes unnecessary suffering, suffering that could be easily prevented by painlessly euthanizing the infant.

Of all his views, Singer's arguments about euthanasia for disabled infants have raised the most vociferous objections. Unfortunately, the criticisms, predominantly made by disability rights activists, miss the mark. Singer is not singling out infants with disabilities as those that it may be morally permissible to painlessly kill – as we have seen, painless killing of all non-persons may be justified, or even morally required, depending on the circumstances. The ethical imperative to try to prevent needless suffering would justify euthanasia in many instances – for severely brain-damaged adults, for those who are terminally ill and wish to die, as well as to severely disabled infants. The criticism that disability rights advocates have made, that Singer would have them killed, is clearly mistaken, as preference utilitarianism would judge the killing of those who can express a desire for continued existence as minimally *prima facie* wrong. Singer's preference utilitarianism, unlike hedonistic utilitarianism, recognizes not just pleasures and pains in the moral calculus, but the satisfaction of preferences as well. If an individual has a preference for continued existence (with all the other preferences that a continued existence could satisfy), then it would be wrong, other things being equal, to painlessly kill that individual. Had the parents of these disabled adults and their doctors determined before these individuals had any preferences that their lives would not be worth living, then their deaths before they became persons may have been justified. But that determination would depend on the broader consequences as well as the expected life prospects for the infant and her family.

Imagine that you have given birth to an infant with a severe case of spina bifida. During prenatal testing your doctor informed you that your fetus had a neural tube defect, but no one knew with certainty how severe the disability would be and, since children with more moderate forms of spina bifida can now lead meaningful, relatively happy lives, you decided not to terminate the pregnancy. Sadly, it turned out that the area of the spine that failed to close in your infant was closer to the neck, which means the infant will be completely paralyzed from the waist down, the digestive tract and abdominal muscles will be weak, and she will be unable to use her bowels and bladder. In addition, the infant is hydrocephalic – that is, there is a build up of spinal fluid on the brain that has already caused some brain damage and will be fatal if surgery isn't performed to implant a cerebral shunt. Your infant's condition is severe enough that the prospects of her leading a meaningful, independent life are rather slim. In addition, the infant will be subjected to multiple surgeries and will spend much of her time in discomfort and pain.

You have to decide whether you want the doctor to perform the surgery to implant a shunt or not.

As you are making your decision, you hear a baby crying in the room next door. You walk past and smile at the new mother and her family and overhear them lamenting the fact that their otherwise healthy newborn has a heart defect and will die in a matter of days if a new heart isn't found. You then learn that your child's heart is compatible with and would provide this other child with an opportunity to live a full, healthy life. After careful thought, you decide that you will not have the shunt surgery performed and thus will allow your baby to die and will ask that your infant's heart be given to the baby from the room next door.

Singer never doubts that these decisions are painful for the parents, families, doctors, and other healthcare providers who make them. What he challenges is the notion that good always results from keeping humans alive no matter what the cost. He argues that quality of life is more important from an ethical point of view than the often indefensible absolutist belief in the sanctity of human life. Adherence to the doctrine of the sanctity of life has caused, and will continue to cause, unnecessary suffering. When faced with the prospect of lifetime care and expense for individuals who will only suffer, or individuals who are unaware of themselves or their family and care-givers, Singer argues that parents and medical staff should be able to terminate those lives. The permissibility of killing certain humans in certain carefully monitored circumstances is even stronger when the death can contribute to the quality of life of another.

Poverty[10]

For Singer and many utilitarians, the goal of ethical action, to reduce suffering and promote well-being, is the responsibility of those who are in a position to do something about it, whether those people are directly causally responsible for the suffering or not. For most utilitarians, causing suffering is indistinguishable from failing to prevent it when the consequences are the same. Today, there is a huge amount of suffering and death that isn't being prevented. I've already discussed the unnecessary suffering of non-human animals and the terminal suffering that could be ended through euthanasia. Poverty is another source of human suffering that we are generally not doing much about. While the rich are richer than ever before, an estimated 10 million children die every year, about 30,000 a day, from poverty-related causes. People who are in a position to do something to save these children generally don't do so, because most people don't think helping those in need, even those in desperate need, is an individual moral responsibility. Singer argues that this is wrong. Those of us who are living comfortable lives should do whatever we can to minimize suffering and promote well-being by helping to eliminate poverty, famine, and easily preventable diseases. One way to eliminate, or at least drastically reduce, this suffering is for people with money for leisure goods to give that money to those in need.

In his extremely influential and much anthologized paper, "Famine, Affluence, and Morality," originally published in 1972, Singer presents a clear argument for why those of us who have more than we need should be doing more to help eliminate the suffering that results from poverty. His argument goes like this:

1   Suffering and death from absolute poverty and lack of food, shelter, and medical care are bad.
2   If it is in our power to prevent something bad from happening, without sacrificing anything of comparable importance, we ought to do it.
3   Given our level of affluence, we can do much more without making too great a sacrifice.
4   We ought to be doing more than we are currently.

Singer doesn't argue for premise (1), but assumes that those interested in thinking about our ethical obligations to others would agree that this sort of suffering is indeed bad. To support his claim in premise (2), he asks us to consult our intuitions about a case in which we come across a child drowning in a shallow pond. I may be running a bit late for an appointment and I may be wearing my nicest shoes, but to see this child drowning and to do nothing would be outrageous. The right thing to do in this case is to wade in and pull the child out. I may annoy those I was scheduled to meet and I will have ruined my best shoes, but these are of little moral importance when compared to the life of a child. And even though I had nothing to do with putting the child into this position, not doing something to save her implicates me in a serious moral wrong.[11] Once we accept this, and recognize that our not doing anything to help minimize the suffering caused by poverty is analogous to walking past the child drowning in the pond, it is hard not to accept the conclusion that we ought to be doing more, indeed much more, to prevent suffering and death from poverty-related causes.

Of course, precisely what we should do will require information about the effectiveness of aid organizations, about the chances that our giving money will indeed get to those in need, and about what other individuals, organizations, and states are doing. This has led some to argue that the case of the drowning child is not quite as analogous to the case of children dying from starvation in other parts of the world.[12] When I wade into the pond, I directly save the child and know that my action prevented her death; when I send a check to a poverty relief organization, such as Oxfam (the organization that Singer supports), I don't have an immediate sense that my action actually did any good. Fortunately, many organizations that fight poverty, such as Oxfam, have a very solid track record. It is true that some aid organizations are less effective and spend more on overheads than on directly aiding those in need, so doing a bit of research before sending a check is a good idea. Whether sending the check makes people feel as good as they would have if they had saved a drowning child, however, doesn't undermine the power of Singer's argument. Of course, one's pleasure at doing something right is part of a utilitarian calculus. All consequences of an action must be taken into account, for all those affected by it, and that includes the actor. But the differential amount of personal satisfaction one gets from helping someone near cannot compare to the suffering and death one is able to prevent by helping those in need who happen to be far. As Singer argues, to favor someone close over someone far, other things being equal, is to engage in a form of ethically unjustifiable discrimination. Just as favoring one's own species, or gender, or race is unjustifiable from an ethical point of view, so too is favoring one who is in physical proximity.

That we are not directly causally responsible for easily preventable, poverty-related suffering does not mitigate our responsibility to do something about such suffering.[13] We do not believe that the passer-by who lets the child drown is providing an ethical justification when he says, "but I didn't throw the child in the pond." But what about the passerby who said he thought someone else would take care of the child. Liam Murphy has argued that although we do have an individual moral responsibility for things we may not have directly caused, it is tempered by the equal moral responsibility of others who are in a position to help. We have the responsibility of doing our fair share assuming that others also do their fair share.[14] Singer rejects this fair share view and has us consider a slightly modified version of the scenario in which a child is drowning a pond:

> Imagine it is not one small child who has fallen in, but fifty children. We are among fifty adults, unrelated to the children, picnicking on the lawn around the pond. We can easily wade into the pond and rescue the children. . . . The "fair share" theorists would say that if we each rescue one child, all the children will be saved, and so none of us have an obligation to save more than one. But what

if half the picnickers prefer staying clean and dry to rescuing any children at all? Is it acceptable if the rest of us stop after we have rescued just one child, knowing that we have done our fair share, but that half the children will drown? (WSBG)

We cannot assume that because other people are around they will do the right thing. If they don't and we don't, children will die. And while their failures are certainly blameworthy, the failures of others does not minimize the obligations that individuals have to help save as many as possible.

Nevertheless, there is an important question about just how much one should do given that some people have much more money than others. Singer recently did some calculations based on the wealth of US families and came up with an astonishing discovery – when we start with the super-rich (those who make well over a million dollars a year) and come down to those who make at least $92,000 annually, and we tithe proportionately so that each donation is "unlikely to impose significant hardship on anyone," it turns out that there is an annual total "of $404 billion – from just 10 percent of American families" (WSBG). This amount is three times that of the Millennium Development Goals to halve extreme poverty and halve the proportion of people suffering from hunger by 2015. And this amount doesn't include contributions from governments and other wealthy individuals from around the world. Basically, if those who are well off were to give a mere fraction of their annual income to poverty relief, massive amounts of human suffering and death would be prevented.

3   A Meaningful Life

While there are many details of Singer's theoretical and practical views that have generated criticism, one of the most significant criticisms of his work, and indeed, the work of utilitarians generally, is that the view is too demanding. Simply put, it appears that in order to lead ethical lives, we would have to sacrifice many of the things that currently make our lives meaningful. It looks as though Singer believes that we ought to detach ourselves from our personal concerns, seeing them as located amongst many equally significant concerns, and that this would result in our living impoverished lives, devoid of personal satisfaction, interesting and enjoyable activities, and important relationships. For example, to do what is right, we may be required to act in ways that directly contradict respecting and attending to those who are near and dear to us. When it is the birthday of a lover, or child, or friend, we usually think about buying a gift, but the money we would spend on the gift could certainly do much more good for those less fortunate. Even spending time with our friends and family, going to a movie, or having a holiday dinner could be better spent helping those in need. We may be lucky enough to have family and friends who themselves would prefer it if we sent money to an aid organization or a chimpanzee protection group in their name, rather than receive a gift, or to work at a soup kitchen rather than to go see a movie; but sometimes even these very other-regarding individuals find that getting a personal present from a loved one or spending relaxing time together means more. When an ethical theory tells us that we cannot justify these actions, and that we may even be doing something morally wrong when we buy gifts or go to movies, the theory appears to be too demanding for us mere mortals.

Singer is not unaware of these concerns, and because he is not a purist, nor does he claim to be a moral exemplar, he allows that we should strive to do the best we can. Most people, most of the time, however, are not doing anything near the best they can do. When we reason carefully and impartially about our roles in contributing to a better world, a world with less pain and needless death, we must acknowledge that most of us can do much more to end human and non-human suffering. One need not completely agree with utilitarian philosophy in order to see that there is more that ethics demands of us in a world such as ours.

Philosophers have long challenged commonsense beliefs and often the challenges have made our collective lives better. The challenges that Peter Singer poses may look extreme, may require personal sacrifices, and may involve initial hardship. But if we meet these challenges we will contribute to a world with less pain, less misery, and more happiness. We will truly make the world a better place and, at the same time, will also make our own lives more meaningful.[15]

Notes

1 This epithet is particularly distasteful as three of Singer's grandparents were killed in Nazi concentration camps. See *Pushing Time Away* (2003).
2 The conversation took place in a BBC documentary about the conflict over a new biomedical research facility at the University of Oxford between scientists and animal rights activists. See, for example, www.insidehighered.com/news/2006/12/04/singer.
3 See www.arkangelweb.org/international/uk/20061127singer.php.

4 See *Animal Liberation* (1975), *Animal Factories* (1980), *The Great Ape Project* (1993), *The Way We Eat* (2006).
5 Calculated with information from Worldwatch and Compassion in World Farming.
6 I say assuming the facts are as they are presented, because presumably there were many more animals that were needed in the development of this particular primate model for Parkinson's disease, and more animals needed to train the scientists who perform the brain manipulations. In addition, some monkeys would have died from various complications either from the surgery or from some other source, and they may not have been included in this figure.
7 *Daily Princetonian*, December 8, 2006.
8 See *Practical Ethics* (1979), *Should the Baby Live?* (1985), *Rethinking Life and Death* (1995).
9 Some humans are kept alive in states that are described as "vegetative," not even sentient.
10 See *Practical Ethics* (1979), *How Are We to Live?* (1997), *One World: Ethics and Globalization* (2002), "What Should a Billionaire Give – and What Should You?" (2006).
11 Singer has taken his view about muddied shoes a bit further, "if for the cost of a pair of shoes we can contribute to a health program in a developing country that stands a good chance of saving the life of a child, we ought to do so" (WSBG).
12 Dale Jamieson (ed.), *Singer and His Critics*. Oxford: Blackwell, 1999.
13 Thomas Pogge (*World Poverty and Human Rights*, Cambridge: Polity, 2002) has argued that in fact we are responsible because our affluence springs from the global trade regime and other practices of globalization that perpetuate poverty.
14 Liam Murphy, *Moral Demands in Non-Ideal Theory*. Oxford: Oxford University Press, 2000.
15 I'd like to thank the editors of this volume and Robert C. Jones for helpful comments on previous drafts of this essay.

References

Animal Factories (with James Mason). New York: Crown, 1980.
Animal Liberation: A New Ethics for our Treatment of Animals. New York: New York Review, 1975; 2nd edn, 1990.
Democracy and Disobedience. Oxford: Oxford University Press, 1973.
"Famine, Affluence, and Morality" *Philosophy and Public Affairs* 5/1 (1972).
The Great Ape Project: Equality Beyond Humanity (with Paola Cavalieri). London: Fourth Estate, 1993.
How Are We to Live? Ethics in an Age of Self-interest [*HWL*]. Oxford: Oxford University Press, 1997.
"On Being Silenced in Germany" *New York Review of Books* 38/14 (August 15, 1991); repr. in *Writings on an Ethical Life*.

One World: Ethics and Globalization. New Haven: Yale University Press, 2002.

Practical Ethics [*PE*]. Cambridge: Cambridge University Press, 1979.

The President of Good and Evil: The Ethics of George W. Bush [*PGE*]. New York: Dutton, 2004.

Pushing Time Away: My Grandfather and the Tragedy of Jewish Vienna [*PTA*]. New York: Ecco Press, 2003.

Rethinking Life and Death: The Collapse of Our Traditional Ethics. Oxford: Oxford University Press, 1995.

Should the Baby Live? The Problem of Handicapped Infants (with Helga Kuhse). Oxford: Oxford University Press, 1985.

The Way We Eat: Why Our Food Choices Matter [*WWE*]. New York: Rodale, 2006.

"What Should a Billionaire Give – and What Should You?" [WSBG], *New York Times Magazine*, December 17, 2006.

Writings on an Ethical Life [*WEL*]. New York: Ecco Press, 2000.

INDEX